Construction

4

Editorial Advisory Board

The Career Information Center includes:

Agribusiness, Environment, and Natural Resources / 1

Communications and the Arts / 2

Computers, Business, and Office / 3

Construction / 4

Consumer, Homemaking, and Personal Services / 5

Engineering, Science, and Technology / 6

Health / 7

Hospitality and Recreation / 8

Manufacturing / 9

Marketing and Distribution / 10

Public and Community Services / 11

Transportation / 12

Employment Trends and Master Index / 13

Construction **4**

Career Information Center

Seventh Edition

Macmillan Reference USA

New York

Editorial Staff

Project Director: Frances A. Wiser

Writers: Tom Conklin, Suzanne J. Murdico, Judith Peacock

Researchers/Bibliographers: Christopher D. Binkley, Peter Michael Gee

Editors: Jacqueline Morais, Joseph B. Pirret, Meera Vaidyanathan

Copyediting Supervisor: Maureen Ryan Pancza

Photo Editor: Sara Matthews

Production Supervisors: Devan Paine Anding, William A. Murray

Production Assistant: Jessica Swenson

Interior Design: Maxson Crandall

Electronic Preparation: Cynthia C. Feldner, Fiona Torphy

Electronic Production: Rob Ehlers, Lisa Evans-Skopas, Deirdre Sheean, Isabelle Ulsh

Acknowledgments: It would be impossible to acknowledge the many people who gave their help, their time, and their experience to this project. However, we especially want to thank all the people at unions and trade and professional associations for their help in providing information and photographs. We also wish to thank the U.S. Department of Labor, Bureau of Labor Statistics, for providing up-to-date statistics, salary information, and employment projections for all the job profiles.

Developed and produced by Visual Education Corporation, Princeton, New Jersey

Macmillan Library Reference USA
1633 Broadway
New York, NY 10019

ISSN 1082-703X

ISBN 0-02-864915-X (set)

ISBN 0-02-864905-2 (volume 4)

Printed in the United States of America

printing number
1 2 3 4 5 6 7 8 9 10

This paper meets the requirements of ANSI/NISO Z39.48-1992 (Permanence of Paper).

Contents

Job Summary Chart

Job	Salary	Education/ Training	Employment Outlook	Page
Job Profiles—No Specialized Training				
Air-Conditioning, Heating, and Refrigeration Mechanic	Average—$535 a week	None	Good	27
Bricklayer	Average—$480 a week	None	Good	29
Carpenter	Average—$475 a week	None	Good	32
Cement Mason	Average—$15 to $45 an hour	None	Fair	34
Construction Electrician	Average—$485 to $815 a week	None	Fair	36
Construction Equipment Mechanic	Average—$500 to $760 a week	None	Fair	38
Construction Laborer	Average—$250 to $480 a week	None	Fair	41
Construction Millwright	Starting—$510 to $820 a week	None	Poor	42
Demolition Worker	Varies—see profile	None	Fair	44
Drywall Installer and Finisher	Average—$295 to $630 a week	High school	Fair	46
Elevator Constructor and Repair Worker	Average—$740 to $1,090 a week	High school	Poor	48
Floor Covering Installer	Average—$345 to $660 a week	None	Fair	50
Glazier	Average—$28 to $42 an hour	None	Fair	52
Heavy Equipment Operator	Average—$330 to $605 a week	High school	Fair	54
Insulation Worker	Average—$22 to $48 an hour	None	Good	56
Iron and Steel Worker	Varies—see profile	High school	Good	58
Lather	Average—$23,200	None	Good	60
Manufactured Home Assembler and Installer	Average—$18,000 to $26,000	None	Good	62
Marble, Tile, and Terrazzo Worker	Average—$470 a week	None	Good	63
Painter and Paperhanger	Average—$285 to $515 a week	None	Good	65

★ High-growth job

⭐ **High-growth job**

Job	Salary	Education/ Training	Employment Outlook	Page
Real Estate Developer	Varies—see profile	Varies—see profile	Good	103
Septic Tank Installer	Average—$20,000 to $25,000	Varies—see profile	Varies—see profile	105
Solar Energy Technician	Average—$18,000 to $39,000	High school plus training	Varies—see profile	108
Specification Writer	Starting—$20,000 Average—$22,000 to $30,000	High school plus training	Varies—see profile	110
Water Well Driller	Average—$25,000	High school plus training	Varies—see profile	112

Job Profiles—Advanced Training/Experience

Job	Salary	Education/ Training	Employment Outlook	Page
Architect	Average—$38,900	College plus training; license	Varies—see profile	114
Building Inspector	Average—$25,200 to $43,800	High school plus training	Good	116
Civil Engineer	Starting—$29,400 Average—$43,400	College plus training	Good	119
Construction Supervisor	Average—$35,000 to $110,000	High school	Very good	121
Heavy Construction Contractor	Average—$600 to $675 a week	Varies—see profile	Varies—see profile	123
Highway Contractor	Average—$35,000	Varies—see profile	Good	125
Highway Engineer	Starting—$28,000 Average—$35,000	College	Good	127
Highway Inspector	Average—$31,200	High school plus training	Varies—see profile	129
Landscape Architect	Average—$30,200 to $53,900	College	Good	131
Surveyor	Average—$28,400 to $44,100	2- or 4-year college; license	Fair	133

★ High-growth job

Foreword

The seventh edition of the *Career Information Center* mirrors the ongoing changes in the job market caused by new technological and economic developments. These developments continue to change what Americans do in the workplace and how they do it. People have a critical need for up-to-date information to help them make career decisions.

The *Career Information Center* is an individualized resource for people of all ages and at all stages of career development. It has been recognized as an excellent reference for librarians, counselors, educators, and other providers of job information. It is ideally suited for use in libraries, career resource centers, and guidance offices, as well as in adult education centers and other facilities where people seek information about job opportunities, careers, and their own potential in the workforce.

This seventh edition updates many of the features that made the earlier editions so useful.

- A Job Summary Chart, a quick reference guide, appears in the front section of each volume to help readers get the basic facts and compare the jobs described in the volume. High-growth jobs are highlighted and identified with a star.

- Each volume of the *Career Information Center* begins with an overview of the job market in that field. These "Looking Into . . ." sections have been completely revised and updated. They also include new graphs, charts, and boxes providing information such as industry snapshots and the fastest-growing and top-dollar jobs in the field.

- Each volume has a section called "Getting Into . . . ," which contains useful information on entering the particular field. It offers self-evaluation tips and decision-making help; and it relates possible job choices to individual interests, abilities, and work characteristics. There is also practical information on job hunting, using the Internet and classified ads, preparing resumes, and handling interviews. "Getting Into . . ." also includes a section on employee rights.

- Each volume has a listing of all job profiles in the series and the volumes in which they appear, making access to profiles in other volumes easy.

- *Career Information Center* contains 676 job profiles in which more than 3,000 jobs are discussed. Each profile describes work characteristics, education and training requirements, getting the job, advancement and employment outlook, working conditions, and earnings and benefits.

- Job summaries, provided for each job profile, highlight the education or training required, salary range, and employment outlook.

- Volume 13 has been revised to reflect career concerns of the 1990s and employment trends through the year 2006. This volume includes updated articles on benefits, employment law, health in the workplace, job search strategies, job training, job opportunities at home, adjusting to job loss, and identifying opportunities for retraining.

- More than 560 photographs appear in the *Career Information Center,* including many new photos. Profile photos provide a visual glimpse of life on the job. Photos have been selected to give the reader a sense of what it feels like to be in a specific field or job.

- Updated bibliographies in each volume include recommended readings and World Wide Web sites in specific job areas. Additional titles for the vocational counselor are included in Volume 13.

- Each volume also contains a comprehensive directory of accredited occupational education and vocational training facilities listed by occupational area and grouped by state. Directory materials are generated from the IPEDS (Integrated Postsecondary Education Data System) database of the U.S. Department of Education.

The *Career Information Center* recognizes the importance not only of job selection, but also of job holding, coping, and applying life skills. No other career information publication deals with work attitudes so comprehensively.

Using the Career Information Center

The *Career Information Center* is designed to meet the needs of many people—students, people just entering or reentering the job market, those dissatisfied with present jobs, those without jobs—anyone of any age who is not sure what to do for a living. The *Career Information Center* is for people who want help in making career choices. It combines the comprehensiveness of an encyclopedia with the format and readability of a magazine. Many professionals, including counselors, librarians, and teachers will find it a useful guidance and reference tool.

The *Career Information Center* is organized by occupational interest area rather than in alphabetical order. Jobs that have something in common are grouped together. In that way people who do not know exactly what job they want can read about a number of related jobs. The *Career Information Center* classifies jobs that have something in common into clusters. The classification system is adapted from the cluster organization used by the U.S. Department of Labor. Each volume of the *Career Information Center* explores one of 12 occupational clusters.

To use the *Career Information Center,* first select the volume that treats the occupational area that interests you most. Because there are many ways to group occupations, you may not find a particular job in the volume in which you look for it. In that case, check the central listing of all the profiles, which is located in the front of Volumes 1 through 12. This listing provides the names of all profiles and the volume number in which they appear. Volume 13 also includes a comprehensive index of all the jobs covered in the first 12 volumes.

After selecting a volume or volumes, investigate the sections that you feel would be most helpful. It isn't necessary to read these volumes from cover to cover. They are arranged so that you can go directly to the specific information you want. Here is a description of the sections included in each volume.

- **Job Summary Chart**—This chart presents in tabular form the basic data from all profiles in the volume: salary, education and training, employment outlook, and the page on which you can find the job profile. Jobs with a high growth potential are highlighted and starred.

- **Looking Into . . .**—This overview of the occupational cluster describes the opportunities, characteristics, and trends in that particular field.

- **Getting Into . . .**—This how-to guide can help you decide what jobs may be most satisfying to you and what strategies you can use to get the right job. You will learn, for example, how to write an effective resume, how to complete an application form, what to expect in an interview, how to use networking, and what to do if someone has discriminated against you.

- **Job Summary**—These summaries, located at the beginning of each profile, highlight the most important facts about the job: education and training, salary range, and employment outlook.

Education and Training indicates whether the job requires no education, high school, college, advanced degree, voc/tech school, license, or training.

Salary Range is given as an approximate yearly wage unless "a week" or "an hour" is noted. These are average salaries that may vary significantly from region to region.

Employment Outlook is based on several factors, including the Bureau of Labor Statistics' projections through the year 2006. The ratings are defined as follows: *poor* means there is a projected employment decrease of 1 percent or more; *fair* means there is a projected employment increase of 0 to 13 percent; *good* means there is a projected employment increase of 14 to 26 percent; *very good* means there is a projected employment increase of 27 to 40 percent; and *excellent* means there is a projected employment increase of 41 percent or more. The outlook is then determined by looking at the ratings and other employment factors. For example, a job with excellent projected employment growth in which many more people are entering the field than there are jobs available will have an outlook that is good rather than excellent.

For all categories, the phrase *Varies—see profile* means the reader must consult the profile for the information, which is too extensive to include in the Job Summary.

- **Job Profiles**—The job profiles are divided into three categories based on the level of training required to get the job. Each profile explores a number of related jobs and covers seven major topics: description of the job being profiled, the education and training requirements, ways to get the job, advancement possibilities and employment outlook, the working conditions, the earnings and benefits, and places to go for more information.

Job Profiles—No Specialized Training includes jobs that require no education or previous work experience beyond high school.

Job Profiles—Some Specialized Training/Experience includes jobs that require one, two, or three years of vocational training or college, or work experience beyond high school.

Job Profiles—Advanced Training/Experience includes jobs that require a bachelor's degree or advanced degree from a college or university and/or equivalent work experience in that field.

- **Resources—General Career Information** includes a selected bibliography of the most recent books, audiovisual materials, and web sites on general career information, how-to books on such topics as resume writing and preparing for tests, and useful computer software. In addition, there are special sections of readings for the career counselor in Volume 13.

- **Resources**—Each volume also contains a bibliography of books, audiovisual materials, and web sites for specific fields covered in that volume.

- **Directory of Institutions Offering Career Training**—This listing, organized first by career area, then by state, includes the schools that offer occupational training beyond high school. For jobs requiring a bachelor's degree or an advanced degree, check a library for college catalogs and appropriate directories.

- **Index**—This index, which is located at the end of each volume, lists every job mentioned in that volume. It serves not only to cross-reference all the jobs in the volume but also to show related jobs in the field. For example, under the entry LICENSED PRACTICAL NURSE, you will find Home Health Aide, Nurse's Aide and Orderly, and Ward Clerk. In addition, the "profile includes" part of an entry lists other jobs that are mentioned in the profile, in this case Licensed Vocational Nurse and Registered Nurse.

- **Volume 13, Employment Trends and Master Index**—This volume includes several features that will help both the job seeker and the career counselor. A useful correlation guide provides the *DOT (Dictionary of Occupational Titles)* number of most of the job profiles in the *Career Information Center*. There is also a special section on career information for Canada. The updated and revised "Employment Trends" section contains articles on health in the workplace; employment projections through the year 2006; job search strategies; employment trends for women, minorities, immigrants, older workers, and the physically challenged; employment demographics; benefits programs; training; employment opportunities at home; employment law; adjusting to job loss; identifying opportunities for retraining. All articles have been written by authorities in these fields. The articles provide job seekers and career professionals with an overview of current employment issues, career opportunities, and outlooks. Finally, there is a master index to all the jobs included in all 13 volumes.

The *Career Information Center* is exactly what it says it is—a center of the most useful and pertinent information you need to explore and choose from the wide range of job and career possibilities. The *Career Information Center* provides you with a solid foundation of information for getting a satisfying job or rewarding career.

Comprehensive Job Profile List

The following list includes job profiles and the corresponding volume number.

Accountant, 3
Accountant, Public, 3
Actor, 2
Actuary, 3
Acupuncturist, 7
Administrative Assistant, 3
Admitting Clerk, 7
Adult Education Worker, 11
Advertising Account Executive, 10
Advertising Copywriter, 2
Advertising Manager, 10
Aerospace Engineer, 6
Aerospace Industry, 9
Aerospace Technician, 6
Agricultural Engineer, 1
Agricultural Supply Sales Worker, 1
Agricultural Technician, 1
Agronomist, 1
AIDS Counselor, 7
Air Pollution Control Technician, 1
Air Traffic Controller, 12
Air-Conditioning and Heating
    Technician, 4
Air-Conditioning Engineer, 6
Air-Conditioning, Heating, and
    Refrigeration Mechanic, 4
Aircraft Mechanic, 12
Airline Baggage and Freight Handler, 12
Airline Dispatcher, 12
Airline Flight Attendant, 12
Airline Reservations Agent, 12
Airline Ticket Agent, 12
Airplane Pilot, 12
Airport Manager, 12
Airport Utility Worker, 12
All-Round Machinist, 9
Alternative Fuels Vehicle Technician, 6
Aluminum and Copper Industry, 9
Ambulance Driver, 7
Amusement and Recreation
    Attendant, 8
Anatomist, 6
Anesthesiologist, 7
Animal Caretaker, 8
Announcer, 2
Anthropologist, 6
Apparel Industry, 9
Appliance Service Worker, 5
Appraiser, 5
Archaeologist, 6
Architect, 4
Architectural Drafter, 4
Architectural Model Maker, 4
Armed Services Career, 11
Art Director, 2
Art and Music Therapist, 7
Artificial Intelligence Specialist, 6
Artist, 2

Assembler, 9
Astronomer, 6
Athletic Coach, 8
Athletic Trainer, 8
Auctioneer, 10
Auditor, 3
Auto Body Repairer, 12
Auto Parts Counter Worker, 10
Auto Sales Worker, 10
Automated Manufacturing Manager, 9
Automobile Driving Instructor, 12
Automotive Exhaust Emissions
    Technician, 12
Automotive Industry, 9
Automotive Mechanic, 12
Avionics Technician, 12

Bank Clerk, 3
Bank Officer, 3
Bank Teller, 3
Barber and Hairstylist, 5
Bartender, 8
Bicycle Mechanic, 12
Biochemist, 6
Biological Technician, 6
Biologist, 6
Biomedical Engineer, 6
Biomedical Equipment Technician, 7
Blacksmith and Forge Shop Worker, 9
Blood Bank Technologist, 7
Boat Motor Mechanic, 12
Boiler Tender, 9
Boilermaking Worker, 9
Bookbinder, 2
Bookkeeper, 3
Border Patrol Agent, 11
Botanist, 6
Bricklayer, 4
Broadcast Technician, 2
Brokerage Clerk, 3
Building Custodian, 11
Building Inspector, 4
Business Family and Consumer
    Scientist, 5
Business Machine Operator, 3

Cable Television Engineer, 2
Cable Television Technician, 2
CAD Specialist, 6
Cafeteria Attendant, 8
CAM Operator, 9
Camera Operator, 2
Candy, Soft Drink, and Ice Cream
    Manufacturing Worker, 1
Car Rental Agent, 12
Car Wash Worker, 12
Cardiac-Monitor Technician/
    Perfusionist, 7

Cardiology Technologist, 7
Carpenter, 4
Cartographer, 1
Cartoonist, 2
Cashier, 10
Casino Worker, 8
Caterer, 8
Cement Mason, 4
Ceramic Engineer, 6
Ceramics Industry, 9
Chauffeur, 5
Cheese Industry Worker, 1
Chemical Engineer, 6
Chemical Technician, 6
Chemist, 6
Child Care Worker, Private, 5
Chiropractor, 7
Choreographer, 2
City Manager, 11
Civil Engineer, 4
Civil Engineering Technician, 4
Claim Adjuster, 3
Claim Examiner, 3
College Student Personnel Worker, 11
College/University Administrator, 3
Commercial Artist, 2
Companion, 5
Comparison Shopper, 10
Compensation Specialist, 3
Composer, 2
Composite Technician, 9
Computer Artist, 2
Computer Consultant, 3
Computer Database Manager, 3
Computer Network Technician, 3
Computer Operator, 3
Computer Programmer, 3
Computer Security Engineer, 3
Computer Servicer, 3
Computer Software Documentation
    Writer, 3
Construction Electrician, 4
Construction Equipment Dealer, 4
Construction Equipment Mechanic, 4
Construction Laborer, 4
Construction Millwright, 4
Construction Supervisor, 4
Consumer Advocate, 5
Consumer Credit Counselor, 5
Controller, 3
Convention Specialist, 8
Cook and Chef, 8
Cooperative Extension Service Worker, 1
Corrections Officer, 11
Correspondence Clerk, 3
Cosmetologist, 5
Court Clerk, 11
Craftsperson, 2

Looking Into Construction

onstruction is one of our nation's most vital industries, providing jobs for more than 5.4 million workers. More than 4.5 percent of the nation's total workforce is involved in some aspect of building, renovation, or demolition. The products of this industry include everything from single-family houses to apartment buildings, from suspension bridges to electric power plants, to tunnels far beneath the earth's surface.

Construction activity is also one of the cornerstones of the U.S. economy. The value of new construction accounted for more than 8 percent of the gross domestic product (GDP) in 1995. There are hundreds of thousands of construction firms in the United States today, accounting for billions of dollars in new construction activity each year.

The construction industry is extremely volatile, however, as it is constantly shaped and reshaped by new technologies, environmental regulations, and economic trends. Interest rates, mortgage rates, real estate finances, and equipment and material costs are just some of the economic factors that have an impact on the industry. In addition, federal budget negotiations have an effect on federal spending, often limiting the funds spent on public works projects.

The construction industry is generally divided into four separate subindustries—residential, commercial, industrial, and public works. These subindustries differ from one another in the types of jobs they offer and in the clientele they serve.

Employment in the construction field is very different from that in other industries. First, employees are usually hired for specific jobs, so they tend to move on to other employers and other projects after a job is completed. Second, workers are associated more with a specialized trade than with a particular

Workers in the construction industry specialize in a particular trade and are hired by different employers for temporary, often perilous jobs.

employer or company. Construction work requires workers with a wide range of skills and talents. From the civil engineer to the general contractor to the stonemason, each worker brings particular abilities and knowledge to the construction process. Third, working conditions in some areas of construction can be perilous. Finally, employment prospects are often unpredictable.

FROM SHACKS TO SKYSCRAPERS

Construction has been an integral part of human expression since the dawn of recorded history. For thousands of years people have built shelters, roads, schools, and other structures in which to carry on the functions and pursuits of society. Although ancient builders lacked the technology and heavy equipment fundamental to modern construction, they were nevertheless able to build edifices of great beauty and durability.

Because they lacked modern transportation and construction technology, ancient builders had to rely on the materials on hand, as well as a staggering number of laborers. It took more than 100,000 workers many years to build the Great Pyramid in ancient Egypt. Although they had no cranes with which to lift the giant limestone blocks, the workers were able to create an awe-inspiring structure that still stands thousands of years later. Similarly, the Romans used their resources to build incredibly sophisticated structures, such as the aqueducts. Many principles of ancient Greek and Roman architecture are still applied today.

Throughout history, construction has played a central role in human society. Many ancient structures were built not only for a specific practical function but also as expressions of humankind's deepest artistic instincts or spiritual beliefs. Structures built to house rulers or to glorify gods were often physical manifestations of the importance of the ruler or deity.

The construction process did not change a great deal from the days of ancient Rome to the mid-19th century. Traditional building techniques developed in the ancient world were used throughout the Middle Ages and the Renaissance. Because there were no railroads or automobiles, building materials usually consisted of those that were available locally.

The Industrial Revolution rapidly transformed the construction process in the 19th century. Whereas builders had traditionally been dependent on locally available materials, the advent of the railroad enabled them to obtain materials from far away. Newly developed construction materials, such as steel, quickly grew into huge industries. With the change from an agricultural to an industrial society, large cities sprang up across the United States. Waves of immigration at the turn of the century created a need for more urban housing and provided the country with a large, capable workforce.

Construction and the Economy

Throughout the 20th century the construction industry has reflected the expansion and contraction of the U.S. economy. There have been periods of sharp decline and years of rapid growth. During wartime the government has traditionally put restrictions on nonessential construction activity so that the nation's resources can be committed to the war effort.

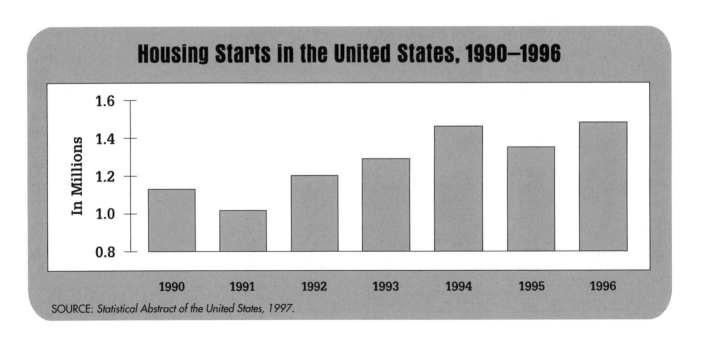

Housing Starts in the United States, 1990–1996

SOURCE: *Statistical Abstract of the United States, 1997.*

During the first two decades of the 20th century, U.S. construction grew at a brisk pace. Then—with the stock market crash and the Great Depression—the industry fell into a severe slump. As the economy recovered, so too did the construction industry. By the time the United States entered World War II, the industry was thriving.

Following World War II, the industry entered a period of dramatic growth. U.S. materials, labor, and technology were needed to build or repair infrastructures throughout war-torn Europe. In the United States, there was a population explosion as many returning GIs started families and bought new houses. The children of this population explosion would come to be known as baby boomers. During the next 40 years, construction activity mirrored the business cycle, dropping at periodic intervals and recovering with the economy in general. Overall, the industry saw steady growth.

THE INDUSTRY TODAY

In the mid-1980s commercial construction and multi-family home construction were booming businesses, making up about one-third of total construction spending. As the decade drew to a close, real estate developers realized that the supply of new buildings greatly exceeded the demand. This led to layoffs and unemployment in the construction industry as fewer new projects were undertaken.

The U.S. economy was in recession as the 1990s began. Unemployment rates rose and consumers had less money to spend on new homes. The savings and loan (S&L) crisis of the early 1990s, during which hundreds of lending institutions folded, caused many banks to grow apprehensive about lending funds or giving credit. As a result, the demand for new housing fell sharply. Department of Housing and Urban Development figures show that during the recession, multifamily housing starts fell to their lowest level in 35 years.

The credit crunch affected not only private consumers but also small businesses. Commercial and industrial construction requires heavy financial backing from lending institutions. During the first part of the 1990s, many institutions were not willing to take such risks. The poor performance of commercial and industrial construction during the recession accounted for a significant drop in the GDP during that period.

In the mid-1990s the economy began to recover from the recession and the S&L crisis. The construction industry rebounded with the economy. Banks and other institutions were more willing to lend money and extend credit for real estate projects. Residential construction was the first sector of the industry to recover.

The recovery of the industry as a whole also has been slow, and total yearly revenue has been low

Industry Snapshots

ARCHITECTURE
Although the industry has entered a period of steady growth, many architects are currently involved in renovation and rehabilitation projects. Workers without training in computer-aided design will most likely have difficulty finding work in this field.

COMMERCIAL CONSTRUCTION
Growth in commercial construction will be steady but slow throughout the decade. The lack of further growth is due mainly to an overabundance of existing commercial buildings. Renovation and repair work, including adapting buildings to meet current safety standards, will be the growth areas in this field.

PUBLIC WORKS
The market for public works construction is strong. Increased attention to the aging infrastructure, coupled with increased government spending, has resulted in an abundance of public works projects across the country. The market for institutional construction, including health care facilities and prisons, remains strong.

RESIDENTIAL CONSTRUCTION
This segment of the industry fluctuates with the economy. The affordability of new homes depends greatly on the current mortgage rates. New residential construction is expected to grow slowly for the remainder of the decade, but spending on home maintenance and remodeling will grow substantially.

INDUSTRIAL CONSTRUCTION
Most capital spending in the industrial market continues to be committed to new equipment rather than to the construction of new buildings. However, like the rest of the industry, this sector is growing at a moderate pace.

by traditional standards. Mortgage rates hit bottom in 1993 and had not increased significantly in the 5 years afterward. This should keep the demand for new homes slow but steady until the year 2000.

The Shape of the Industry

The construction industry is unique in a number of important ways. First, each product—or structure—is custom-made, requiring a unique combination of skills and resources. Second, each structure carries its own price based on the ever-changing costs of labor, materials, and land. Third, many laborers are employed on a project-by-project basis, with long-term job security available only for workers who are employed as managers of construction firms.

Owners A construction project is usually commissioned by an individual, a business, or the government. The person commissioning the project is called the owner. In most cases the owner hires professionals, such as architects and engineers, to design the building or structure. Then the owner hires a general contractor or a construction management company to take care of the actual construction.

General Contractors General contractors are skilled workers who specialize in a particular type of construction work, such as commercial construction.

The general contractor of a construction project hires subcontractors to carry out specific functions such as plumbing, carpentry, masonry, and cement work.

They take responsibility for coordinating an entire project, including everything from locating building materials to hiring specialty trade contractors such as plumbers, carpenters, and electricians.

Construction Managers Construction managers are usually hired by companies to supervise large construction projects. They oversee the architect, engineers, and general contractors hired to complete the project.

Contracting

Owners often choose general contractors through a bidding system. First, the owner places an advertisement describing the project. Next, interested contractors contact the owner and request documents that list the goals and objectives of the project. The contractor then submits a cost estimate for the project, taking into consideration the necessary materials, labor, and time. The contractor also calculates a profit margin. The owner considers competing bids from different contractors and hires the one who has submitted the most appealing offer. Because many factors influence a contractor's bidding decisions, competing bids can differ greatly. The general contractor who has been awarded the contract usually hires subcontractors to carry out specific functions on the project. Many construction jobs—usually government projects—are awarded through closed bids. Only those general contractors who are invited by the owner are allowed to bid on the project.

Subcontractors Also called specialty trade workers, subcontractors are usually skilled in a specific trade. For example, plumbers, stonemasons, and carpenters are subcontractors. On very small projects, subcontractors may do the work themselves. On large jobs, however, many subcontractors hire their own work crews, and these crews join them at a construction site.

Heavy Construction Contractors Other construction workers, called heavy construction contractors, specialize in building and repairing highways, bridges, and similar structures. Many of these workers are skilled at operating dangerous and hard-to-manage machinery. Many heavy construction contractors are hired by the government to complete large-scale projects.

Worker Training A large number of construction workers learn their trades by participating in union programs. They often start out as apprentices, working alongside skilled workers. Other workers attend vocational programs to learn their skills. Many colleges and universities across the country now offer undergraduate and graduate degrees in construction science. A college degree in civil engineering is highly desired by large construction companies.

Residential Construction

Some people consider the building of homes to be the most fragmented industry in the United States. One industry survey revealed that, in 1993, the country's largest 100 residential construction firms accounted for only 13 percent of all new housing starts. The majority of single-family and multifamily homes are built by smaller local contracting firms, many with only a few employees. Whereas this means that many opportunities exist in residential construction for the small business entrepreneur, it also means that competition is keen.

Although traditional "site-built" homes have always been the primary type of residential construction, manufactured housing is another sector of the industry. Manufactured homes, also called mobile homes, are assembled in one setting and then moved to their permanent site. In 1993 and 1994, the number of mobile homes in use rose significantly. By 1996, however, the increase had slowed considerably. Modular homes, also called prefabricated homes, are gaining in popularity as well. Modular homes are built to meet state building codes, whereas manufactured homes are subject to federal standards.

Jobs in Residential Construction Carpenters are by far the largest single group of skilled workers employed in residential construction. Increasingly, contractors are looking for educated individuals skilled at carpentry who can also help manage a construction site. Bricklayers, painters, plumbers, and electricians are some of the other workers who contribute to a construction project. Because the industry is projected to grow slowly over the next decade, many of the opportunities in residential construction will probably involve renovation rather than new construction.

Commercial Construction

Commercial construction involves the building of restaurants, shopping centers, office buildings, banks, and other business-oriented establishments. Many commercial construction projects involve large work crews and may last for more than a year.

Excessive commercial construction during the 1980s resulted in millions of square feet of vacant and unwanted office space. After remaining stagnant from 1992 to 1995, new commercial construction was up 13 percent in 1996. This should continue to increase as the economy improves and stabilizes.

Jobs in Commercial Construction Many commercial construction firms are much larger than their residential counterparts. Opportunities in this area of construction exist for specialty trade workers such as glaziers, carpenters, painters, paperhangers, and ironworkers. Large firms often employ civil engineers, architects, and other design professionals.

Industrial Construction

Industrial construction includes the building of manufacturing plants and the renovation of existing plants. Many of these projects are complex and require the skills of hundreds of workers and personnel. To meet this need, huge industrial construction firms employ thousands of workers such as engineers, drafters, and labor relations experts.

Jobs in Industrial Construction Like other areas of the industry, industrial construction was hit hard by the recession. Although it has since rebounded, industrial construction continues to grow quite slowly. Opportunities in this area of construction exist for heavy construction contractors and ironworkers, as well as for many of the specialty trade workers involved in commercial and residential construction. Many large corporations hire construction managers to oversee their various construction projects.

Public Works

The U.S. government is the largest employer of workers and the largest funder of projects in the entire construction industry. Public works projects include highways, bridges, dams, hospitals, and airports. Prisons, schools, and mass transit facilities are also part of this category. Public works construction is essential to maintaining the country's infrastructure. Without continual renovation and replacement, our roads, bridges, and tunnels would not be safe for traveling.

The U.S. government continually employs construction workers to renovate and maintain public areas so they are safe and attractive.

Jobs in Public Works Construction Bridge and highway construction provides the greatest opportunities in this field. Opportunities also exist for heavy construction contractors, ironworkers, glaziers, electricians, and other skilled trade workers, especially in the building of prisons and other correctional facilities. As the baby boomer population grows older, the need for building and renovating hospitals and health care facilities will increase. The "echo boom"—the population surge of the 1980s, as baby boomers started families—will also require the building and renovation of schools to continue.

Construction Management

Managing a construction project can be an arduous task. Deadlines must be met, strict building codes adhered to, and numerous supplies and workers organized. A project's workforce often consists of specialty trade workers who are required to focus only on their own specific functions. Without proper guidance, even a small project can become disorganized and chaotic, resulting in wasted time, wasted resources, and an over-budget project.

The Site Who is in charge at the construction site? In some cases it is the general contractor; in others it is the design professional hired by the owner. Some design firms employ engineers, inspectors, and surveyors who are trained in construction management. Some states have laws that dictate who can be in charge at a construction site, as well as who is responsible for safety and emergency work stoppage.

Scheduling Managing a construction project's schedule has traditionally been a complex task. Running even a small project involves keeping track of a multitude of deadlines, mounting costs, and employee payment schedules.

The industry has developed management techniques to coordinate the complex network of workers, companies, resources, and payment schedules involved in a project. One such scheduling system is

Construction managers run large and small projects. They manage the site and keep track of deadlines, mounting costs, and payment schedules.

called the critical path method (CPM). CPM is used to reduce the time, cost, and difficulties that can occur in a construction project. Nevertheless, even this type of scheduling is time-consuming and complicated, requiring industry workers to spend long hours designing flowcharts and diagrams.

Recent developments in computer software programs now make the CPM technique much easier to use. In addition, there are many other scheduling software programs to select from. Computers are commonly used at construction sites, and workers interested in managing construction sites should be computer literate.

THE FUTURE OF THE INDUSTRY

The construction industry is changing as rapidly as the rest of our society. A variety of outside influences affect the industry. The most significant of these influences is fluctuating economic conditions. Other influences include new technology, international construction, changing demographics, environmental concerns, and worker safety and health care.

Technology

Just as the railroad and steel mills revolutionized the construction industry more than 100 years ago, new building materials, sophisticated computer software, and space-age tools are fundamentally changing construction as we enter the 21st century.

Every year, new building materials are developed and existing ones are improved. For example, high-performance concrete is now used to build stronger and more durable structures that are able to support more weight than those built with standard concrete. High-performance steel and fiber-reinforced plastic are just two of the other materials changing the industry. In addition to these new resources, recycling provides builders with a plentiful source of building materials. One house—built by the National Association of Home Builders—incorporates a slew of recycled

Summer Jobs in Construction

ARCHITECTURE

Architecture firms and government agencies offer summer internships with opportunities for designing, drafting, lettering, and model building. Other summer jobs include clerical work, landscape architecture, interior design, and historic building preservation. Contact:

- architecture firms
- government agencies
- contractors
- interior designers
- corporate in-house architecture departments

Sources of Information

Profile
American Institute of Architects
1735 New York Avenue, NW
Washington, DC 20006-5292
www.aiaonline.com

ENGINEERING

Summer internships are available with many engineering firms. Summer jobs in civil engineering include field measuring, blueprint preservation, surveying, drafting, and site work. Summer mechanical engineering jobs include stress analysis and analysis of heating and ventilation systems. General office work is also available. Contact:

- engineering firms
- local planning offices
- construction companies
- surveyors

Sources of Information

Job Choices (engineering, science, and other technical employment)
National Association of Colleges and Employers
College Placement Council, Inc.
Highland Avenue
Bethlehem, PA 18017
www.jobweb.org

Job Opportunities in Engineering and Technology 1995
Peterson's Guides
P.O. Box 2123
Princeton, NJ 08540-2123

CONSTRUCTION

Construction activity increases in the summer when the weather is favorable for outdoor work. Positions are generally available for carpenters, painters, roofers, masons, road crews, technicians, and other general construction workers. Contact:

- building contractors
- unions
- building suppliers
- newspapers

materials in its construction. Even the house's steel frame is made from junkyard leftovers.

For years, design professionals have used computer-aided design (CAD) software in their work. Today, CAD is used on virtually every type of construction project. CAD software programs enable designers to create computer images of the structures being planned. Using this software, designers can design a three-dimensional object, then rotate the image on the screen. This allows them to view objects from different angles, catching potential problems at a much earlier phase of construction.

Even the tools that industry workers use are being transformed by the technological revolution now sweeping the globe. Engineers are producing lighter, sturdier power tools that run more quietly than their predecessors. Saw blades are constructed of new alloys that remain razor sharp. Laser-optic technology is being applied to tools such as power saws and high-tech levels that shoot laser beams for precise measurement and alignment. Instead of batteries, some new tools are powered by magnets made from rare organic materials. Technology also plays an important role in on-site safety. Soon many cranes will use sensors to warn operators if loads are too heavy. Other devices in development include remote-controlled vehicles that fill potholes and seal cracks in road pavement.

International Construction

In the 1970s U.S. firms expanded their overseas operations. By the early 1990s, U.S. companies were regularly awarded about half of all international construction contracts. In addition to working for foreign clients, many U.S. construction firms are hired by American companies undertaking construction projects overseas. Prefabricated homes constructed in the United States are also exported to many countries including Mexico, Japan, Saudi Arabia, and Russia. Mexico is a major consumer of U.S. construction and housing materials, and the North American Free Trade Agreement (NAFTA) has further opened this lucrative construction market to U.S. firms. South Africa is another emerging market for U.S. materials.

Changing Demographics

Most home buyers are between the ages of 20 and 49. Predictably, home buying increases when a larger percentage of the population fits into this age group. Over the next few years, however, fewer people will fit into this category. This is one reason why industry experts predict a slowdown in housing starts for the next decade. The beginning of the next century, however, should witness a different trend.

Middle- and upper-class retirees are another group that tend to buy new homes. This is evident in states such as Florida, which has traditionally had a healthy housing market. Retirement communities are likely to be a plentiful resource for the building of new homes in the first two decades of the next century, when baby boomers (people born between 1946 and 1964) will be senior citizens. Government figures project that the population age 85 and older will grow four times as fast as the total population by the year 2006. This will increase the demand for health care and undoubtedly for nursing homes and health-related facilities.

Top-Dollar Jobs in Construction

These are high-paying jobs described in this volume. The figures represent typical salaries or earnings for experienced workers.

$50,000 plus	Construction Supervisor
	Real Estate Developer
$35,000–$50,000	Architect
	Civil Engineer
	Highway Engineer
	Landscape Architect
$27,000–$35,000	Air-Conditioning and Heating Technician
	Plumber and Pipe Fitter

Immigration is an additional factor increasing the demand for new housing. Between 1980 and 1990, immigration in the United States rose by about 7 million people. This was the largest increase since the beginning of the 20th century. Immigration is projected to be even higher between 1990 and the year 2000. Industry observers suggest that this increase will partially compensate for the decreased housing demand resulting from the aging population.

Environmental Concerns

Over the past 20 years the construction industry has become much more environmentally aware. New technologies—combined with a growing appreciation of the limited availability of natural resources—have led industry workers to rely more on recycled materials and on "earth-friendly" practices.

Although government environmental regulations have made construction more costly, they also have helped industry workers develop valuable new skills. Construction workers in the United States are among the world's best at environmental management. Workers have developed new systems for disposing of hazardous waste and have become skilled at solving problems at construction sites where toxic substances taint the soil or groundwater.

Worker Safety and Health Care

Even though on-site safety has improved dramatically in recent years, areas of concern remain. Some construction materials once thought to be safe, such as asbestos insulation, have proven to be dangerous. Although such materials are no longer used in new construction, older structures may contain them. Workers involved in the renovation of such structures may encounter these toxic substances.

A related issue in the construction industry is that of rising health care costs for workers. In a recent industry survey, construction firms reported that their greatest challenge is meeting insurance costs, particularly in health insurance and workers' compensation. Such increasing expenses may eventually be passed on to the consumer, thus affecting the demand for new housing. Possible future health care legislation will not only affect industry costs but also may have an effect on the demand for new health care facilities.

EMPLOYMENT OPPORTUNITIES

The construction industry employs a great number of people, and industry observers project that between the years 1992 and 2006, the number of construction workers will increase from 4.5 million to 5.6 million. Many of these jobs will most likely shift from residential construction to public works construction and will involve repairing the nation's aging infrastructure.

The future may also bring a more competitive job market. In 1992 the average age of workers was 37.2 years. By the year 2006 the average age will be 40.5 years. As a result, more experienced workers will probably be vying for the same positions.

One of the fastest-growing construction careers between now and the year 2006 will be that of construction manager. The increased size and complexity of many construction projects, along with the use of new methods and materials, will necessitate an increased demand for experienced people to manage these complex projects.

Jobs for Women and Minorities

Although women and minorities have made great strides in the construction industry, they are still trying

In construction, as in other male-dominated fields, women are beginning to make themselves known.

Construction

Projected Change in Employment for Selected Occupations, 1996–2006

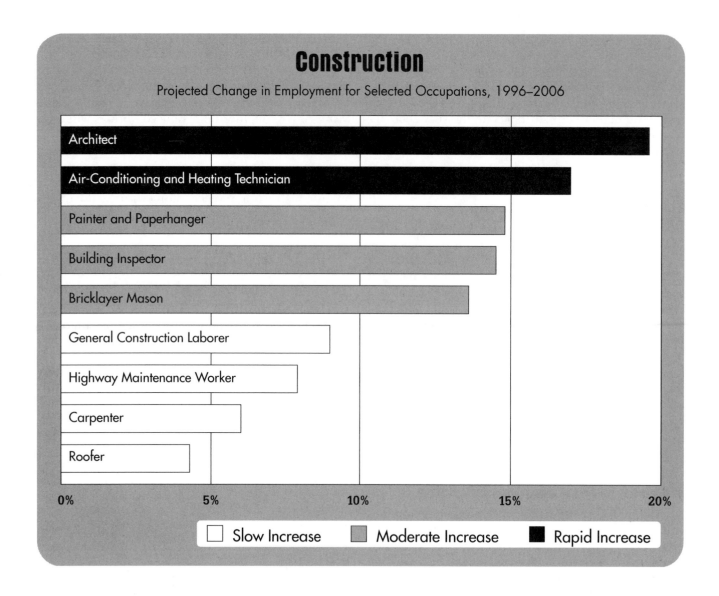

to make inroads into certain types of jobs. During the recessions of the 1980s and 1990s, there were fewer apprenticeship programs, so fewer minorities could prepare for construction jobs. Those already in the industry were often among the workers with the least experience. When jobs were scarce, they lost out to senior workers. However, many large construction companies are currently making special efforts to hire women and minorities.

African Americans, Hispanics, and other minorities have been entering the construction trades in greater numbers since the civil rights laws were enacted in the 1960s and 1970s. Some experts say that one possibility for women and minorities looking for jobs in construction is to seek self-employment and entrepreneurial roles. Today, women and African Americans account for half of those entering professional design programs.

Good jobs rarely, if ever, just fall out of the sky. As anybody who has ever been in the job market knows, getting the right job takes planning, perseverance, and patience. There are, however, a number of ways to make the process easier and more rewarding. This is true whether you are looking for your first job, reentering the job market, trying to get a new job, or planning a mid-career change.

This essay is designed to serve as your guide to the process of finding a job in the field of construction. It starts off with the basics—helping you define your career objectives. Then it takes you through a number of steps you can use to work out a strategy to achieve these goals.

EVALUATING YOURSELF

Most people enjoy doing a job well. Apart from any praise from employers or fellow workers, there is an inner satisfaction in knowing that you've taken on a challenge and then succeeded in accomplishing something worthwhile. If you are unhappy or dissatisfied in your job and are just trying to do enough to get by, you may not be in the right job or the right field.

Making a Self-Inventory Chart

Before you make any career decisions, think about areas that interest you and things you do well. One way to go about this is to compile a self-inventory chart. Such a chart will be helpful when you decide what jobs you want to consider. It will also save time when you write cover letters and resumes, fill in applications, and prepare for job interviews.

Begin your self-inventory chart by listing all the jobs you have ever had, including summer employment, part-time jobs, volunteer work, and any freelance or short-term assignments you have done. Include the dates of employment, the names and addresses of supervisors, and the amount of money you earned. Then add a similar list of your hobbies and other activities, including any special experiences you have had, such as travel. Next, do the same for your education, listing your schools, major courses of study, grades, special honors or awards, courses you particularly enjoyed, and extracurricular activities.

In determining what you do well and what you enjoy doing, you may find a career pattern beginning to develop. If the picture still lacks detail or focus, try making a list of aptitudes, and then rate yourself *above average, average,* or *below average* for each one. Some of the qualities you might include in your list are administrative, analytic, athletic, clerical, language, leadership, managerial, manual, mathematical, mechanical, sales, and verbal abilities. You might also rate your willingness to accept responsibility and your ability to get along with people.

Compiling a Work Characteristics Checklist

Another way to choose a career path is to compile a checklist. Go through the questions in the "Work Characteristics Checklist" and then make a list of the work characteristics that are most important to you.

Do not expect a job to meet all your requirements. You have to consider which job characteristics are most important to you. If the characteristics of a job match most of your preferences, you might want to give the position serious consideration.

Work Characteristics Checklist

Do you want a job in which you can

- work outdoors?
- be physically active?
- work with your hands?
- be challenged mentally?
- work with machines?
- work independently?
- work on a team?
- follow clear instructions?
- earn a lot of money?
- have a chance for quick promotion?
- have good benefits?
- travel in your work?
- work close to home?
- work regular hours?
- have a flexible schedule?
- have a variety of tasks?
- have supervisory power?
- express your own ideas?
- be a decision maker?

Evaluating Your Career Options

It's important to evaluate yourself and your career options realistically. If you need help doing this, you can consult an experienced career counselor or take on-line aptitude tests.

Most guidance and counseling departments of high schools, vocational schools, and colleges provide vocational testing and counseling. Some local offices of the state employment services affiliated with the federal employment service offer free counseling. Career centers also offer these services.

Although vocational interest and aptitude testing can be done with paper and pencil, a variety of on-line programs can be used to test your interests and aptitudes. The results are measured against job skills and your personal profile is matched with potential jobs to show the training that is necessary. Some of these programs are self-administered on a personal computer whereas others must be administered and interpreted by a counselor.

Most major cities have professional career consultants and career counseling firms. You should, however, check their reputations before paying for their services. A list of counseling services in your area is available from the American Counseling Association, 5999 Stevenson Avenue, Alexandria, VA 22304 (www.counseling.org). (If you write, send a stamped, self-addressed envelope.)

You can also use the World Wide Web for services that career counselors would provide. Some sites have on-line counselors who can help you with a variety of tasks, such as obtaining information on jobs, careers, and training. They may be able to provide information on available services, including housing assistance, day care facilities, and transportation.

EVALUATING SPECIFIC JOBS

After you have taken a good look at what you do well and what you enjoy doing, you need to see how different jobs measure up to your abilities and interests. First, make a note of all the jobs in this volume that interest you. Then examine the education and training required for these jobs. Decide whether you qualify and, if not, whether you have the resources available to gain the qualifications. If possible, talk with someone who has such a job. Firsthand information can be invaluable. Also look through the appropriate trade and professional journals listed at the end of this essay and check the sections in this volume called "Resources" for books, audiovisual materials, and web sites that contain more detailed information about the job. In addition, counselors usually have helpful information on careers in construction. For more detailed information, you can call or write to any of the trade and professional associations listed at the end of each occupational profile.

Once you have found out all you can about a particular job, compare the features of the job with your work characteristics checklist. See how many characteristics of the job match your work preferences. By completing these steps for all the jobs that appeal to you, you should be able to come up with a list of jobs that match your interests and abilities.

WAYS TO FIND JOB OPENINGS

Once you've decided what kind of job suits you, the next step is to look for available positions. Obviously, the more openings you can find, the better your chance of landing a job. People usually apply for a number of job openings before they are finally accepted.

There are many ways to find out about job openings. A number of job-hunting techniques are explained on the pages that follow and information is given on how you can follow up on job leads.

Applying in Person

For some jobs, especially entry-level positions, your best method may be to apply directly to the company or companies for which you would like to work. If you are looking for a position as a bricklayer or painter, for example, you might make an appointment to see the person responsible for hiring. This is a good method to use when jobs are plentiful or when a company is expanding. However, applicants for professional or supervisory positions generally need to send a cover letter and resume to the company first.

Applying in person will sharpen your interviewing techniques and give you a look at different places of employment. However, in most fields, it is not the method to use unless you are directed to do so.

Phone and Letter Campaigns

To conduct a phone campaign, use the Yellow Pages of your telephone directory to build a list of companies for which you might like to work. Call their personnel departments and find out whether they have any openings. This technique is not useful in all situations, however. If you're calling from out of town, a phone campaign can be very expensive. You may not be able to make a strong impression by phone. You also will not have a written record of your contacts.

Letter-writing campaigns can be very effective if the letters are well thought-out and carefully prepared. Your letters should always be typed. Handwritten letters and photocopied letters convey a lack of interest or motivation.

You may be able to get good lists of company addresses in your field of interest by reading the trade and professional publications listed at the end of this essay. Many of the periodicals publish directories or directory issues. Other sources you can use to compile lists of companies are the trade unions and professional organizations listed at the end of each job profile in this volume. The reference librarian at your local library can also help you find appropriate directories.

You can e-mail letters to human resource departments of companies with web sites, too. Be sure, however, that you follow all the same guidelines as you would for a letter you mail.

Your letters should be addressed to the personnel or human resources department of the organization. If possible, send it to a specific person. If you don't know who the correct person is, try to find the name of the personnel director through the directories in the library. You can also call on the phone and say, "I'm writing to ask about employment at your company. To whom should I address my letter?" If you can't find a name, use a standard salutation. It's a good idea to enclose a resume (described later in this essay) with the letter to give the employer a brief description of your education and work experience.

Keep a list of all the people you write to, along with the date each letter was mailed, or keep a photocopy of each letter. Then you can follow up by writing a brief note or calling people who do not reply within about 3 weeks.

Job Databases on the Web

The latest tool to use in looking for a job is the World Wide Web. The Internet currently has thousands of career-related sites to use to find job openings and to post your resume. Some sites, such as The Monster Board (www.monsterboard.com), help you build a resume and post it on-line as well as allow you to search through a massive database of help-wanted listings. Others, including E.span (www.espan.com), employ a search engine to find jobs that match your background, then post your resume on-line for employers. Another site called CareerBuilder (www.careerbuilder.com) has an interactive personal search agent that lets you key in job criteria such as location, title, and salary, and then it e-mails you when a matching position is posted in the database.

If you find a job that interests you in an ad on the web, you can respond by sending your resume and cover letter directly to the employer. Many companies even post job openings of their own in their company's human resource web pages. This allows you to target specific firms. Job hunters in many fields can also use professional associations to find jobs.

Some states, such as New Jersey, even have a home page (www.wnjpin.state.nj.us) designed to meet the needs of four groups: job seekers, students looking to make career choices, career counselors, and employers looking for workers. This one-stop career center has direct links to a variety of job listing sites on the web. You can post your resume, get information on training and education required for various jobs, read about occupations in demand, and even find out about job fairs.

Job Finder's Checklist

The following list of job-hunting tips may seem obvious, but getting all the bits and pieces in order beforehand helps when you're looking for a job.

Resume. Find out whether you will need a resume. If so, bring your resume up to date or prepare a new one. Assemble a supply of neatly typed copies or have a resume ready to e-mail to prospective employers.

References. Line up your references. Ask permission of the people whose names you would like to use. Write down their addresses, phone numbers, and job titles.

Contacts. Put the word out to everyone you know that you are looking for a job.

Job market. Find out where the jobs are. Make a list of possible employers in your field of interest.

Research. Do a little homework ahead of time—it can make a big difference in the long run. Find out as much as you can about a job—the field, the company—before you apply for it. A well-informed job applicant makes a good impression.

Organization. Keep a file on your job-hunting campaign with names and dates of employers contacted, ads answered, results, and follow-up.

Appearance. Make sure that the clothes you plan to wear to an interview are neat and clean. You may need to dress more formally than you would on the job, particularly if you are visiting a personnel office or meeting with a manager. Keep in mind that people may form an opinion of you based on their first impressions.

Help-Wanted Ads

Many people find out about job openings by reading the help-wanted sections of newspapers, trade journals, and professional magazines. Many employers and employment agencies use help-wanted classifieds to advertise available jobs.

Classified ads have their own telegraphic language. You will find some common abbreviations in the chart in this essay entitled "Reading the Classifieds." You can usually decode the abbreviations by using common sense, but if one puzzles you, call the newspaper and ask for a translation. Classified ads explain how to contact the employer, and they usually list the qualifications that are required.

As you find openings that interest you, follow up on each ad by using the method requested. You may be asked to call a specific person or send a resume. Record the date of your follow-up, and if you don't hear from the employer within 2 to 3 weeks, place another call or send a polite note asking whether the job is still open. Don't forget to include your phone number and address.

Some help-wanted ads are "blind ads." These ads give a box number but no name, phone number, or address. Employers and employment agencies may place these ads to avoid having to reply to all of the job applicants. In other words, you may not receive a response after answering a blind ad.

Situation-Wanted Ads

Another way to get the attention of potential employers is with a situation-wanted ad. You can place one of these in the classified section of your local newspaper or of a trade journal in your field of interest. Many personnel offices and employment agencies scan these columns when they're looking for new employees. The situation-wanted ad is usually most effective for people who have advanced education, training, or experience, or who are in fields that are in great demand.

A situation-wanted ad should be brief, clear, and to the point. Its main purpose is to interest the employer enough so you are contacted for an interview. It should tell exactly what kind of job you want, why you qualify, and whether you are available for full-time or part-time work. Use abbreviations that are appropriate.

If you are already employed and do not want it known that you are looking for a new position, you can run a blind ad. A blind ad protects your privacy by listing a box number at the publication to which all replies can be sent. They are then forwarded to you.

Reading the Classifieds

HELP WANTED	CLASSIFIED ABBREVIATIONS		SITUATION WANTED

HELP WANTED

Air-Conditioning Mechanic
Top mechanic for installation & service. Min. 3-yrs. exp. on commercial equipment. Chauffeurs license a must. Top pay per hr. & overtime. Gd. bnfts. 000-0000.

ARCHITECT
Architectural firm seeks senior architect experienced in shopping malls. Must possess management capabilities. Please forward resume to
Myers & Steele, Inc.
Long Avenue, City, State 12345
An Equal Opportunity Employer

BRICKLAYERS WANTED—Apply on job site. Lexington Industrial Park, Route 40W. Experienced, long job, good pay.

CONSTRUCTION—Purchasing & Contracting Agent. Major builder is seeking a purchasing & contracting agent with min. 4–5 yrs. exp. Responsibilities will include all purchasing & contracting activities, estimating, budgeting, and cost control. Excel. sal. & bnfts. Send resume with references to Eastwood Homes, Sweeney Avenue, City, State 12345.

CONSTRUCTION WORKERS—available for temp. work. Could lead to perm. job. Reply self-addressed stamped envelope. T 74631 Chronicle.

ELECTRICAL ESTIMATOR
with contractor experience in substations & switchgear.
Send resume to Box 72, City, State 12345.

ESTIMATOR—A firm of Engineers/Constructors requires an estimator thoroughly familiar with all constr. trades. Must be able to do take-offs and pricing for complete bid packages. Computerized estimating exp. pfd. Excellent growth potential. Call or send resume to Frank Hall, 000-0000, Starlight Co., 17 Ocean St., City, State 12345.

PLUMBER SUPERVISOR
for building maintenance co. Exp. in heating, sprinkler, genl. repairs & preventive maintenance programs. Call Mr. Camps 000-0000.

CLASSIFIED ABBREVIATIONS

a/c	air conditioning
bkgd.	background
co.	company
col.	college
constr.	construction
elect.	electrical
excel.	excellent
exp., expd.	experience, experienced
ext.	phone extension
fee neg.	fee negotiable (fee can be worked out with employer)
figs.	figures
f/p., f/pd.	fee paid (agency fee paid by employer)
f/t	full time
genl.	general
gd. bnfts.	good benefits
grad.	graduate
incl.	including
K	thousand
M	thousand
mech.	mechanic, mechanical
mfr.	manufacturer
mgr.	manager
min.	minimum
oppty.	opportunity
perm.	permanent
pfd.	preferred
p/t	part time
pvt.	private
refrig.	refrigeration
refs.	references
sal.	salary
skls.	skills
supvr.	supervisor
temp.	temporary
trnee.	trainee
w/	with

SITUATION WANTED

ARCHITECT
NCARB
4 yrs. Seeks design exp. For resume write P.O. Box 1692, City, State 12345.

BRICKLAYER—Cement work. Call anytime. 000-0000.

CARPENTER
Paneling, roofing, plumbing, masonry, general remodeling. 20 yrs. exp. 000-0000.

CONSTRUCTION
Jr. Estimator, or superintendent. 000-0000 after 6.

ESTIMATOR
Painting—new & alterations takeoff for bidding, commercial & pvt. projects.
X 473 Chronicle.

EXPERIENCED DRAFTER
Desires full-time permanent drafting or drafting related position. Have experience in architectural and structural drawings. CAD literate.
Contact M 147 Tribune.

MASON desires stone work, patio, bricklaying. Call Charlie, 000-0000.

MECHANIC
Elect. Mech. weld, pneumatic. Supvr. Can adapt. 000-0000.

PAINTER, expd.—new look in painting. Also wallpapering. Insured. **Free estimates.** Call 000-0000.

PLUMBER, service work, exp., Lincoln area. Call 000-0000.

TRAINED HELPERS
Available. No fee. A/C-Refrig.-Plumbing-Electrical-Carpentry.
MADISON AGENCY
000-0000

You do not need to give your name, address, or phone number in the ad.

Networking

A very important source of information about job openings is networking. This means talking with friends and acquaintances about jobs in your area of interest. For example, if you would like to work in architecture, get in touch with all the people you know who work as architects, drafters, engineers, or surveyors. Speak with people you know who have friends or relatives in the field.

There's nothing wrong with telling everyone who will listen that you are looking for a job—family, friends, counselors, and former employers. This will multiply your sources of information many times over.

You can use the web to make contacts, too. You can meet people with similar interests in news groups, which are organized by topic. Then you can write to them by e-mailing back and forth. Many fields have professional organizations that maintain web sites. You might use them to keep current on news affecting your field.

Sometimes a contact knows about a job vacancy before it is advertised. You can have an advantage, then, when you get in touch with the employer. Don't, however, use the contact's name without permission. Don't assume that a contact will go out on a limb by recommending you, either. Once you have received the inside information, rely on your own ability to get the job.

Placement Services

Most vocational schools, high schools, and colleges have a placement or career service that maintains a list of job openings and schedules visits from companies. If you are a student or recent graduate, you should check there for job leads. Many employers look first in technical or trade schools and colleges for qualified applicants for certain jobs. Recruiters often visit colleges to look for people to fill technical and scientific positions. These recruiters usually represent large companies. Visit your placement office regularly to check the job listings, and watch for scheduled visits by company recruiters.

State Employment Services

Another source of information about job openings is the local office of the state employment service. Many employers automatically list job openings at the local office. Whether you're looking for a job in private industry or with the state, these offices, which are affiliated with the federal employment service, are worth visiting.

Notes on Networking

Let people know you're looking. Tell friends, acquaintances, teachers, business associates, former employers—anyone who might know of job openings in your field.

Read newspapers and professional and trade journals. Look for news of developments in your field and for names of people and companies you might contact.

Use the World Wide Web. Make contacts through news groups, or find out information on web sites for professional organizations in your field.

Join professional or trade associations in your field. Contacts you make at meetings could provide valuable job leads. Association newsletters generally carry useful information about people and developments in the field.

Attend classes or seminars. You will meet other people in your field at job-training classes and professional development seminars.

Participate in local support groups. You can gain information about people and places to contact though support groups such as Women in Business, Job Seekers, Forty Plus, Homemakers Reentering the Job Market, as well as through alumni associations.

Be on the lookout. Always be prepared to make the most of any opportunity that comes along. Talk with anyone who can provide useful information about your field.

State employment service offices are public agencies that do not charge for their services. They can direct you to special programs run by the government in conjunction with private industry. These programs, such as the Work Incentive Program for families on welfare, are designed to meet special needs. Some, but not all, of these offices offer vocational aptitude and interest tests and can refer interested people to vocational training centers. The state employment service can be a valuable first stop in your search for work, especially if there are special circumstances in your background. For example, if you did not finish high school, if you have had any difficulties with the law, or if you are living in a difficult home environment, your state employment service office is equipped to help you.

Private Employment Agencies

State employment services, though free, are usually very busy. If you are looking for more personal service and want a qualified employment counselor to help you find a job, you might want to approach a private employment agency.

Private employment agencies will help you get a job if they think they can place you. Most of them get paid only if they're successful in finding you a job, so you need to show them that you are a good prospect. These agencies will help you prepare a resume if you need one, and they will contact employers they think might be interested in you.

Private employment agencies are in the business of bringing together people who are looking for jobs and companies that are looking for workers. For some positions, usually middle- and higher-level jobs, the employment agency's fee is often paid by the employer. In such cases, the job seeker pays no fee. In other cases, you may be required to pay the fee, which is usually a percentage of your annual salary. Paying a fee is a worthwhile investment if it leads to a rewarding career. In addition, the fee may be tax deductible.

Some agencies may also ask for a small registration fee whether or not you get a job through them. Some agencies may demand that you pay even if you find one of the jobs they are trying to fill through your other contacts. Just be sure to read and understand the fine print of any contract you're about to sign, and ask for a copy to take home. Since the quality of these agencies varies, check to see if an agency is a certified member of a state or national association.

Some employment agencies, called staffing services, operate in a different way. They are usually paid by employers to screen and refer good candidates for job openings. They earn money when they refer a candidate who is hired by the employer. The employee pays no fee. Staffing firms, however, only spend time on candidates they think they may be able to place.

Private employment agencies are usually helping many people at one time. They may not have the time to contact you every time they find a job opening. Therefore, you may need to phone them at reasonable intervals after you have registered.

Computer Placement Services

Computer placement services are basically data banks (computerized information files) to which you send your resume or employment profile. When a company that subscribes to the service has a job to fill, it can call up on its computer a certain combination of qualifications and quickly receive information on qualified candidates.

Computer placement is very limited in scope and in the number of users. It seems to be most useful for people looking for technical or scientific jobs.

Civil Service

In your search for work, don't forget that the civil service—federal, state, and local—may have many construction jobs. You may contact the state employment office or apply directly to the appropriate state or federal agency. The armed services also train and employ civilians in many fields, including construction. Don't neglect these avenues for finding jobs.

Civil service positions usually require you to take a civil service examination. Books are available to help you prepare for these examinations, and your local civil service office can give you information, too.

Unions

In many areas of construction, unions can be useful as sources of information. If you are a member of a union in your field of interest, you may be able to find out about jobs in the union periodical or through people at the union local. If you do not belong to a union, contact a union in the field you are interested in. In many fields in construction, contractors and the unions run apprenticeship programs that combine on-the-job training with classroom instruction. To find out about these, contact a local contractor or union in your field of interest.

Temporary Employment

A good way to get a feel for the job market—what's available and what certain jobs are like—is to work in a temporary job. Many construction projects require part-time help on a seasonal basis to take advantage of good weather and to meet deadlines. Carpenters, roofers, electricians, and other workers are all needed. To learn about part-time jobs, contact contractors or look for help-wanted ads.

Temporary employment can increase your job skills, your knowledge of a particular field, and your chances of hearing of permanent positions. In today's tight labor market, many companies are using the services of temporary workers in increasing numbers. In fact, temporary agencies may sign multimillion-dollar contracts to provide businesses with a range of temporary workers. In some cases, temporary workers are in such demand that they may receive benefits, bonuses, and the same hourly wages as equivalent full-time workers. Some temporary agencies are even joining with companies to create long-term career paths for their temporary workers.

PRESENTING YOURSELF ON PAPER

An employer's first impression of you is likely to be based on the way you present yourself on paper. Whether it is in an application form or on a resume, you will want to make a good impression so that employers will be interested in giving you a personal interview. A potential employer is likely to equate a well-written presentation that is neat with good work habits and a sloppy, poorly written one with bad work habits.

Writing an Effective Resume

When you write to follow up a lead or to ask about job openings, you should also send information about yourself. The accepted way of doing this is to send a resume with a cover letter.

The work *resume* is derived from the French word *résumer,* meaning "to summarize." A resume does just that—it briefly outlines your education, work experience, and special abilities and skills. A resume may also be called a curriculum vitae, a personal profile, or a personal data sheet. This summary can act as your introduction by mail or e-mail, as your calling card if you apply in person, and as a convenient reference for you to use when filling out an application form or when being interviewed.

A resume is a useful tool in applying for almost any job in the field of construction. It is valuable, even if you use it only to keep a record of where you have worked, for whom, and the dates of employment. A resume is usually required if you are being considered for positions at the professional or executive level. Prepare it carefully. It is well worth the effort.

The goal of a resume is to capture the interest of potential employers so they will call you for a personal interview. Since employers are busy people, the resume should be as brief and as neat as possible. You should, however, include as much relevant information about yourself as you can. This is usually presented under at least two headings: "Education" and "Experience." The latter is sometimes called "Employment History." Many people add a third section titled "Related Skills," "Professional Qualifications," or "Related Qualifications."

If you prepare a self-inventory such as the one described earlier, it will be a useful tool in preparing a resume. Go through your inventory, and select the items that show your ability to do the job or jobs in which you are interested. Plan to highlight these items on your resume. Select only those facts that point out your relevant skills and experience.

Once you have chosen the special points to include, prepare the resume. At the top, put your name, address, and phone number. After that, decide which items will be most relevant to the employer you plan to contact.

State Your Objective Some employment counselors advise that you state a job objective or describe briefly the type of position for which you are applying. The job objective usually follows your name and address. Don't be too specific if you plan to use the same resume a number of times. It's better to give a general career goal. Then, in a cover letter, you can be more specific about the position in which you are interested.

Describe What You've Done Every interested employer will check your educational background and employment history carefully. It is best to present these sections in order of importance. For instance, if you've held many relevant jobs, you should list your work experience first, followed by your educational background. On the other hand, if you are just out of school with little or no work experience, it's probably best to list your educational background first and then, under employment history, to mention any part-time and summer jobs or volunteer work you've done.

Under educational background, list the schools you have attended in reverse chronological order, starting with your most recent training and ending with the least recent. Employers want to know at a glance your highest qualifications. For each educational experience, include years attended, name and location of the school, and degree or certificate earned, if any. If you have advanced degrees (college and beyond), it isn't necessary to include high school and elementary school education. Don't forget to highlight any special courses you took or awards you won, if they are relevant to the kind of job you are seeking.

Chronological and Functional Resume Information about your employment history can be presented in two basic ways. The most common format is the chronological resume. In a chronological resume, you summarize your work experience year by year. Begin with your current or most recent employment and then work backward. For each job, list the name and location of the company for which you worked, the years you were employed, and the position or positions you held. The order in which you present these facts will depend on what you are trying to emphasize. If you want to call attention to the type or level of job you held, for example, you should put the job title first. Regardless of the order you choose, be consistent. Summer employment or part-time work should be identified as such. If you held a job for less than a year, specify months in the dates of employment.

It is important to include a brief description of the responsibilities you had in each job. This often reveals more about your abilities than the job title. Remember, too, that you do not have to mention the names of former supervisors or how much you earned. You can discuss these points during the interview or explain them on an application form.

The functional resume, on the other hand, emphasizes *what you can do* rather than *what you have done*. It is useful for people who have large gaps in their work history or who have relevant skills that would not be properly highlighted in a chronological listing of jobs. The functional resume concentrates on qualifications—such as familiarity with construction equipment, organizational skills, or managerial experience. Specific jobs may be mentioned, but they are not the primary focus of this type of resume.

Explain Special Skills You may wish to include a third section called "Related Skills," "Professional Qualifications," or "Related Qualifications." This is

DO YOU KNOW YOUR RIGHTS?

JOB DISCRIMINATION—WHAT IT IS

Federal and State Law

An employer cannot discriminate against you for any reason other than your ability to do the job. By federal law, an employer cannot discriminate against you because of your race, color, religion, sex, or national origin. The law applies to decisions about hiring, promotion, working conditions, and firing. The law specifically protects workers who are over the age of 40 from discrimination on the basis of age.

The law also protects workers with disabilities. Employers must make their workplaces accessible to individuals with disabilities—for example, by making them accessible to wheelchairs or by hiring readers or interpreters for blind or deaf employees.

Federal law offers additional protection to employees who work for the federal government or for employers who contract with the federal government. State law often provides protection also, for instance, by prohibiting discrimination on the basis of marital status, arrest record, political affiliations, or sexual orientation.

Affirmative Action

Affirmative action programs are set up by businesses that want to make a special effort to hire women and members of minority groups. Federal employers and many businesses that have contracts with the federal government are required by law to set up affirmative action programs. Employers with a history of discriminatory practices may also be required to establish affirmative action programs.

Discrimination Against Job Applicants

A job application form or interviewer may ask for information that can be used to discriminate against you illegally. The law prohibits such questions. If you are asked such questions and are turned down for the job, you may be a victim of discrimination. However, under federal law, employers must require you

to prove that you are an American citizen or that you have a valid work permit.

Discrimination on the Job

Discrimination on the job is illegal. Being denied a promotion for which you are qualified or being paid less than coworkers are paid for the same job may be forms of illegal discrimination.

Sexual, racial, and religious harassment are forms of discrimination and are prohibited in the workplace. On-the-job harassment includes sexual, racial, or religious jokes or comments. Sexual harassment includes not only requests or demands for sexual favors but also verbal or physical conduct of a sexual nature.

JOB DISCRIMINATION— WHAT YOU CAN DO

Contact Federal or State Commissions

If you believe that your employer practices unfair discrimination, you can complain to the state civil rights commission or the federal Equal Employment Opportunity Commission (EEOC). If, after investigating your complaint, the commission finds that there has been unfair discrimination, it will take action against the employer. You may be entitled to the job or promotion you were denied or to reinstatement if you were fired. You may also receive back pay or other financial compensation.

Contact a Private Organization

There are many private organizations that can help you fight job discrimination. For example, the American Civil Liberties Union (ACLU) works to protect all people from infringement on their civil rights. The National Association for the Advancement of Colored People (NAACP), National Organization for Women (NOW), and Native American Rights Fund may negotiate with your employer, sue on your behalf,

useful if there are points you want to highlight that do not apply directly to educational background or work experience. Be sure these points are relevant to the kind of work you are seeking. This section is most effective if you can mention any special recognition, awards, or other evidence of excellence. It is also useful to mention if you are willing to relocate or can work unusual hours.

Have References Available Employers may also want to know whom they can contact to find out more about you. At the start of your job search, you should ask three or four people if you may use them as references. If you haven't seen these people for a while, you may want to send them a copy of your resume and let them know what kind of position you're seeking. Your references should be the kind of people your potential employer will respect, and they should be able to comment favorably on your abilities, personality, and work habits. You should indicate whether these people are personal references or former work supervisors. Avoid using any

or start a class action suit—a lawsuit brought on behalf of all individuals in your situation.

WHAT TO DO IF YOU LOSE YOUR JOB

Being Fired and Being Laid Off

An employer usually has the right to fire an employee at any time. In many cases, however, an employer can fire you only if there is good cause, such as your inability to do the job, violation of safety rules, dishonesty, or chronic absenteeism.

Firing an employee because of that employee's race, color, religion, sex, national origin, or age (if the employee is over 40) is illegal. Firing an employee for joining a union or for reporting an employer's violation (called whistle-blowing) is also prohibited. If you believe you have been wrongfully discharged, you should contact the EEOC or the state civil rights commission.

At times, employers may need to let a number of employees go to reduce costs. This reduction in staff is called a layoff. Laying off an employee has nothing to do with the employee's job performance. Federal law requires employers who lay off large numbers of employees to give these employees at least two months' notice of the cutback.

Unemployment Compensation

Unemployment insurance is a state-run fund that provides payments to people who lose their jobs through no fault of their own. Not everyone is entitled to unemployment compensation. Those who quit their jobs or who worked only a few months before losing their jobs may not be eligible.

The amount of money you receive depends on the amount you earned at your last job. You may receive unemployment payments for only a limited period of time and only so long as you can prove that you are actively looking for a new position.

Each claim for unemployment compensation is investigated before the state makes any payments. If the state unemployment agency decides to deny you compensation, you may ask the agency for instructions on how to appeal that decision.

OTHER PROTECTIONS FOR EMPLOYEES

Honesty and Drug Testing

Many employers ask job applicants or employees to submit to lie-detector tests or drug tests. Lie-detector tests are permitted in the case of high-security positions, such as police officers. Some states prohibit or restrict the testing of applicants or employees for drug use. Aptitude and personality tests are generally permitted.

Other Federal Laws

The Fair Labor Standards Act prescribes certain minimum wages and rules about working hours and overtime payments. Workers' compensation laws provide payment for injuries that occur in the workplace and wages lost as a result of those injuries.

The Occupational Safety and Health Act sets minimum requirements for workplace safety. Any employee who discovers a workplace hazard should report it to the Occupational Safety and Health Administration (OSHA). The administration will investigate the claim and may require the employer to correct the problem or pay a fine.

Rights Guaranteed by Contract

Not every employee has a written contract. If you do, however, that contract may grant you additional rights, such as the right to severance pay in the event you are laid off. In addition, employees who are members of a union may have certain rights guaranteed through their union contract.

Before you sign any contract, make sure you understand every part of it. Read it thoroughly and ask the employer questions. Checking the details of a contract before signing it may prevent misunderstanding later on.

LEON C. DAVIES

203 Walnut Street
Lansing, MI 54321
(000) 555-2424 Home
(000) 555-1234 Message
lcdavies.thom.com

RESUME SUMMARY:

Ten years' experience in construction engineering.

EXPERIENCE:

1995 to present

Supervisory Engineer, Thomson Group Architects and Planners, Lansing, MI.
Consult with clients and designers: prepare proposals including detailed sketches, estimates, and schedules; supervise preparation of all drawings and materials lists. Consult with contractors and prepare organization plans. Conduct regular site visits to inspect and report on construction.

1990 to 1995

Associate Engineer, Eagle Construction Company, Inc., Detroit, MI.
Supervised construction site. Responsible for implementation of plans for building structure, electricity, heating and ventilation, and other systems. Inspected each phase of project. Solved structural problems as they arose. Consulted with clients, architects, design engineers, technicians, and crew supervisors.

1987 to 1990

Junior Engineer, Tyler & Wells Design Associates, Detroit, MI.
Prepared drawings and plans for company projects. Consulted with estimators, contractors, and senior engineers to prepare reports that accompanied plans.

PROFESSIONAL QUALIFICATIONS:

State license: Registered Civil Engineer in Michigan.
Member: American Society of Civil Engineers.

EDUCATION:

1987

Bachelor of Science in Civil Engineering, Ur
Charlottesville, VA. Courses included therm
electric circuits, stress analysis, and struc

REFERENCES:

Available upon request.

- State your name, address, and telephone number first.
- State job objective or general career goal in a few words.
- List education and work experience in reverse chronological order, with most recent item first.

MARISSA ONO
612 St. Martin's Road, Raleigh, NC 02345   *(000) 325-4848*

OBJECTIVE: Position as construction electrician.

EXPERIENCE:

1993 to 1998   **ASSISTANT ELECTRICIAN**
Dependable Electrical Contractors, Inc., Raleigh, NC.
Completed assembly, installation, and wiring of electrical systems. Worked on lighting, heating, and power systems. Acquired knowledge of state and local building and electrical codes, blueprints, and wiring diagrams.

1992 to 1993   **ASSISTANT**
Sherman Electric, Charlotte, NC.
Assisted with electrical installations and repairs for residential clients. Repaired and serviced electrical appliances. Responsible for cleaning and maintaining tools and company vehicle. Part-time.

EDUCATION:

1994   Completed apprenticeship as union electrician.

1990   **GRADUATE**
Tri-County Technical High School, Charlotte, NC.
Courses in math, physics, and electronics.

**RELATED
QUALIFICATIONS:**   Currently preparing for master electrician's license examination.

Valid driver's license.

**PROFESSIONAL
EQUIPMENT:**   Complete set of electrician's hand tools.

REFERENCES: Available upon request.

- List your work experience first if it is more important than your educational background.
- Keep descriptions of your education and work experience brief.
- List special skills and qualifications if they are relevant to the job.

relatives. You can list the names and addresses of your references at the end of your resume or in a cover letter. Or, you can simply write, "References available upon request." Just be sure you have their names, addresses, and phone numbers ready if you are asked.

Present Yourself Concisely Tips for making your resume concise include using phrases instead of sentences and omitting unnecessary words. When appropriate, start a sentence with a verb, such as *maintained* or *coordinated*. There is no need to say "I"—that is obvious and repetitive.

Present Yourself Well Employment counselors often recommend that resumes be no longer than one page because employers won't take the time to read a second page. If you've held many positions related to your occupation, go on to the second page, but don't include beginning or irrelevant jobs. If you have a lot of work experience, limit the education section to just the essentials.

You should also concentrate on the appearance of your resume. It should be typed on a good grade of 8½" × 11" white bond paper. If you can't type, a professional typist can do it for you for a small charge. Be sure that it is neatly typed with adequate margins. The data should be spaced and indented so that each item stands out. This enables a busy executive or personnel director to see at a glance the facts of greatest interest.

You will probably need many copies of your resume during your job search. Each copy should be as neat and as clear as your original. If possible, input your resume on a computer and print copies on a good-quality printer. You may want to have your resume reproduced professionally. A photo-offset printer can make several hundred excellent copies for a moderate fee. A photocopying machine may be more economical for smaller quantities.

These suggestions for writing a resume are not hard-and-fast rules. Resumes may be adapted to special situations. For example, people with a variety of work experience often prepare several versions of their resume and use the experience that's most relevant when applying for a particular job.

If this is your first resume, show it to someone else, perhaps a guidance counselor, for constructive advice. No matter what, be truthful while emphasizing your assets. You can do that by showing the abilities, skills, and specific interests that qualify you for a particular job. Don't mention any weaknesses or deficiencies in your training. Do mention job-related aptitudes that showed up in previous employment or in school. Don't make up things about yourself; everything that's in your resume can, and sometimes will, be checked.

Writing Cover Letters

When you send your resume through the mail or the Internet, you should send a cover letter with it. This is the same whether you are writing to apply for a specific job or just to find out if there are any openings.

A good cover letter should be neat, brief, and well written with no more than three or four short paragraphs. Since you may use your resume for a variety of job openings, your cover letter should be very specific. Try to get the person who reads it to think that you are an ideal candidate for a particular job. If at all possible, send the letter to a specific person, either to the personnel director or to the person for whom you would be working. If necessary, call the company and ask to whom you should write.

Start your letter by explaining why you are writing. Say that you are inquiring about possible job openings at the company, that you are responding to an advertisement in a particular publication, or that someone recommended that you should write. (Use the person's name if you have received permission to do so.)

Let your letter lead into your resume. Use it to call attention to your qualifications. Add information that shows why you are well suited for that specific job. The engineer in the sample letter points out that he is a registered engineer and emphasizes his interest in major construction development projects. In the second sample letter, the applicant for a position as an electrician explains her interest in the construction industry and indicates that she is taking steps to qualify for the necessary license.

Completing the Application Form

Many employers ask job applicants to fill out an application form. This form usually duplicates much of the information on your resume, but it may ask some additional questions. Give complete answers to all questions except those that are discriminatory. If a question doesn't apply to you, put a dash next to it.

You may be given the application form when you arrive for an interview, or it may be sent to your home. When filling it out, print neatly in ink. Follow the instructions carefully. For instance, if the form asks you to put down your last name first, do so.

The most important sections of an application form are the education and work histories. As in your resume, many applications request that you write these in reverse chronological order, with the most recent experience first. Unlike your resume, however, the application form may request information about your earnings on previous jobs. It may also ask what rate of pay you are seeking on this job.

LEON C. DAVIES

203 Walnut Street
Lansing, MI 54321
(000) 555-2424 Home
(000) 555-1234 Message
lcdavies.thom.com

February 18, 1999

Ms. Deborah Shapiro
Personnel Manager
Poe, Carter, and Sanchez
18 Rowan Avenue
Lansing, MI 54321

Dear Ms. Shapiro:

I am writing in response to the advertisement in *The Sunday City News* for a civil engineering
project manager. I am a registered professional engineer in the state of Michigan.

I am currently a supervisory engineer and have been involved in the planning and supervision of
building projects. I would like to move on to more complex development projects. I am familiar
with the work Poe, Carter, and Sanchez has done at the state office complex and the downtown
shopping area, and I feel that projects of this type would b

I enclose my resume as requested. I can be available any
reached at my office during business hours. I look forward

Very truly yours,

Leon C. Davies

Leon C. Davies

Enclosure

MARISSA ONO

612 St. Martin's Road, Raleigh, NC 02345   *(000) 325-4848*

July 22, 1999

Mr. Geoffrey Turner
Warner Corporation
State Highway Number 2
Raleigh, NC 02344

Dear Mr. Turner:

I am writing in reply to the advertisement in the *Evening Herald* for an electrician
to work on a hospital project. I am familiar with the city and state electrical codes
and have experience in installation and wiring.

I am very interested in continuing in the construction industry because I enjoy the
variety of electrical work involved. I am currently preparing for the master
electrician's license examination and expect to qualify in September.

I enclose my resume and hope that you will schedule an interview for me during
your interview day on August 5.

Very truly yours,

Marissa Ono

Marissa Ono

Enclosure

Be prepared to answer these and other topics not addressed on your resume. Look at the sample application form, and make note of the kinds of questions that you are likely to be asked—for example, your Social Security number, the names of previous supervisors, your salary, and your reason for leaving. If necessary, carry notes on such topics with you to an interview. You have a responsibility to tell prospective employers what they need to know to make an informed decision.

Neatness Counts Think before you write on an application form so you avoid crossing things out. An employer's opinion of you may be influenced just by the general appearance of your application form. A neat, clearly detailed form may indicate an orderly mind and the ability to think clearly, follow instructions, and organize information.

Know Your Rights Under federal and some state laws, an employer cannot demand that you answer any questions about race, color, creed, national origin, ancestry, sex, marital status, age (with certain exceptions), number of dependents, property, car ownership (unless needed for the job), or arrest record. Refer to the information on job discrimination in this essay for more information about your rights.

PRESENTING YOURSELF IN AN INTERVIEW

An interview is the climax of your job-hunting efforts. On the basis of this meeting, the prospective employer will decide whether or not to hire you, and you will decide whether or not you want the job.

Prepare in Advance

Before an interview, there are a number of things you can do to prepare. Begin by giving some more thought to why you want the job and what you have to offer. Then review your resume and any lists you made when you were evaluating yourself so that you can keep your qualifications firmly in mind.

Learn as much as you can about the organization. Check with friends who work there, read company brochures, search the Internet, or devise other information-gathering strategies. Showing that you know something about the company and what it does will indicate your interest.

Try to anticipate some of the questions the interviewer may ask and think of how you would answer. For example, you may be asked: Will you work overtime when necessary? Are you ready to go to night school to improve some of your skills? Preparing answers in advance will make the process easier for you. It is also wise to prepare any questions you may

have about the company or the position for which you are applying. The more information you have, the better you can evaluate both the company and the job.

Employers may want you to demonstrate specific skills for some jobs. Employers may ask to see licenses held by electricians or surveyors indicating that they have passed standard examinations in their fields.

On the appointed day, dress neatly and in a style appropriate for the job you're seeking. When in doubt, it's safer to dress on the conservative side, wearing a tie rather than a turtleneck or wearing a dress or blouse and skirt rather than pants and a T-shirt.

Be on time. Find out in advance exactly where the company is located and how to get there. Allow extra time in case you get lost, get caught in a traffic jam, can't find a parking spot, or encounter another type of delay.

Maintain a Balance

When your appointment begins, remember that a good interview is largely a matter of balance. Don't undersell yourself by sitting back silently and don't oversell yourself by talking nonstop about how wonderful you are. Answer all questions directly and simply, and let the interviewer take the lead.

Instead of saying, "I'm reliable and hardworking," give the interviewer an example. Allow the interviewer to draw conclusions from your example.

It's natural to be nervous before and during a job interview. However, you need to try to relax and be yourself. You may even enjoy the conversation. Your chances of being hired and being happy if you get the job are better if the employer likes you as you are.

Avoid discussing money until the employer brings it up or until you are offered the job. Employers usually know in advance what they are willing to pay. If you are the one to begin a discussion about the salary you want, you may set an amount that's either too low or too high.

Be prepared to ask questions, but don't force them on your interviewer. Part of the purpose of the interview is for you to evaluate the company while you are being evaluated. For instance, you might want to ask about the company's training programs and its policy on promotions.

Don't stay too long. Most business people have busy schedules. It is likely that the interviewer will let you know when it's time for the interview to end.

Don't expect a definite answer at the first interview. Employers usually thank you for coming and say that you will be notified shortly. Most employers want to interview all the applicants before they make a hiring decision. If the position is offered at the time of the interview, you can ask for a little

1. Always print neatly in blue or black ink. When completing an application at home, type it, if possible.

2. Read the application carefully *before* you start to fill it out. Follow instructions precisely. Use standard abbreviations.

3. If you aren't applying for a specific job, indicate the kind of work you're willing to do.

4. You don't have to commit to a specific rate of pay. Write "open" or "negotiable" if you are uncertain.

5. Traffic violations and so on do not belong here. Nor do offenses for which you were charged but not convicted.

6. If a question doesn't apply to you, write "NA" (for not applicable) or put a dash through the space.

7. Take notes along to remind you of school names, addresses, and dates.

8. If you're short on "real" employment, mention jobs such as babysitting, lawn mowing, or any occasional work.

9. Your references should be people who can be objective about you, such as former employers, teachers, and community leaders.

10. Under the heading "Reason for Leaving," a simple answer will do. Avoid saying "better pay"—even if it's so.

APPLICATION FOR EMPLOYMENT

NAME (LAST)	(FIRST)	(MIDDLE)	SOCIAL SECURITY NO.

PRESENT ADDRESS	CITY	STATE	ZIP CODE	AREA CODE	TELEPHONE NO.

PERMANENT ADDRESS	(IF DIFFERENT FROM ABOVE)	AREA CODE	TELEPHONE NO.

POSITION APPLIED FOR	DATE AVAILABLE
SALARY OR WAGE DESIRED	WILL YOU RELOCATE?	REFERRED BY
ARE YOU A U.S. CITIZEN? YES _____ NO _____	IF NOT A U.S. CITIZEN, LIST VISA NUMBER AND EXPIRATION DATE: NUMBER _____ DATE _____

WITHIN THE LAST FIVE YEARS HAVE YOU BEEN CONVICTED OF A FELONY?	☐ YES ☐ NO	IF YES, GIVE DETAILS ON BACK PAGE	HAVE YOU EVER BEEN EMPLOYED BY OUR COMPANY? IF YES, GIVE DETAILS ON BACK PAGE	☐ YES ☐ NO

EDUCATION	INSTITUTION NAME AND ADDRESS	DID YOU GRADUATE?	MAJOR FIELD OF STUDY	CLASS STANDING
HIGH SCHOOL				
COLLEGE OR UNIVERSITY				
GRADUATE STUDY				
OTHER				

EMPLOYMENT RECORD

PLEASE LIST ALL EMPLOYMENT STARTING WITH MOST RECENT. ACCOUNT FOR ALL PERIODS (INCLUDING U.S. ARMED FORCES, PERIODS OF UNEMPLOYMENT, AND VOLUNTARY SERVICES).

LIST YOUR MOST RECENT POSITION HELD	MAY WE CONTACT YOUR PRESENT EMPLOYER? ☐ YES ☐ NO	
EMPLOYER'S NAME AND COMPLETE ADDRESS/PHONE	DATES EMPLOYED	POSITION TITLE
	FROM TO	NAME AND TITLE OF SUPERVISOR
	SALARY	
	START FINAL	REASON FOR LEAVING
EMPLOYER'S NAME AND COMPLETE ADDRESS/PHONE	DATES EMPLOYED	POSITION TITLE
	FROM TO	NAME AND TITLE OF SUPERVISOR
	SALARY	
	START FINAL	REASON FOR LEAVING
EMPLOYER'S NAME AND COMPLETE ADDRESS/PHONE	DATES EMPLOYED	POSITION TITLE
	FROM TO	NAME AND TITLE OF SUPERVISOR
	SALARY	
	START FINAL	REASON FOR LEAVING

PERSONAL REFERENCES

NAME	ADDRESS	PHONE NUMBER
1.		
2.		
3.		

time to think about it. If the interviewer tells you that you are not suitable for the job, try to be polite. Say, "I'm sorry, but thank you for taking the time to meet with me." After all, the company may have the right job for you next week.

Follow Up After the Interview

If the job sounds interesting and you would like to be considered for it, say so as you leave. Follow up after the interview by writing a brief thank-you note to the employer. Express your continued interest in the position and thank the interviewer for taking the time to meet with you.

It's a good idea to make some notes and evaluations of the interview while it is still fresh in your mind. Write down the important facts about the job—the duties, salary, promotion prospects, and so on. Also evaluate your own performance in the interview. List the things you wish you had said and things you wish you had not said. These notes will help you make a decision later. They will also help you prepare for future interviews.

Finally, don't hesitate to contact your interviewer if you haven't heard from the company after a week or two (unless you were told it would be longer). Write a brief note or make a phone call in which you ask when a decision might be reached. Making such an effort will show the employer that you are genuinely interested in the job. Your call will remind the interviewer about you and could work to your advantage.

TAKE CHARGE

The field of construction offers many job opportunities. Job hunting is primarily a matter of organizing a well-thought-out campaign. Scan the classified ads, search through online job banks, watch for trends in local industry that might be reported in the news, and check with people you know in the field. Take the initiative. Send out well-crafted resumes and cover letters. Respond to help-wanted advertisements. Finally, in an interview, state your qualifications and experience in a straightforward and confident manner.

TRADE AND PROFESSIONAL JOURNALS

The following is a list of some of the major journals in the field of construction. These journals can keep you up-to-date with what's happening in your field of interest. These publications can also lead you to jobs through their own specialized classified advertising sections.

Construction Planning, Architecture, and Management

Architectural Record, 1221 Avenue of the Americas, New York, NY 10020.
www.mcgraw-hill.com/corporate/news-info/locator
Architecture, 1130 Connecticut Avenue, NW, Suite 625, Washington, DC 20036.
www.bpi.com
Building Design and Construction, 1350 East Touhy Avenue, P.O. Box 5080, Des Plaines, IL 60018-5080.
www.bdcmag.com
Construction Equipment, 1350 East Touhy Avenue, P.O. Box 5080, Des Plaines, IL 60018-5080.
www.pacdigest.com/mathmag/cc.htm
Construction Specifier, 601 Madison Street, Alexandria, VA 22314.
www.csinet.org
Constructor, 1957 E Street, NW, Washington, DC 20006.
agc.org
Interior Design, 245 West 17th Street, New York, NY 10011.

Finishing Trades

Woodwork, P.O. Box 1529, Ross, CA 94957.
Workbench, KC Publishing Inc., 700 West 47th Street, Suite 310, Kansas City, MO 64111.

Mechanical Trades

Airconditioning, Heating & Refrigeration News, P.O. Box 2600, Troy, MI 48007.
www.bup.com/the news
ASHRAE Journal, American Society of Heating, Refrigerating, and Air-Conditioning Engineers, Inc., 1791 Tullie Circle, NE, Atlanta, GA 30329.
www.ashrae.org
Construction Equipment, 1350 East Touhy Avenue, P.O. Box 5080, Des Plaines, IL 60018-5080.
www.packdigest.com/mainmag/ce.htm
Electrical Construction and Maintenance, 9800 Metcalf, Overland Park, KS 66212.
www.intertec.com/pubs/ecm.htm
Heating-Piping-Air Conditioning, 1100 Superior Avenue, Cleveland, OH 44114-2543.

Structural Trades

Aberdeen's Concrete Construction, 426 South Westgate Street, Addison, IL 60101.
www.wochet.com/mags/cc.htm
Builder, 1 Thomas Circle, NW, Suite 600, Washington, DC 20005.
www.builderonline.com
Wood & Wood Products, 400 Knightsbridge Parkway, Lincolnshire, IL 60069.

Air-Conditioning, Heating, and Refrigeration Mechanic

Definition and Nature of the Work

Air-conditioning, heating, and refrigeration mechanics install, maintain, and repair cooling and heating equipment. Air-conditioning and heating equipment makes the air inside buildings cool in summer and warm in winter. This equipment is also used in cars, buses, and trains. Refrigeration machines are used in restaurants, hotels, supermarkets, and homes to make ice and to keep food cool or frozen. Without mechanics to install the proper equipment and fix it when it breaks down, many comforts of modern life would not exist.

Mechanics may specialize in one type of equipment. These specialists are called air-conditioning and refrigeration mechanics, furnace installers, oil burner mechanics, and gas burner mechanics. They may also specialize in installation or in maintenance and repair. Many workers are qualified in more than one of these areas.

Air-conditioning and refrigeration mechanics install and repair many different sizes of machines. A machine or unit may be large enough to cool an entire building or small enough to fit into a window to cool only one room. These mechanics follow blueprints and manufacturers' instructions to install the motors, compressors, condensing units, evaporators, pipes, and ducts that make up refrigeration or air-conditioning units. Since they must connect ducts and refrigerant (cooling) lines, mechanics must know how to weld and fit pipe. To do the necessary electrical work, mechanics must handle soldering irons and read wiring diagrams. The mechanics also put in refrigerant, the substance that makes refrigeration systems work. The refrigerant flows through the system and transfers heat from the inside of the refrigerator to the outside air. Finally, the mechanics check to see that the unit is working properly.

When air-conditioning or refrigeration equipment breaks down, mechanics determine the cause and make repairs. They test the equipment, electrical circuits, and control box, and they look for leaks in the system. They may remove worn parts, repair or replace them, seal leaks, and add refrigerant. In the winter, air-conditioning mechanics inspect the systems and do required maintenance work, such as overhauling compressors.

Furnace installers follow blueprints and manufacturers' instructions to put in oil, gas, electric, and multifuel heating systems. The installers must know how to install fuel lines, pumps, air ducts, and fans. They must know how to connect the electrical wiring, control box, timer, and temperature regulator. Once the furnace or heating unit is in place, the installer must test it to make sure it is working properly.

Oil burner mechanics service and maintain heating units that burn oil. The mechanic must check all the parts of an oil burner. These parts include the electrical controls, the burner nozzles and feed lines, the blower fan, and the air ducts or water pipes and radiators.

Gas burner mechanics fix and adjust heating systems that use natural gas. These systems include everything from large industrial furnaces and heating units to relatively small household stoves, clothes dryers, and water heaters.

Education and Training
None

Salary Range
Average—$535 a week

Employment Outlook
Good

During the summer, when heating systems are not used, mechanics do mainte-nance work, such as replacing filters and vacuuming vents, ducts, and other parts of the system that may accumulate dirt, soot, or ash.

Tools used by air-conditioning, heating, and refrigeration mechanics include hammers, wrenches, metal cutters, screwdrivers, electric drills, pipe cutters and threaders, welding torches, and electrical testing devices.

Education and Training Requirements

Air-conditioning, heating, and refrigeration systems are becoming more sophis-ticated. Most employers prefer to hire workers with technical school or appren-ticeship training. However, you can still enter this field informally with on-the-job training.

A high school education is important. While in school you should take classes in mathematics, mechanical drawing, physics, blueprint reading, machine shop, and electricity. You should also know something about microelectronics, the miniaturization of electronic circuits and components, since this technology is being used in equipment controls.

After high school you can join either a union apprenticeship or an on-the-job training program. To enter an apprenticeship you may have to pass a test and be approved by a joint labor-management committee. Apprenticeships usually last 4 years. Once in the program, you will work under a qualified mechanic. You will also take courses to learn the more technical aspects of your trade. After completing your apprenticeship, you will become a fully qualified mechanic.

Contractors and other employers run on-the-job training programs. Like union apprenticeships, the programs include both classroom study and supervised work experience. In both programs you are paid for your work, but you do not earn as much as a fully qualified mechanic. Generally your wages increase as your skill grows. Many vocational/technical schools and junior colleges offer courses in air-conditioning, heating, and refrigeration that may reduce the length of the training period or, in some cases, qualify you for a beginning job.

Getting the Job

There are many places to look for a job in the air-conditioning, heating, and re-frigeration industry. A good place to start is the Yellow Pages of your phone book. Check such headings as "Air-Conditioning—Equipment and Service," "Heating Equipment," and "Gas Furnaces." Listed under these and related head-ings will be companies you can contact about a beginning job. Be sure to check with fuel oil dealers and gas utility companies, too. Also, contact the appropriate labor union and ask about the apprenticeship program. Watch the classified ads in local newspapers. Check your state employment office for job listings.

Advancement Possibilities and Employment Outlook

Air-conditioning, heating, and refrigeration mechanics are already at the top of their craft. They may, however, become supervisors. They may be put in charge of a work crew or made responsible for servicing all of the units in a certain area. Some mechanics own their own service and repair shops, or they may be-come contractors or equipment suppliers.

Currently, approximately 256,000 workers are employed as air-conditioning, heat-ing, and refrigeration mechanics. This number is expected to increase as fast as the average for all occupations through the year 2006. As the population and econ-omy expand and new residential, commercial, and industrial structures are built, more air-conditioning, heating, and refrigeration mechanics will be needed to install climate-control systems. Most job openings will result from the need to replace workers who transfer to other occupations or leave the workforce.

The growth of the economy will determine the level of activity in the construction industry. However, repairs and general maintenance are always needed. The growing need to replace old air-conditioning, heating, and refrigeration systems with new, energy-efficient ones will also have an impact on the job outlook for air-conditioning, heating, and refrigeration mechanics.

Working Conditions

Air-conditioning, heating, and refrigeration mechanics work on construction job sites, in repair shops, and in homes—anywhere there is climate-control equipment. They may work outside in any kind of weather or inside in buildings that are too hot or too cold because the equipment is broken. They often work in cramped positions and are sometimes required to work in high places. They may be exposed to electrical shocks and may suffer burns, muscle strains, and other injuries from handling heavy equipment.

The number of weekly working hours varies within the field. For those who work for a contractor, equipment supplier and installer, utility company, or other firm, a 40-hour week is normal. Extra pay is earned for overtime. Mechanics who own and manage their own businesses often work longer hours, including nights and Saturdays. The season of the year also makes a difference. In hot weather, for example, more air-conditioners are used and more break down. During the winter months, heaters must be repaired most often. Mechanics who provide repair service must be prepared to make emergency house calls.

Earnings and Benefits

Earnings for mechanics vary, depending on where they work. The average salary earned is $535 a week. The lowest wages earned are $285 a week and the highest reach $885 a week. Apprentices start at about 50 percent of the experienced worker's wage and receive regular increases. Mechanics may receive health and life insurance, paid vacations, and pension plans.

Where to Go for More Information

Air-Conditioning and Refrigeration Institute
1650 South Dixie Highway, Fifth Floor
Boca Raton, FL 33432
(561) 338-3495

Industrial Heating Equipment Association
1901 North Fort Myer Drive
Arlington, VA 22209
(703) 525-2513
www.ihea.org

Refrigeration Service Engineers Society
1666 Rand Road
Des Plaines, IL 60016
(847) 297-6464
www.rses.org

Bricklayer

Definition and Nature of the Work

Bricklayers build walls, chimneys, fireplaces, and other structures made of brick. They also work with concrete and cinder blocks, stone, tile, marble, and terra cotta. Terra cotta is a ceramic material used for decoration. Bricklayers can do both construction and maintenance work. In construction, bricklayers build walls and partitions in private homes and public buildings. In maintenance, bricklayers repair existing structures, such as the brick linings in industrial furnaces, kilns, and fireplaces.

To build a brick wall, bricklayers construct the corners of the wall first. Then they stretch string from one corner of the wall to the other. This line is usually

Education and Training
None

Salary Range
Average—$480 a week

Employment Outlook
Good

A bricklayer uses a trowel—a flat, pointed tool made of metal—to spread a bed of mortar before putting the bricks into place.

called a gauge or course line. It is used as a guide so that the bricklayers build the wall straight. The bricklayers move the string up the wall with each row of bricks laid. Before bricklayers put the bricks in place, they spread a bed of mortar with a trowel. A trowel is a flat, pointed tool made of metal. Mortar is a kind of cement. They place the brick on the mortar and tap it into place. Bricklayers cut the brick to fit around doors, windows, and other openings.

Bricklayers use many tools, including trowels, brick hammers, chisels, levels, and rulers. Helpers do the heavy work, such as carrying materials and mixing the mortar. These helpers are known as *hod carriers*. Bricklayers and hod carriers generally work together on large projects. Bricklayers read blueprints and other specifications to be sure their work is accurate. They constantly check for both horizontal and vertical straightness with a mason's level. Bricklayers often specialize in specific materials. Some of these specialists include the terra cotta mason, the concrete block mason, and the hollow partition erector.

Education and Training Requirements

The best way to become a bricklayer is to complete a 3-year apprenticeship program, which may be sponsored by a union or a contractor. A high school diploma is desirable, especially for those who want to become apprentices. Apprentices should be at least 17 years of age. They should also have a good eye for straightness and a certain degree of manual dexterity. The 3-year program combines on-the-job training with at least 144 hours of classroom instruction each year.

On the job, apprentices work as helpers. They learn to mix and spread mortar, as well as how to handle and use the other materials and tools of the trade. By observing the qualified craft workers, the apprentices soon learn to build walls and partitions and to lay, point, and set blocks. In the classroom, they are taught to read blueprints, sketches, and layouts. They are also taught measurements.

Apprentices learn welding and the relationship of bricklaying to the other building trades.

Many bricklayers learn their trade while working as helpers, or hod carriers, for experienced bricklayers. This type of informal training is equivalent to an apprenticeship but usually takes much longer.

Getting the Job

To enter the apprenticeship program, you should apply to a contractor or union. Check with local contractors for a job as a laborer or hod carrier. Helpers who do not join apprenticeship programs must wait for openings before they can become qualified craft workers.

Advancement Possibilities and Employment Outlook

Fully qualified bricklayers are already at the top of their craft. However, experienced bricklayers can become supervisors. They can also become estimators. An estimator computes the duration and cost of labor and materials for projects. Bricklayers can become building inspectors for city or county governments. These workers supervise work on large construction sites. Bricklayers can also become construction superintendents.

The employment outlook for bricklayers is good. Bricklayers will be needed to install precast brick panels, do decorative brickwork on building exteriors, and erect inside walls. Currently about 142,000 bricklayers are employed in the United States. As with most jobs in the construction industry, employment opportunities depend on fluctuations in the economy. However, an emerging shortage of qualified bricklayers and other tradespeople should continue to create a demand for these workers.

Working Conditions

Bricklayers do maintenance bricklaying work in close quarters, usually in cramped positions. The work area is usually dusty or ash-filled. Bricklayers who work in construction generally work outdoors. In cold climates, work time is lost due to bad weather. Bricklayers spend most of the day on their feet in hot or cold weather. They sometimes work on scaffolding, so they risk injury from falls. Lifting and handling heavy, sometimes bulky materials may also cause injury. Bricklayers supply their own hand tools. Contractors supply the power equipment, scaffolding, and ladders. Most bricklayers work 40 hours a week. Many bricklayers belong to labor unions.

Earnings and Benefits

The current average union wage for qualified bricklayers is $480 a week. Wages vary from one part of the country to another, but most bricklayers receive time and a half for overtime work and double their wages for weekend and holiday work. Beginning apprentices earn at least 50 percent of the qualified craft worker's wage and receive periodic raises. Union members generally receive paid holidays, life insurance, and hospitalization and pension plans. Vacation days are determined by the number of days worked each year. Other benefits are negotiated separately for each contract.

Where to Go for More Information

Brick Industry of America
11490 Commerce Park Drive
Reston, VA 22091-1525
(703) 620-0010
www.bia.org

International Union of Bricklayers and
   Allied Craftsmen of America
815 Fifteenth Street, NW, Third Floor
Washington, DC 20005
(202) 783-3788

Mason Contractors Association of America
1910 Highland Avenue, Suite 101
Lombard, IL 60148-6147
(630) 705-4200

Carpenter

Education and Training
None

Salary Range
Average—$475 a week

Employment Outlook
Good

Definition and Nature of the Work

Carpenters work throughout the construction industry. They are the largest group of the building trades workers. They saw, shape, and fasten wood in order to build houses and other buildings. They also build cabinets, doors, and other objects made of wood. They work on construction sites, inside buildings, in factories, and in small woodworking shops. Carpenters use both power and hand tools, such as hammers, saws, drills, and chisels. They fasten wood with nails, screws, bolts, and glue.

Carpentry work can be divided into two categories—rough carpentry and finish carpentry. *Rough carpenters* often work outdoors where they begin projects using unfinished wood and other building materials. They frame houses, build scaffolding, and make forms to be filled with concrete. Forms are used to mold concrete for bridges, highways, and house foundations. *Finish carpenters* include those who cut and fit doors, windows, and interior molding. They also build and install cabinets, lay hardwood floors, and panel rooms.

Some carpenters build sets for theaters and television studios. Others build wharves and docks. *Millworkers,* or carpenters who work in factories, make prefabricated, or ready-made, parts for buildings, such as window frames, cabinets, and partitions. These parts are shipped already assembled to the construction site. Other millworkers are employed by lumberyards, cutting lumber and building prefabricated structures such as walls, floors, and ceilings. Some carpenters specialize in cabinetmaking. *Cabinetmakers* custom design cabinets, counters, shelves, and other fixtures for homes, stores, and restaurants. A few cabinetmakers specialize in building fine furniture by hand. Some carpenters work with other materials in addition to wood. They apply drywall or prefinished coverings such as vinyl to ceilings, walls, and partitions. Carpenters can also specialize in installing acoustical panels to soundproof rooms.

Most carpenters are employed by contractors and builders. Those who work in cities often specialize in one kind of carpentry, while carpenters working in rural areas may do many kinds of rough and finish work.

Education and Training Requirements

A high school diploma is preferred but not required. While in school, you should take courses in woodworking, mechanical drawing, and mathematics. The best way to become a carpenter is to complete a union-contractor apprenticeship program. Applicants should be at least 17 years of age. Apprentices are chosen on the basis of written tests and interviews. You should have manual dexterity and the ability to imagine how things will look when assembled. You must be able to do simple arithmetic. You should also be strong and in good health. The formal apprenticeship program takes about 3 to 4 years to complete. It consists of about 8,000 hours of on-the-job training and at least 144 hours of classroom instruction each year. In the classes, apprentices learn structural design, common framing systems, how to read blueprints, and simple layouts. On the job, apprentices learn all the techniques and operations of carpentry from experienced carpenters on a less formal basis. A formal apprenticeship is a good way to find out whether carpentry is the trade you really want.

Getting the Job

Those who can obtain an all-around knowledge of construction through high school courses will have a better chance of joining an apprenticeship program.

Carpenters spend a lot of time squatting, bending, and climbing. They must have a good sense of balance because they often risk falling from buildings.

People who have experience in semiskilled work related to carpentry also have a good chance to become apprentices. Carpenters may also learn the trade by working as helpers for contractors. However, this kind of training takes longer and is not as thorough as the 4-year apprenticeship program. Furthermore, carpenters who have taken part in the formal program earn union wages, which are generally higher than the wages earned by nonunion carpenters.

Advancement Possibilities and Employment Outlook

Experienced carpenters can become supervisors of crews of carpenters. Eventually, they can become general superintendents of construction sites. Some carpenters become estimators and analyze the duration and costs of materials and labor for a job. Often carpenters become contractors. Almost one-third of all carpenters own their own businesses. This percentage is higher than the average for all construction trades. Self-employed carpenters make cabinets and furniture, do repair work, and remodel houses.

Currently 996,000 people are employed as carpenters. However, the introduction of prefabricated structures has reduced the job opportunities for carpenters, especially for those doing rough carpentry. But since carpenters also build prefabricated structures, many will still be employed in factories. The employment outlook remains good through 2006. However, employment opportunities in the construction industry do vary with changes in the economy.

Working Conditions

Rough carpenters work outdoors most of the time. They can expect to lose work time in winter and when the weather is bad. While most people work 2,000 hours a year, carpenters can count on working only 1,400 hours a year. Both finish carpenters and rough carpenters can expect to lose time because of layoffs and material shortages.

Carpenters take pride in their workmanship. They must be precise and pay attention to detail. They must be willing to follow set standards and rules in their work. Carpenters must have a good deal of stamina, because their work is active and somewhat strenuous. It requires standing, squatting, stooping, bending, and climbing. They must have a good sense of balance; there is always the risk of falling. Carpenters use rough materials, sharp tools, and powerful equipment and must be aware of the hazards.

Most carpenters work 40 hours a week. Higher wages are paid for overtime work. Overtime is generally available depending on the job and its deadline for completion. Many carpenters belong to labor unions.

Earnings and Benefits

The average salary for union workers is $475 a week. Nonunion pay is usually lower. Apprentices begin by earning 50 percent of the qualified craft worker's wage. Every 6 months their pay is increased by 5 percent until, in their fourth year, they earn 85 percent to 90 percent of the experienced worker's salary. Highly skilled and experienced carpenters may earn as much as $875 a week. Union benefits include paid holidays, vacations determined by the number of days worked, and hospitalization and pension plans. Other benefits are negotiated separately for each union contract.

Where to Go for More Information

Associated General Contractors of America
1957 E Street, NW
Washington, DC 20006-5199
(202) 393-2040

United Brotherhood of Carpenters and
    Joiners of America
101 Constitution Avenue, NW
Washington, DC 20001
(202) 546-6206

United States Department of Labor
Bureau of Apprenticeship and Training
200 Constitution Avenue, NW,
    Room North 4649
Washington, DC 20210
(202) 219-5921

Cement Mason

Education and Training
None

Salary Range
Average—$15 to $45 an hour

Employment Outlook
Fair

Definition and Nature of the Work

Cement masons smooth and finish poured concrete. They work on foundations of buildings, in highway construction, and on sidewalks, driveways, and patios. They help make concrete beams, columns, and panels. Cement masons are needed wherever a finished surface of concrete is poured. They also apply latex and epoxy to floors. Cement masons can create colored surfaces by applying tinted cement.

Many cement masons work for general contractors in charge of constructing highways and large buildings. Some work for concrete contractors. A small number of masons work for firms that do their own construction, such as public works departments. Others are self-employed and work on small jobs, such as driveways and patios.

Masons use wood or plastic forms to shape the concrete and hold it until it is dry. First the masons check the forms into which the concrete is to be poured to be sure they are set at the right depth and angle. Under the mason's watchful eye, laborers pour and spread the concrete. Then they level the concrete. Next the masons use leveling tools such as floats or darbies to smooth high spots and fill depressions. Floats are also used to produce an even, but not smooth, texture.

When the cement areas begin to dry, the masons put boards across them. Then the masons kneel on the boards so that their weight is evenly distributed across the cement. Sitting this way allows them to work on the cement without damaging the surface. The masons then go over the cement with a trowel to smooth the area before it dries completely. A power-operated trowel can be used on open areas, but corners and edges must be finished by hand.

Cement masons finish concrete surfaces by leveling and smoothing them.

Cement masons must smooth the rough surfaces left by the pouring forms after they have been removed. The masons prepare the rough surface with a hammer and chisel. Then they rub the high spots with brick to smooth them. A rich mixture of cement is then rubbed in with a sponge-rubber float or with burlap. This operation is called finishing.

Cement masons sometimes use chemical additives to slow or speed up the setting time. In order to prevent defects, masons must know what effects heat and cold have on the concrete.

Education and Training Requirements

A 3-year apprenticeship program is the best way to train to become a cement mason. You do not need a high school diploma, but you should take a high school math course if you want to enter a formal apprenticeship program. Blueprint reading and mechanical drawing courses are also helpful. You should be at least 18 years old, in good health, and able to work well with your hands. Masons work alone or as part of a team.

During the 3 years of on-the-job training, apprentices work with the materials and tools of the trade and learn finishing, layout, and safety procedures. While working on the job, apprentices attend school. They must have at least 144 hours of classroom instruction during the year. In these classes, apprentices learn drafting, mathematics, and basic science. They study local building codes and learn to estimate material costs. They also learn to read blueprints. Some cement masons learn their craft while working as helpers for experienced masons.

Getting the Job

To get a job as a cement mason, you should contact a local contractor or union office and inquire about the apprenticeship program. Another good way to gain knowledge and experience is to get a job at a construction site working as a laborer and assisting cement masons.

Advancement Possibilities and Employment Outlook

Many cement masons open their own contracting businesses. These masons install sidewalks, curbs, and driveways. An experienced mason can also become a supervisor or estimator. Estimators figure out the duration and costs of labor and materials before jobs are begun.

The employment outlook for cement masons is fair. However, opportunities will depend on the growth of the construction industry. Concrete walls continue to be used widely due to their strength and fire resistance. New products such as epoxy and latex flooring will broaden the mason's job possibilities.

Working Conditions

As in all the building trades, some work time is lost due to poor weather. But since heated plastic shelters for workers have been used, the amount of work time lost has been reduced. Overtime in cement masonry is frequent because once the concrete is poured, it must be finished regardless of the hour. Higher wages are paid for overtime hours. Cement masonry is strenuous work. Masons must stoop, bend, and kneel all day. Layoffs may occur during slow seasons. Masons sometimes travel from construction site to construction site in order to keep working. Many cement masons belong to labor unions.

Earnings and Benefits

Currently the average union wages for experienced cement masons range from $15 to $45 an hour, including benefits. Wages vary from one part of the country to another. Apprentices start at 50 to 60 percent of the rate paid to experienced workers. Union workers generally receive paid holidays, life insurance, and hospitalization and pension plans. The number of vacation days they receive depends on the number of days they work each year.

Where to Go for More Information

Mason Contractors Association of America
1910 Highland Avenue, Suite 101
Lombard, IL 60148-6147
(630) 705-4200

Operative Plasterers and Cement Masons
 International Association of the United
 States and Canada
14405 Laurel Place
Laurel, MD 20707
(301) 470-4200

United States Department of Labor
Bureau of Apprenticeship and Training
200 Constitution Avenue, NW,
 Room North 4649
Washington, DC 20210
(202) 219-5921

Construction Electrician

Education and Training
None

Salary Range
Average—$485
to $815 a week

Employment Outlook
Fair

Definition and Nature of the Work

Construction electricians assemble, install, and wire the electrical systems in new homes and buildings. Light, heat, power, air-conditioning, and refrigeration operate through electrical systems. Electricians usually install the wiring after the building is partially built. They follow blueprints and wiring diagrams. They also install electronic equipment and signal communication systems.

When electricians wire new homes or buildings, they first run conduit, which is metal tubing or pipe, inside walls and ceilings. They must cut the conduit to the proper length. Once the conduit is in place, electricians pull the wires through the tubing. To complete the circuit, they attach these wires to switches and outlets. Then they solder or screw wires to the fuse box, circuit breakers, or transformers. For safety reasons, electricians must follow state, county, and municipal codes in wiring.

Electricians usually install the electrical wiring when the building is partially completed.

Electricians use several hand tools including screwdrivers, pliers, knives, and hacksaws. Employers usually supply the conduit benders, pipe threaders, power tools, and test meters.

Education and Training Requirements

Some electricians learn the trade by working as a qualified electrician's helper. You can also enter a formal apprenticeship program, which requires a high school diploma. While in high school, you should take courses in math and physics. One of the best ways to get formal training is through the 4-year apprenticeship program developed by the International Brotherhood of Electrical Workers and the National Electrical Contractors Association. This program is conducted under a written agreement between the apprentice and the local union-management committee. The committee decides how many apprentice electricians are needed for the area. It also establishes apprenticeship standards and plans a varied work program that gives you the chance to work with different contractors.

Along with 4 years of on-the-job training, apprentices must receive at least 144 hours of classroom instruction each year. In the classroom, apprentices learn applied mathematics, wiring layout, electrical theory, electronics, and blueprint reading. Many experienced electricians also take classroom instruction because there are always new developments in this field and they must keep up with new information. In most areas you need a master electrician's license. To get such a license you must pass a test that examines your knowledge of the trade; the National Electric Code; and the state, local, and municipal building and electrical codes.

Getting the Job

The best way to enter this field is through the joint union-management apprenticeship program. You can also apply to electrical contractors for work as a helper.

Advancement Possibilities and Employment Outlook

Experienced electricians often advance to become superintendents or supervisors of construction jobs. Some electricians become estimators. Their job is to figure the project duration and labor and material costs and submit bids for jobs. Construction electricians can transfer to related jobs, such as maintenance electricians in factories or electricians for aircraft or shipbuilding companies. They can also start their own contracting businesses.

Currently more than 575,000 electricians are employed in the United States, of which more than 50 percent are in construction-related jobs. By the year 2006 this figure is expected to grow slower than the average for all jobs. However, the outlook for highly skilled electricians is very good through 2006. The sophisticated wiring in computers and electronic devices will provide more jobs for electricians in the future. More electricians will also be needed to install and repair communication devices used in commerce and industry. However, employment in the construction industry depends on the general economy.

Working Conditions

Electricians generally work 40 hours a week. They earn extra wages for overtime work. Generally they work indoors, but they may be exposed to the elements working in partially built structures. They often stand for many hours at a time on ladders and scaffolding, or kneel in tight quarters. The risk of electrical shock is always present, although it has been lessened by strict safety procedures. Many electricians belong to labor unions.

Earnings and Benefits

Apprentices receive 30 to 50 percent of the experienced electrician's wage at the start of their training. The wages increase periodically until the end of the apprenticeship. At this point, apprentices earn 80 to 90 percent of the qualified craft worker's wage. Most workers earn between $485 and $815 a week. Union workers generally receive paid holidays, life insurance, and hospitalization and pension plans. The number of vacation days they receive depends on the number of days they work each year.

Where to Go for More Information

Independent Electrical Contractors
2010A Eisenhower Avenue
Alexandria, VA 22314
(703) 549-7351

International Brotherhood of
  Electrical Workers
1125 Fifteenth Street, NW
Washington, DC 20005
(202) 833-7000

National Electrical Contractors Association
3 Bethesda Metro Center, Suite 1100
Bethesda, MD 20814-3299
(301) 657-3110

Construction Equipment Mechanic

Education and Training
None

Salary Range
Average—$500
to $760 a week

Employment Outlook
Fair

Definition and Nature of the Work

Construction equipment mechanics repair and service many kinds of machines. These machines include bulldozers, earthmovers, tractors, paving machines, pile drivers, cranes, and concrete mixers. A mechanic's job is very important because a broken machine can slow down or even stop construction work.

Many construction machines are powered by engines that use diesel rather than gasoline. Mechanics must have special skills to work on diesel engines. Mechanics inspect and test the engine, looking for the cause of the trouble. Once the problem has been discovered, mechanics repair or replace the broken part or make the needed adjustments. This work is done either at the job site or in a repair shop.

Construction equipment mechanics repair and service machines including bulldozers, tractors, cranes, and concrete mixers.

Mechanics also do routine maintenance. They inspect and adjust machines regularly. Often they apply oil, tighten bolts, and replace parts before they wear out.

Other duties may include working on a machine's brake and steering system. Mechanics also repair various controls and levers, as well as some of the rods and cables found in many machines. Some mechanics can even make new parts in a machine shop.

Construction equipment mechanics use tools such as screwdrivers, wrenches, and pliers. Power hoists and small cranes may also be used for moving heavy equipment.

Education and Training Requirements

There are several ways to learn about construction equipment. Many mechanics begin by working in an automobile repair shop. Working on gasoline-powered car engines and other automobile systems is good background for a future construction equipment mechanic. Other mechanics begin by taking courses in trade, vocational, and correspondence schools. These courses teach them how to repair diesel engines and other equipment. Still other mechanics begin by working as trainees for construction companies. Often a combination of work experience and classroom instruction is involved in each of these situations.

Perhaps the best way to become a construction equipment mechanic is through a formal apprenticeship. Apprenticeships are supervised by local unions. The program usually takes 3 years. Apprentices are trained to repair and maintain universal equipment, such as hoists, shovels, cranes, grading and paving equipment, and plant equipment, such as mixing and crushing machines. The apprentice also receives at least 144 hours of classroom instruction each year. A high school education is generally required to enter an apprenticeship program.

To work in this field you must be able to use many different tools, read and understand diagrams, and be mechanically inclined. You should also be in good physical condition since you may have to do some lifting and moving. You should be able to work as a member of a team.

Getting the Job

All beginning jobs in this field are trainee positions. On-the-job training that allows you to work on the machinery is the best experience. If possible, enter an apprenticeship program. Contact a local construction firm to find out which union supervises the apprenticeship program in your area. You will probably have to pass a test and be approved by a joint labor-management committee. Apprentices are chosen by the number of openings in the program and by their qualifications.

You can also contact construction firms, building contractors, and excavating contractors. Check the newspaper classifieds and contact contractors listed in the Yellow Pages of your local phone book.

You might begin by working in a repair shop or for an equipment supplier. If you attend a trade or vocational school, ask about its job placement service.

Advancement Possibilities and Employment Outlook

With experience in fixing different machines and with the proper technical knowledge and classroom background, a mechanic can advance to the position of lead operator. The lead operator is in charge of a work crew. Mechanics with proven ability can become supervisors. Mechanics who learn to operate the machines used in construction can become heavy equipment operators. More experienced heavy equipment operators earn a slightly higher rate of pay than mechanics.

The need for mechanics is directly related to the number of construction projects. But construction activity is related to the economy. Periods of unemployment may occur. The employment outlook for these jobs is fair. However, jobs are expected to grow more slowly than the average for all jobs through 2006.

Working Conditions

Much of the mechanic's work takes place outdoors. Mechanics may have to inspect and repair equipment when the weather is very hot or very cold.

Construction sites are usually dirty and noisy. Some mechanics wear special earmuffs to protect their hearing. Working in a repair shop is usually more comfortable, but even repair shops can be dirty and noisy, and ventilation can be a problem. Mechanics also handle greasy tools and have to work in cramped positions for long periods of time.

A 5-day, 40-hour week is normal. However, if the weather is bad, construction crews may not be able to work. Sometimes mechanics must work at night or on weekends to make necessary repairs. A higher rate of pay is usually given for weekend and overtime work.

Earnings and Benefits

Earnings for construction equipment mechanics vary, depending on the location of the work. Currently mechanics can earn an average of $500 to $760 a week. Construction equipment mechanics may also receive benefits, such as paid vacations, health and life insurance, and pension plans.

Where to Go for More Information

International Union of Operating Engineers
1125 Seventeenth Street, NW
Washington, DC 20036
(202) 429-9100

National Association of Women
    in Construction
327 South Adams Street
Fort Worth, TX 76104
(817) 877-5551
www.nawic.org

United States Department of Labor
Bureau of Apprenticeship and Training
200 Constitution Avenue, NW,
    Room North 4649
Washington, DC 20210
(202) 219-5921

Construction Laborer

Definition and Nature of the Work

Construction laborers work in every phase of building activity. Although laborers are unskilled workers, no building project could get off the ground without their work. Laborers are usually the first workers to arrive at the job site and are the last to leave the completed project. They work on the construction sites of homes and high-rise buildings, airports and highways, dams and bridges, and water and sewer projects. They perform many tasks that require great physical strength. Laborers load and unload equipment, put up and take down scaffoldings, clear work areas, and carry materials to skilled workers.

Some laborers specialize in certain kinds of work. Laborers who work with bricklayers or plasterers are known as *hod carriers*. These workers help bricklayers and plasterers by mixing materials and setting up scaffolding. Some work closely with cement masons. When concrete is mixed at a construction site, construction laborers unload materials and fill hand-loaded cement mixers. They set up the forms into which the concrete is poured. They also spread the concrete and vibrate or spade it to prevent air pockets. To keep the newly poured pavement from drying out so quickly that it cracks, laborers cover it with straw or burlap.

All laborers must have a general knowledge of the building trades in which they work. Laborers who work for certain kinds of skilled workers must be trained and experienced. For example, some construction laborers work in rock blasting, rock drilling, and tunnel construction. They must know what effects explosives will have on different kinds of rock so they can prevent injury and damage to property. Laborers who work on tunnel construction and on the foundations of bridges and dams must be able to bore and mine the tunnels.

Laborers learn through experience and instruction from skilled workers and supervisors. Construction laborers generally work for construction contractors. Some laborers work for state and local governments and public utility companies.

Education and Training Requirements

You need very little training to become a laborer. A high school diploma is not a requirement. However, you should have good judgment and an alert mind. You should be in good health and have a strong body, especially a strong back. Inexperienced laborers first do simple tasks, such as clearing lumber. As laborers gain experience, they do more complex jobs. For instance, they may pour concrete forms or work as hod carriers. Some contractors now have 4- to 8-week training programs so that trainees can become familiar with the construction trade.

Getting the Job

The best way to get a job as a laborer is to contact local contractors about openings in their businesses.

Construction laborers work in every phase of building activity, performing tasks that require great physical strength.

You can also contact a local union about job opportunities, check the newspaper classifieds, and contact small construction companies listed in the Yellow Pages in your local phone book.

Advancement Possibilities and Employment Outlook

Construction laborers advance very little within their own trades. However, those who get construction experience while working as laborers have a good chance of getting into an apprenticeship program.

The employment outlook for laborers is fair and growth is expected to be slower than the average for all jobs through 2006. Laborers will continue to be needed on most construction sites, but mechanized equipment has taken over many jobs. This equipment can do the work of a laborer faster and less expensively. Competition for unskilled jobs is keen. A laborer with any skill or training to offer has a clear advantage over an unskilled worker.

Working Conditions

The work demands heavy lifting and much stooping, carrying, and bending. Construction laborers usually work a 40-hour week. Extra wages are paid for overtime hours. Laborers spend a good deal of time outdoors, even in bad weather. Construction work is seasonal. More jobs are available in some months than in others. Winter is the industry's slowest season. Many construction laborers belong to unions.

Earnings and Benefits

Currently the average salary for laborers is $250 to $480 a week. Experienced workers may earn more. Union workers generally receive paid holidays, life insurance, and hospitalization and pension plans. The number of vacation days they receive depends on the number of days worked each year. Other benefits are negotiated separately for each union contract.

Where to Go for More Information

Laborers International Union of
    North America
905 Sixteenth Street, NW
Washington, DC 20006-1765
(202) 737-8320

National Association of Women
    in Construction
327 South Adams Street
Fort Worth, TX 76104
(817) 877-5551
www.nawic.org

Construction Millwright

Education and Training
None

Salary Range
Starting—$510
to $820 a week

Employment Outlook
Poor

Definition and Nature of the Work

Millwrights move and install heavy machinery. They work for industrial plants, construction companies, firms that make machinery, and companies that specialize in installing heavy equipment.

Millwrights must be skilled in many construction activities. Bricklaying, painting, plumbing, welding, and electrical work may all be part of a millwright's job. Millwrights use these and other skills to build concrete foundations for heavy equipment, to assemble new machines, and to replace worn parts. They must have a knowledge of building materials. They must know how to operate hoists, jacks, and other rigging devices.

In smaller construction plants millwrights also do much of the plumbing, electrical work, carpentry, and routine repair work. In larger plants millwrights often specialize in one area. One person may be an expert machine mover and installer, while another may be a maintenance specialist. Some millwrights work for firms that specialize in installing one type of machinery, such as paper mill equipment or automobile assembly line conveyors.

Education and Training Requirements

A high school diploma is recommended for this job. While in school you should take courses in mathematics, science, mechanical drawing, and electricity, as well as wood, metal, and machine shop. Since a millwright must often give and follow directions, any course that develops communication skills, such as English or speech, is also a good idea.

One of the best ways to become a millwright is through a formal union apprenticeship program. More than 50 percent of the millwrights belong to unions. Contact the union to which millwrights in your area belong and ask about its apprenticeship program. The program usually involves 4 years of on-the-job training and classroom instruction. Shop instruction in electricity, welding, rough carpentry, handling structural steel, and servicing equipment is also included.

Millwrights move and install heavy machinery. They must be skilled in bricklaying, painting, plumbing, welding, and electrical work.

Another way to become a millwright is through an informal trainee program. In this type of program a person starts as a helper under the supervision of a skilled millwright. As various jobs come up, the helper learns the skills required to complete each one. After several years of experience the helper can become a fully qualified millwright.

Getting the Job

You can enter the field by joining an apprenticeship or a trainee program. If you want to begin as an apprentice, you should contact the appropriate union. If you want to start as a trainee, you should check with firms in your area employing millwrights. Apply directly to manufacturing plants, companies that build heavy machinery, local construction companies that specialize in building plants, and industries that install machines. Also, check your state employment office and scan the newspaper classified ads.

Advancement Possibilities and Employment Outlook

Advancement in this field depends on skill and experience. The more skilled you become, the higher your earnings will be. Some millwrights become supervisors.

Currently more than 78,000 people are employed as millwrights. The demand for millwrights is expected to decline slightly through the year 2006. Employment in the construction industry is sensitive to changes in economic conditions, and the demand for jobs fluctuates with the level of building activity. Therefore, the number of millwrights needed will depend on the economy and industrial expansion.

Working Conditions

Conditions vary with the job, but most millwrights work indoors. Millwrights must handle oil, grease, sharp pieces of metal, and heavy objects. Physically, a millwright should be strong and quick. The job often calls for a lot of lifting, climbing, and physical force. A millwright should also be able to come up with feasible solutions to problems.

A 40-hour workweek is normal. Sometimes millwrights may have to work longer to complete a job on time. Usually time and a half is paid for any overtime hours and double time for work on Sundays and holidays. Employment is generally steady for those who work in factories, but millwrights who work for construction companies and contractors may experience periods of unemployment.

Earnings and Benefits

Wages vary depending on the experience of the worker and the location of the job. Currently the average salary for beginning millwrights ranges from $510 to $820 a week. Experienced millwrights who work in large cities and are members of labor unions earn more. In general, apprentices start at wages that are 50 percent of those of qualified workers. They receive periodic raises as they progress through the training period. Benefits such as life insurance, savings plans, health benefits, and paid vacations usually depend on the individual company or union.

Demolition Worker

Education and Training
None

Salary Range
Varies—see profile

Employment Outlook
Fair

Definition and Nature of the Work

In the construction industry, destroying old structures is just as important as building new ones. Demolition workers tear down anything from high-rise apartment buildings to bridges or factories. Demolition includes blasting, which is the use of explosives, and wrecking, or the use of machinery and equipment. Operating engineers, also called heavy equipment operators, and hand laborers usually work for wrecking contractors. Blasters work for wrecking and blasting contractors. They may also work for general contractors helping to build roads, bridges, and dams.

The method of destroying a structure depends on many factors. Demolition workers must take into account what the building is made of—brick, lumber, concrete, or metal. For instance, they may have to use an oxyacetylene torch to cut steel braces in addition to using other wrecking equipment. They also consider the structure's surroundings. Using explosives in urban areas may be too dangerous. Also, local ordinances may restrict or ban the use of explosives.

When it is safe to use explosives, *blasters* plant and set off explosive charges. They first look at the structure to be blown up. Based on its size, makeup, and location, they decide what kind of and how much explosive to use, and where to plant the charges. They mark the correct places and drill holes where the charges are to be placed. Blasters then put together the explosive, place it in the hole, and fill in the remaining space with sand, dirt, or some other material. When the area has been cleared of workers and equipment, blasters set off the explosion.

Where it is unsafe or illegal to use explosives, structures are demolished by hand or with wrecking equipment. Wrecking a structure is basically the reverse of

Although demolition workers often destroy buildings by operating wrecking balls and other machines, sometimes workers take apart buildings by hand, using wrecking bars, sledgehammers, axes, and shovels.

building a structure. First laborers "gut" the building. "Gutting" means stripping the inside of anything of value, such as pipes, radiators, and light fixtures. Then starting at the top of the building, *crane operators,* also called *ball and chain operators,* knock the building down. *Frontend machine operators* pick up debris and dump it into trucks to be hauled away. *Compressor* or *air gun operators* break up concrete. Smaller brick or wooden structures may be demolished by hand laborers using wrecking bars, sledgehammers, axes, and shovels. Brick buildings are usually taken apart by hand, since brick is very valuable. Demolition companies may sell any materials they salvage.

Education and Training Requirements

Many demolition workers are trained on the job. There are no set requirements for hand laborers, although you have to join a union to work for a union contractor. You may become an operating engineer through a union training program or learn on the job through a nonunion contractor.

If you are interested in becoming a blaster, you should take science and math courses in high school. Electronics and electricity are also important courses, since many explosives are set off with electronic devices. Blasters begin as helpers, carrying explosives to blast sites, drilling and filling charge holes, and connecting wires and fuses. Experienced blasters teach trainees what type and quantity of explosives to use and safety practices and laws. Blasters must be licensed by the state. Your state licensing agency may require you to take a written test and submit letters of recommendation from a licensed blaster.

Getting the Job

Union wrecking contractors hire workers directly through unions. Apply directly to unions to find out about training programs and job openings. For nonunion work, apply directly to wrecking or blasting contractors listed in the Yellow Pages. Also check with your state employment service and read the newspaper classifieds for job openings.

Advancement Possibilities and Employment Outlook

With training, hand laborers can become operating engineers. Operating engineers can advance to a machine requiring more skill. Crane operators are highly skilled workers. Some operating engineers become supervisors or field superintendents. Blasters usually advance by increasing their skills. As blasters learn how to handle a greater variety of jobs, their chances of employment increase. Some blasters and wreckers open their own demolition businesses.

The future for demolition workers is fair. Available space for new buildings is relatively scarce in heavily populated areas. Builders must tear down factories and other old buildings to increase the amount of usable land. Demolition workers will also be in demand as cities continue to modernize and redevelop older sections.

Working Conditions

Demolition workers spend most of their time outdoors. Laborers' work is fairly strenuous. Although demolition workers work with explosives, heavy equipment, and large chunks of falling debris, job hazards are greatly reduced when safety precautions are taken. The noise of wrecking sites may affect workers' hearing.

Blasters must be especially careful and have a responsible attitude toward the property and lives of others. Demolition workers work 40 hours a week. Some overtime work may be necessary.

Earnings and Benefits

Earnings for demolition workers often depend on experience and geographical location. Currently union wages for experienced blasters range from $825 to $1,270 a week. Highly skilled blasters are among the highest paid workers in the demolition field. Operating engineers earn salaries that average between $455 and $575 a week, depending on their experience, the type of machine they operate, and the difficulty of the job. Less skilled helpers earn about $8 to $10.50 an hour.

Benefits may include life and health insurance, overtime pay, accident insurance, pension plans, and paid vacations. Union workers usually receive all these benefits and others as part of a labor-management contract.

Where to Go for More Information

International Society of Explosives
 Engineers
29100 Aurora Road
Solon, OH 44139-1800
(440) 349-4004
www.isee.org

International Union of Operating Engineers
1125 Seventeenth Street, NW
Washington, DC 20036
(202) 429-9100

National Association of Women
 in Construction
327 South Adams Street
Fort Worth, TX 76104
(817) 877-5551
www.nawic.org

Drywall Installer and Finisher

Education and Training
High school

Salary Range
Average—$295
to $630 a week

Employment Outlook
Fair

Definition and Nature of the Work

For the past 30 years, installation of drywall, or sheetrock, has been the most popular method of constructing the inner walls of buildings. Drywall was developed as a substitute for wet plaster. It consists of a thin layer of gypsum sandwiched between two pieces of heavy paper made in standard-size panels of 4 feet by 8 or 12 feet. Installers cut the panels to fit, then nail or screw to the frames. Finishers fill in joints with a paste and prepare the walls for paint or wallpaper.

Drywall installation requires careful measuring and cutting to fit pieces into small spaces above doors or below windows. Installers also saw holes in the panels for electrical outlets and plumbing. Because drywall is heavy, an assistant works with the installer to position and secure the panels. A lift may be used to install ceiling panels.

A drywall finisher uses an automatic taping tool to apply joint compound and tape between the panels of drywall.

After installing the drywall, finishers use a compound to fill joints between panels. Using the tip of a wide trowel, they spread the compound along each side of the joint. They then press a perforated paper tape into the wet compound and scrape away excess material. Finishers may use automatic taping tools to apply the joint compound and tape in one step. Further coats may be added to make a smooth surface. Finally, the wall is sanded to ensure uniformity between patched and unpatched areas.

Some finishers create textured surfaces on walls and ceilings with trowels or spray guns. They also repair imperfections caused by installation of heating and other fixtures. Drywall installers and finishers use tape measures, straightedges, keyhole saws, spatulas, hammers, and brushes.

Education and Training Requirements

Most drywall installers and finishers learn their trade on the job, although they may have learned some of the tool skills in wood or metal shop in high school. Some installers learn their trade in a union apprenticeship program.

Getting the Job

You can apply directly to local contractors, who often look for new assistants. State employment services and newspaper ads also list building jobs requiring drywall workers. Regional union offices will provide information about apprenticeships.

Advancement Possibilities and Employment Outlook

Drywall workers with experience may become supervisors of small crews of workers. As they learn to estimate costs of installation and finishing, they become a valuable asset to a construction team. Some workers may start their own drywall contracting businesses.

Currently, there are about 133,000 drywall installers and finishers in the U.S. They work for contractors specializing in drywall installation or for general building contractors. Employment of drywall workers is expected to grow more slowly than the average for all occupations through the year 2006.

Working Conditions

Drywall installation and finishing are completed indoors, so these workers rarely lose time because of inclement weather. However, they may be unemployed between construction projects and during downturns in construction activity.

The work is sometimes strenuous. It requires lifting and maneuvering heavy panels. Flying dust and exposure to fumes are constant hazards.

Earnings and Benefits

At the present time, earnings for drywall workers average $295 to $630 a week. Trainees start at about half the rate of experienced workers. Some contractors pay installers and finishers by the amount of work they do. Those who work for hourly wages receive time and a half for overtime. Benefits may be provided to those who have worked with the same contractor for a long time, but many workers must make their own provisions for health insurance and pensions.

Where to Go for More Information

Associated Builders and Contractors
1300 North 17th Street, Eighth Floor
Rosslyn, VA 22209
(703) 812-2000

International Brotherhood of Painters
and Allied Trades
1750 New York Avenue, NW, Eighth Floor
Washington, DC 20006
(202) 637-0700

National Association of the Remodeling
Industry
4301 North Fairfax Drive, Suite 310
Arlington, VA 22203-3000
(703) 276-7600

Elevator Constructor and Repair Worker

Education and Training
High school

Salary Range
Average—$740
to $1,090 a week

Employment Outlook
Poor

Definition and Nature of the Work

Elevator constructors build elevators, escalators, and dumbwaiters. They repair broken elevators, modernize older models, and perform maintenance duties. They work in all types of buildings, including skyscrapers and low-rise office buildings.

Elevators are installed in new buildings during construction. Elevator constructors put the guide rails on the side walls of the elevator shaft. Then they set the hoisting machine, the frame, and the platform of the passenger car in place. The car frame is attached to the counterweights and cables. Next the body and the roof of the car are installed and the entire elevator system is wired. It is then tested and, if necessary, adjusted.

Elevator constructors use similar methods to install dumbwaiters and escalators. Dumbwaiters are small lifts used to transport food and other things from floor to floor. They are sometimes used in large buildings in which the kitchen and dining rooms are on different floors.

Repair workers fix elevators that are not operating. They may also convert old, manually operated elevators to automatic elevators.

Workers who perform maintenance duties must oil and grease the moving parts of an elevator. Elevator repair workers also adjust or replace control systems, signal systems, and hoisting mechanisms.

Skilled elevator constructors and repair workers have a working knowledge of electricity and electronics. They use hand and power tools and meters and gauges for testing.

Education and Training Requirements

To become an elevator constructor, you must have a high school diploma or its equivalent and be at least 18 years old. You should have a good understanding of mathematics and physics. Mechanical aptitude and an interest in machinery are very important. You can be trained in a joint union-management program that involves on-the-job training and classroom work. Trainees usually become helpers after 6 months of experience. They learn from experienced craft workers. They also attend classes in mathematics, physics, safety techniques, and electrical and electronics theory. Within 4 years helpers can become fully qualified workers. Many repairers continue training to keep up with the latest changes in the industry.

Getting the Job

The best way to become an elevator constructor is to get a job as a helper on an elevator construction crew. Most elevator manufacturing firms employ such crews to install, modernize, and repair their equipment. Contact the appropriate union to find out about openings for helpers. Also check the classifieds of your local newspaper.

Advancement Possibilities and Employment Outlook

Experienced elevator constructors can become supervisors in large elevator manufacturing companies. Experienced workers may also start their own contracting businesses. The opportunities, however, are limited.

Currently about 25,000 people are employed as elevator constructors and repair workers in the U.S. This number is expected to grow at a slower rate than the average for all jobs through the year 2006. Because of improvements in elevator manufacturing, some workers will be needed to modernize elevators. However, the number of workers needed depends on the general economy.

Working Conditions

Elevator constructors and repair workers must lift and carry heavy equipment. Usually helpers do most of the strenuous work. Most of the work is done indoors, so little work time is lost because of the weather. Elevator constructors and repair workers work in cramped quarters, usually in awkward positions. They usually work in small crews. Generally they work 40 hours a week. Extra wages are paid for overtime work. Many elevator constructors and repair workers belong to labor unions.

Earnings and Benefits

Earnings for elevator constructors and repair workers vary, depending on the worker's experience and the location of the work. Currently the average salary for unionized elevator constructors and repair workers is $865 a week. Nonunion workers earn $740 to $1,090 a week depending on the place and the complexity of their jobs. Apprentices and helpers earn 50 percent of the rate experienced workers receive. This rate increases to 70 percent as they gain experience on the job.

Union members generally receive paid holidays, life insurance, and hospitalization and pension plans. The number of vacation days they receive depends on the number of days they work each year. Other benefits are negotiated separately for each union contract.

Where to Go for More Information

International Union of Elevator Constructors
5565 Sterrett Place, Clark Building,
   Suite 310
Columbia, MD 21044
(410) 997-9000

National Association of Elevator Contractors
1298 Wellbrook Circle
Conyers, GA 30207
(770) 760-9660

National Elevator Industry
185 Bridge Plaza, North
Fort Lee, NJ 07024
(201) 944-3211

Floor Covering Installer

Education and Training
None

Salary Range
Average—$345
to $660 a week

Employment Outlook
Fair

Definition and Nature of the Work

Floor covering installers are people who put down carpet, linoleum, and tile in older buildings as well as those under construction. They also install materials made of cork, asphalt, rubber, and vinyl. In addition to floors, they sometimes cover walls and countertops. Floor covering installers work for retail installers and installing contractors. They install floor coverings in homes, offices, factories, stores, and other buildings.

Floor coverings fall into two basic types: carpetlike materials and more resilient coverings, such as linoleum and asphalt tile. Some floor finishers are able to install both types, but they generally specialize in either carpet or resilient installation.

The first step in the installation of either type is the same: preparation of the subfloor. The subfloor is what lies beneath all floor coverings. It can be wood, concrete, stone, or other material. If it is a rough or uneven floor, the installer must fill in the cracks and go over it with a power sander. A smooth, clean, dry subfloor can mean the difference between a good floor covering and one that does not lie flat.

To install sheet goods (rolls of flooring) and tile, the floor installer carefully prepares the subfloor. Next the installer applies a strong glue or adhesive. The installer then carefully sets the floor covering in place. An installer finishes the job by going over the glued area with a rubber roller designed to create a smooth, even surface.

If wall-to-wall carpet is to be installed, an installer puts down special spiked strips called tackless strips near the walls. The spikes or tiny pins help to hold the carpet in place. Next the installer rolls out the padding and then the carpet. Carpet installers may sew large parts of carpeting together if necessary. The carpet is then stretched tightly over the floor and hooked to the pins. The stretching prevents ripples and bulges. Sometimes carpet is glued to the subfloor in the same way as sheet goods.

When installing any kind of floor covering, the floor finishers must cut pieces to fit around pipes, radiators, support posts, and other obstacles. Matching patterns is also an important part of the job. To avoid wasting material, the floor installer must plan the job very carefully before beginning work.

Education and Training Requirements

A high school education is good preparation for this field. Courses in geometry, algebra, business arithmetic, mechanical drawing, and shop will give you a good start.

There are several ways to enter this trade. Formal apprenticeships usually teach you how to handle many different floor covering materials and tools. The more materials you can install, the easier it will be to find a job. Apprenticeship classes include learning layouts, architectural drawings, and other skills for the trade. Apprenticeship programs are supervised by various trade unions.

Many vocational and trade schools offer courses in floor covering installation. If there are no apprenticeships available in your area, these schools offer a way to get the necessary training. You can get on-the-job training by working for a floor covering installing firm. You will begin as a helper and learn the trade by working under a skilled worker. Summer work as a helper or floor covering salesperson is also a good way to prepare for this career.

A carpet installer uses a variety of tools to stretch the carpet tightly over the floor and hook it to the pins or spikes that hold the carpet in place.

Getting the Job

There are a number of ways to become an installer. You can find out about apprenticeship programs. Then check with the union of floor installers about job openings and requirements. You can also contact local floor covering contractors.

Another option is to apply for a job with an installing firm. Try to find one that handles many different kinds of floor coverings. Ask if they could use you as a helper or trainee. Also, consider working for a floor covering manufacturer. Knowing how coverings are made can be helpful. Register with your state employment service and check the newspaper classifieds and the Yellow Pages.

Advancement Possibilities and Employment Outlook

Fully qualified workers can become job or work crew supervisors. They can also become district service managers. Some installers become salespeople or estimators. It is even possible to open a business.

The employment opportunities for floor covering installers are expected to grow somewhat slower than the average for all jobs through the year 2006. However, there will always be a need for floor covering installers. Worn-out floor coverings must be replaced. People frequently remodel their homes or businesses. When the construction industry is active, the need for floor covering installers increases. The number of jobs in this field, as with almost every other industry, depends on the economy.

Working Conditions

Most jobs take place indoors, so weather is not usually a factor. Some jobs do require working in new, unheated buildings, however. An installer may occasionally get knee or back injuries since floor installers do a lot of bending, kneeling, and lifting in the course of their work.

An 8-hour day and 40-hour week are common. Overtime work may be necessary on certain jobs. Evening and weekend work may also be necessary when a store or office floor is being covered and normal business hours cannot be interrupted.

Where to Go for More Information

Association of Specialists in Cleaning and
   Restoration International
10830 Annapolis Junction Road, Suite 312
Annapolis Junction, MD 20701-1120
(301) 604-4411
www.ascr.org

International Brotherhood of Painters and
   Allied Trades
1750 New York Avenue, NW, Eighth Floor
Washington, DC 20006
(202) 637-0700

United Brotherhood of Carpenters and
   Joiners of America
101 Constitution Avenue, NW
Washington, DC 20001
(202) 546-6206

Earnings and Benefits

Floor covering installers work either for a fixed salary for one company or as subcontractors for many companies and construction firms. Floor covering installers earn a weekly salary ranging from $345 to $660. Experienced workers can make up to $875 a week. Subcontractors often earn more than salaried employees earn; however, they have no guaranteed income. Also, subcontractors must maintain a truck and equipment.

Floor installers may be paid by the number of square feet they install instead of on an hourly or weekly basis. Bonuses for speed and efficiency are not uncommon. In addition, some stores also pay commissions to workers for selling floor care products to customers.

People who work for one company usually receive vacation pay, pension plans, insurance, and other benefits. Benefits vary among small subcontractors. Self-employed people may have to make their own arrangements.

Glazier

Education and Training
None

Salary Range
Average—$28
to $42 an hour

Employment Outlook
Fair

Definition and Nature of the Work

Glaziers install glass. They work with sheet glass, plate glass, mirrors, and special products, such as leaded glass panels. They install sheet glass windows in private homes; plate glass in store windows, office buildings, and factories; and structural glass in building fronts, ceilings, and walls. Other glaziers work in factories installing glass in mirror frames, doors, and partitions.

To install glass in a window, the glazier must first measure the window frame. The glazier either cuts a sheet of glass to the proper size or uses a piece of precut glass. Then putty is applied to the edges of the frame. The glazier puts the glass into the frame. The glass is secured in place with triangular points or metal clips. Then the glazier flattens the putty with a putty knife to seal out moisture.

Structural glass is handled differently. The glazier installs it by pressing it against cement that has been applied to the backing that supports the glass.

Glaziers install shower and tub enclosures, mirrors, and automatic glass doors. Their tools include suction cups for holding glass plates, glass cutters, putty knives, power cutters, and grinders.

Education and Training Requirements

The best way to become a glazier is to complete a 3-year apprenticeship program. You must have a high school diploma and be at least 17 years of age to enter the

Glaziers install windows and various types of glass products including frames, doors, and partitions.

program. The apprenticeship program combines on-the-job training with at least 144 hours of classroom instruction each year.

On the job, apprentices learn to use materials and tools. In the classroom, apprentices are taught to read blueprints and job specifications, plan designs and layouts, and understand the mathematics related to the trade. Since working with large pieces of glass can be dangerous, an important part of the classroom instruction deals with safety measures and first aid. Glaziers learn their trade by working as helpers for experienced glaziers. In small towns, some painters and paperhangers learn to do glazier's work as part of their training.

Getting the Job

The best way to enter the trade is to apply to a local contractor or union for entry into an apprenticeship program. Another way to enter the field is to ask local glaziers about job opportunities as a helper. You can also try the Yellow Pages and the classified sections of newspapers.

Advancement Possibilities and Employment Outlook

Most glaziers are employed in the construction industry. Experienced glaziers can become supervisors or estimators. Many glaziers own their own businesses.

Glass is a favorite material of today's builders and architects. It is used in large buildings and skyscrapers as wall paneling. Glaziers will be needed to install this material.

Currently about 36,000 glaziers are employed in the construction industry in the U.S. Employment opportunities are expected to grow more slowly than the average for all jobs, which means the outlook is fair through the year 2006. The number of employment opportunities in the construction industry also varies with fluctuations in the economy.

Working Conditions

Since most glaziers work indoors, they seldom lose work time because of bad weather. Glaziers can be hurt by sharp glass edges and cutting tools. They risk injury from falls, since they work on scaffolds and ladders. In an effort to reduce injuries, contractors and unions stress safety methods. Glaziers generally work a standard 40-hour week. They are paid higher wages for overtime work. Many glaziers are unionized.

Earnings and Benefits

Apprentice glaziers earn 50 to 60 percent of the qualified craft worker's salary at the beginning of their training. As the training continues, apprentices receive periodic wage increases. Currently the average wage for unionized glaziers is $28 an hour, with experienced workers earning up to $42 an hour. Wages vary from one part of the country to another.

Union workers receive paid holidays, life insurance, and hospitalization and pension plans. The number of vacation days they receive depends on the number of days they work each year. Other benefits are negotiated separately for each union contract.

Where to Go for More Information

National Glass Association
8200 Greensboro Drive, Suite 302
McLean, VA 22102
(703) 442-4890

United Steelworkers of America
5 Gateway Center
Pittsburgh, PA 15222
(412) 562-2400

Heavy Equipment Operator

Education and Training
High school

Salary Range
Average—$330
to $605 a week

Employment Outlook
Fair

Definition and Nature of the Work

Heavy equipment operators drive and control bulldozers, trench diggers, cranes, and other large pieces of machinery. These machines are used at building sites. Some machines are complex; some are simple. Operators use bulldozers, backhoes, and tractors for moving large amounts of dirt. They use cranes and derricks to move heavy equipment and materials. Heavy equipment operators know a great deal about different machines and different kinds of construction. Operators are sometimes called operating engineers.

Operators sit in the cabs of the machines. They control the machinery with pedals and levers. Their job at a worksite may be to hoist concrete or steel. They also level roads for paving, and dig holes for plumbing and foundations. One machine they use often is the crane. The crane can do many jobs because different parts can be attached to it. The crane can dig out and lift dirt or drive steel beams into the ground. When a wrecking ball is attached to it, the crane can knock down walls. To run the crane, or any construction machine, operating engineers must be able to judge spaces correctly and handle many controls at the same time. If they want to keep working regularly, operating engineers should know how to use a number of machines.

Many heavy equipment operators work at the construction sites of highways, tunnels, high-rise buildings, and airports. Others have regular jobs in factories, steel mills, and mines.

Education and Training Requirements

You must have a high school diploma to enter an apprenticeship program. These programs are the best way to learn the trade. They combine 3 years of on-the-job

Heavy equipment operators use bulldozers, backhoes, and tractors to move large amounts of dirt and other materials.

training with at least 144 hours of classroom instruction each year. As an apprentice, you are taught how to operate and repair bulldozers, hoists, shovels, cranes, and crushing machines. You learn about different kinds of oils and greases, how to weld and cut materials, and how to read plans. To apply for these programs, you must be at least 18 years old. You must also be in top physical condition and have good hand-eye coordination. The ability to work as part of a team is very important.

Some heavy equipment operators learn their trade while they are helpers or repair assistants. These helpers are called oilers. Some large contracting firms may train oilers to become operators of simple machines, such as pumps or dirt borers. However, since machines are dangerous if not used properly, a 3-year apprenticeship program is recommended.

Getting the Job

Working as a helper for a heavy equipment repair worker is a good way to learn about the craft. If you already know how to use farm equipment, you might get a job operating simple construction machinery. The best way to enter the trade is through an apprenticeship program. Contact local contractors or unions for information about such programs. You can also check the classified sections of newspapers for job openings.

Advancement Possibilities and Employment Outlook

Experienced operators may become supervisors. Some buy their own equipment and start contracting businesses. Still others leave the construction field to work in factories or mines.

The employment outlook for equipment operators is fair. Employment is expected to increase more slowly than the average for all jobs through the year 2006 due to mechanization and computerization of equipment. The work can be seasonal and depends on the health of the economy as a whole.

Working Conditions

Heavy equipment operators work with more regularity during the summer than in the winter. Rain or snow causes a good deal of lost work time. Operators work in very cold as well as warm weather. Physical stamina is an important asset because the bucking, jolting, and vibrating of the machines can be extremely tiring. Operators generally work 40 hours a week. They earn extra wages for overtime work. Many heavy equipment operators belong to labor unions.

Where to Go for More Information

Associated General Contractors of America
1957 E Street, NW
Washington, DC 20006-5199
(202) 393-2040

International Union of Operating Engineers
1125 Seventeenth Street, NW
Washington, DC 20036
(202) 429-9100

National Association of Women in
    Construction
327 South Adams Street
Fort Worth, TX 76104
(817) 877-5551
www.nawic.org

Earnings and Benefits

Apprentices in this trade begin at 50 to 70 percent of the qualified craft worker's hourly wage. The pay is increased as the apprentices progress through training. Earnings for qualified workers vary depending on the location and the nature of the work. Currently the wages of heavy equipment operators generally average $330 to $605 a week. Crane operators are at the top of the pay scale as the most highly ranked workers in the trade. The wages for operators of other kinds of equipment, such as bulldozers and air compressors, are at the lower end of the salary range. Take-home pay is affected by loss of work due to bad weather. Union workers generally get paid holidays, life insurance, and hospitalization and pension plans. The number of vacation days they receive depends on the number of days they work each year. Other benefits are negotiated separately for each union contract.

Insulation Worker

Education and Training
None

Salary Range
Average—$22 to $48 an hour

Employment Outlook
Good

Definition and Nature of the Work

Insulation workers apply insulation to pipes, boilers, furnaces, and other building equipment. Insulation conserves heat or cold and absorbs sound. Insulation workers use cork, felt, fiberglass, and other materials to insulate any equipment in which loss of heat or cold would lessen efficiency.

Insulation workers can work in either maintenance or construction. Those who do maintenance work are employed at chemical plants, oil refineries, cold storage facilities, and atomic energy stations. There they check pipes that carry steam or freezing liquids for proper insulation. Where necessary, insulation workers alter or replace inadequate insulation. Insulators also take part in the actual construction of such plants. To insulate equipment, workers first cover the area with a base insulator and attach it with wire clips. Then they clip, sew, or staple a canvas, tar paper, or cloth covering over the insulation.

To insulate equipment, workers first cover the area with a base insulator. Then they clip, sew, or staple a canvas, tar paper, or cloth covering over the insulation.

Many types of insulation are used. In oil refineries insulation workers use a magnesium-cork compound. Rockwool, sheet metal, and mineral compounds are also used in other types of work.

Workers apply the insulation by wiring, taping, stud welding, spraying, blowing, or pasting. They use trowels, hammers, brushes, pliers, stapling guns, saws, knives, and scissors. They may also use power equipment such as welding machines and compressors.

Education and Training Requirements

You do not need to be a high school graduate to enter the insulation trade, though contractors prefer to hire workers with a high school diploma. In order to enter a 4-year "improvership" program, you must have a high school diploma or its equivalent. Trainees learn from experienced workers. To be eligible, you must be in good health, fairly strong, and at least 18 years old.

At the end of the improvership program, trainees must pass a test in order to become qualified insulation workers. Many insulation workers learn their trade in an informal way. Starting as helpers, they learn the craft by observing and working with experienced craft workers. A license is not required to work in this trade.

Getting the Job

The best way to enter this trade is to contact a local insulation contractor. Contractors know of openings in improvership programs. A contractor may also be able to help you find a job. If there are no insulation contractors in your area, contact the appropriate union. You can also check the newspaper classifieds for job openings.

Advancement Possibilities and Employment Outlook

Insulation workers are already at the top of their craft. However, experienced insulation workers can become supervisors or shop superintendents. These workers oversee the insulation work on large jobs. Insulation workers can also become cost and material estimators. Some insulators become contractors and own their own businesses.

The employment outlook for insulation workers is good. More than 65,000 insulation workers are employed in the United States. This number is expected to increase as fast as the average for all occupations through the year 2006. As fuel costs increase, there will be a demand for more workers to install insulation to help conserve energy. Moreover, the use of piping in industry is increasing. Cold storage facilities for food, furs, and other items are becoming more popular. The increased use of air-conditioning in businesses, homes, and schools may also provide more jobs for insulation workers.

Working Conditions

Insulation workers must bend and stoop a great deal. Workers spend a lot of time in cramped quarters and on ladders, using their arms and hands for reaching and holding. Since construction insulators sometimes work outdoors, work time may be lost due to poor weather. On the other hand, maintenance insulators work indoors. They must be able to cope with dirt and dust when replacing old insulation. Serious lung diseases can result from long-term exposure to asbestos fibers found in the insulation of older buildings. Generally, insulation workers work 40 hours a week. Overtime work brings extra pay. Many insulation workers belong to labor unions.

Earnings and Benefits

Trainees earn 50 percent of a qualified craft worker's wage at the beginning of the improvership program. The percentage is increased every few months until they complete the program. Currently, insulation workers earn an average hourly salary ranging from $22 to $48. Union workers average $30 an hour, and generally receive paid holidays and life insurance, as well as hospitalization and pension plans. The number of vacation days received depends on the number of days worked each year. Other benefits are negotiated separately for each union contract.

Where to Go for More Information

International Association of Heat and Frost Insulators and Asbestos Workers
1776 Massachusetts Avenue, NW, Suite 301
Washington, DC 20036-1989
(202) 785-2388

National Insulation and Abatement Contractors Association
99 Canal Center Plaza, Suite 222
Alexandria, VA 22314-1538
(703) 683-6422

United States Department of Labor
Bureau of Apprenticeship and Training
200 Constitution Avenue, NW, Room North 4649
Washington, DC 20210
(202) 219-5921

Iron and Steel Worker

Education and Training
High school

Salary Range
Varies—see profile

Employment Outlook
Good

Definition and Nature of the Work

Bridges and skyscrapers, bank vaults and elevators, fences and stairways—iron and steel workers construct them all. Those who erect bridges, framework for buildings, and other supports for heavy equipment are called *structural iron workers*. They raise, pry, push, and pull huge steel girders and beams into place. Work on large structures, such as bridges, is done in crews. Each crew member specializes in a certain operation.

Once cranes and derricks raise girders into place, a detail crew joins parts temporarily using steel driftpins. A second crew then uses crowbars, jacks, wedges, turnbuckles, and cables to level and align all the structural parts. Finally, iron workers weld, bolt, or rivet the girders permanently together.

Working closely with the structural iron workers are people known as *rod workers* or *reinforcing iron workers*. They reinforce the concrete used in building bridges and highways with steel rods or mesh. They put precut rods inside pouring forms before the forms are filled with concrete. While the concrete is still wet, the rod workers move the rods into position with long, hooked poles. The concrete must be evenly supported, so positioning is very important. Steel mesh is also used. It is spread over a surface to be covered with concrete. The rod workers cut, bend, and hammer the mesh into place.

Ornamental iron workers install all preconstructed metal structures, including elevators, stairways, balconies, and grillwork. They bolt or weld these structures into position.

Education and Training Requirements

The best way to learn the trade is through a 3-year apprenticeship program. Apprentices should be at least 18 years old. A high school diploma is required. The program consists of 3 years of on-the-job training with at least 144 hours a year of classroom instruction. On the job, apprentices are taught by experienced workers. They learn how to put together, install, and repair metal structures. Welding and riveting are also taught. The apprentices learn how to work in crews. In the classroom, apprentices are taught drafting, mathematics, blueprint reading, and other technical skills. Many iron workers who do not go through the apprenticeship program learn their trade by working as helpers.

Steel is made by combining molten iron with scrap metal and selected additives in large furnaces. Workers use steel to construct bridges, skyscrapers, bank vaults, elevators, fences, and stairways.

Getting the Job

To get a job in steel and iron work, you should contact a local contractor or union. Either source can give you information about apprenticeship programs. Another good way to learn the basics is to get a job as a laborer assisting iron and steel workers. Laborers often advance to helpers' positions.

Advancement Possibilities and Employment Outlook

Iron and steel workers are already at the top of their craft. However, experienced iron and steel workers can become supervisors. A few start their own businesses. Experienced iron and steel workers can change jobs within the field. For example, structural workers might choose to do ornamental work.

In the long run, the outlook for iron and steel workers is good, with employment projected to increase as fast as the average for all occupations through the year 2006. However, the number of jobs in the construction industry varies with the general economy.

Iron is being used more and more for ornamental purposes. The increased use of steel in the construction of glass and panel frames also means that more jobs will be available for iron and steel workers. The increased use of reinforced concrete in construction will also open more jobs for these workers.

Working Conditions

Iron and steel workers generally work 40 hours a week. They earn extra wages for overtime work. Since the work takes place outdoors, bad weather can cause lost work time. Therefore, a high hourly wage does not always mean a high annual income. Iron and steel workers use heavy and bulky materials. Above-average strength is required to handle these materials. Structural workers must be agile and have a sense of balance. They spend a lot of time at great heights, walking on narrow footways. Although structural work is still more hazardous than other building trades, the use of safety nets, scaffolding, and helmets has reduced the risk of injury.

Steel and iron workers must sometimes travel long distances for jobs. The local demand for workers is not always large enough to keep crews employed continuously. Some contractors keep crews working by moving them to different parts of the country. Many workers belong to labor unions.

Earnings and Benefits

Wages for iron and steel workers vary according to the worker's experience and the type of job at which the worker is employed. Wages also vary from region to region. Iron and steel workers earn an hourly wage ranging from $20 to $50. Currently the average union wage is $30 an hour, including benefits. Wages for ornamental iron workers are roughly comparable with those of other iron and steel workers.

Union workers generally receive paid holidays, life insurance, and hospitalization and pension plans. The number of vacation days they receive depends on the number of days they work each year. Other benefits are negotiated separately for each union contract.

Where to Go for More Information

Associated General Contractors of America
1957 E Street, NW
Washington, DC 20006-5199
(202) 393-2040

International Association of Bridge,
    Structural, Ornamental and Reinforcing
    Iron Workers
1750 New York Avenue, NW, Suite 400
Washington, DC 20006
(202) 383-4800

United Steelworkers of America
5 Gateway Center
Pittsburgh, PA 15222
(412)562-2400

Lather

Education and Training
None

Salary Range
Average—$23,200

Employment Outlook
Good

Definition and Nature of the Work

Lathers install the metal lath and gypsum lath boards that support the plaster, concrete, and stucco coatings used in construction. Lath is applied to the framework of ceilings and walls. It is also used as a basic frame for the construction of arches and cornices. Metal lath is composed of either wire mesh or strips of expanded metal. When the plaster is mixed properly and to the right consistency, it sticks to the lath. To install metal lath, the lathers first build a metal framework, which they attach to the structure of the building. The framework is called furring. Then they attach the lath to the furring with nails, wire, clips, or machine stapling. After the lathers have finished attaching the lath, they cut holes for the electrical outlets, switches, and plumbing.

Sheets of gypsum board are applied in a similar way. Lathers put this kind of lath up so that it covers the framework of thin wood slats called studs. To cut the board to the proper size, lathers cut lines on one side of the gypsum lath with a lath hatchet. Then they break it along these lines with sharp blows to the other side. They cut openings for electrical outlets and switches and then attach the lath to the wall. Lathers use such tools as drills, shears, hammers, hacksaws, hatchets, wirecutters, and power fastening devices.

Education and Training Requirements

Many lathers gain their knowledge and skill by working as helpers. They learn by watching experienced workers. Another way to learn the craft is to complete a 2-year union-sponsored apprenticeship program. High school graduates are preferred. To become an apprentice, you must be at least 16 years of age. Those who apply must pass tests of manual dexterity before they can be accepted.

Tests are given to apprentices every 6 months to check their progress. On the job, apprentices work with skilled lathers and are taught to use the tools and materials. In the classroom, the apprentices learn welding, applied mathematics, and geometry. They are also taught how to estimate costs and how to read sketches and blueprints. Some classroom time is devoted to safety practices.

Getting the Job

The best way to enter the lathing profession is to contact a local union or contractor for information about the apprenticeship program. You can also ask a local lather or contractor for work as a helper.

Advancement Possibilities and Employment Outlook

Lathers are already at the top of their craft. However, experienced lathers can become supervisors at the job site. Others supervise all lathing work for a general contractor. Some lathers own their own contracting businesses.

Employment is projected to grow slowly through the year 2006, but thousands of job opportunities should still be available annually due to a high turnover rate in the profession. It is expected that there will be more openings in commercial than in residential construction. Lathers are needed to put up the framework for plaster work. Plaster is used chiefly in expensive buildings and on curved surfaces. There may be fewer jobs for lathers, however, in buildings that use drywall materials, which do not require lath.

Working Conditions

Lathers generally work 40 hours a week. They earn extra wages for overtime work. Since lathers usually work indoors, they seldom lose work time because of bad weather. Lathers may become tired from standing, squatting, and stooping. When working on ceilings and other elevated areas, lathers stand on ladders and scaffoldings. Many lathers are unionized.

Earnings and Benefits

Apprentice lathers earn 50 percent of the qualified craft worker's wage at the start of their training program and then earn more as their training progresses. Currently most lathers earn an average salary of $23,200 a year. Experienced workers, employed in large urban areas, can earn much more.

Union workers generally receive paid vacations and life insurance, as well as hospitalization and pension plans. The number of vacation days they receive depends on the number of days they work each year. Other benefits are negotiated separately for each union contract.

A lather installs a metal lath to the frame of a window. After he finishes, the lath will be covered by plaster.

Where to Go for More Information

International Institute for Lath and Plaster
3127 Los Feliz Boulevard
Los Angeles, CA 90039
(213) 660-4411

National Association of the
Remodeling Industry
4301 North Fairfax Drive, Suite 310
Arlington, VA 22203-3000
(703) 276-7600

United Brotherhood of Carpenters and
Joiners of America
101 Constitution Avenue, NW
Washington, DC 20001
(202) 546-6206

Manufactured Home Assembler and Installer

Definition and Nature of the Work

Manufactured home assemblers and installers are factory workers who specialize in building transportable houses. The homes they construct are currently in great demand as efficient, economical alternatives to conventional homes that are built at a construction site. These homes are unlike mobile homes of the past. They are usually moved just once, from the factory to the living site.

Many pieces of the manufactured home are prefabricated to make assembly easy. The assembler's work begins with construction of the chassis that serves as the home's supporting foundation. Below the floor of the home, assemblers install thermal insulation and a network of water and sewer pipes and ducts that will supply heating and air-conditioning. Assemblers then build and install the floor, which they attach to the chassis. Next they secure the walls to the floor, beginning with the innermost walls and working outward to the siding. The upper insulation, beams, and roof are added last.

When the assemblers have finished their work, the installers take over. They install and connect the plumbing, wiring, heating, air-conditioning units, and appliances. They also add finishing touches, such as floor coverings, moldings, and hardware. The house is then ready to be sold and transported by truck or tractor to the designated site.

Education and Training Requirements

Manufactured home assembly and installation work is generally considered semiskilled labor. It has no particular education requirements, although a high school diploma is often preferred. Training is provided on the job.

Manufactured home assemblers use cranes to lift the prefabricated, or factory-produced, pieces of a manufactured home.

Getting the Job

Manufactured home factories are located in nearly all states, so consult your local telephone book or state employment office to find the nearest plants. Beginners are accepted readily if a factory is in need of workers. Also check job listings in your local newspapers.

Advancement Possibilities and Employment Outlook

Workers who learn the various assembly and installation processes thoroughly and have good interpersonal skills may be promoted to group supervisors. Those who earn college degrees may become factory superintendents, engineers, or designers within the industry.

The employment outlook is good, since the number of manufactured homes being purchased is increasing substantially. People are looking for a less expensive alternative to conventional housing. Therefore the future of the industry will depend, in part, on the cost of conventional houses.

Working Conditions

Assemblers and installers generally work a 40-hour, 5-day week. However, they may be subject to layoffs during slow periods. The job entails a moderate amount of physical activity and some discomfort during summer months, when factories become overheated and cannot be air-conditioned sufficiently because of their size. Also, the assembly and installation processes call for workers to repeat the same type of work throughout the day.

Earnings and Benefits

Currently manufactured home assemblers and installers earn an average of $18,000 to $26,000 a year. However, salaries differ according to the geographical area. Workers sometimes have an opportunity to earn overtime pay during busy periods. They may also receive bonuses for exceptionally high output. Benefits usually include paid vacations and holidays, medical insurance, and pension plans.

Where to Go for More Information

Manufactured Housing Institute
2101 Wilson Boulevard, Suite 610
Arlington, VA 22201-3062
(703) 558-0400
www.mfghome.org

Marble, Tile, and Terrazzo Worker

Definition and Nature of the Work

Within the field of construction there are many specialized workers. Marble setters install marble, terrazzo panels, and structural glass in large buildings. Tile setters apply tile to walls, floors, and ceilings in homes and businesses. Terrazzo workers install a decorative concrete mixture used mostly for flooring in schools, office buildings, and hospitals. These workers use a variety of tools including hammers, chisels, trowels, putty knives, power grinders, and polishers. They generally work with at least one helper.

To set marble, marble setters first drill holes in the corners of the marble sheet. They place fasteners, such as bolts or screws, through these holes. Then they press the marble against a plaster mixture that they have applied to the wall. Once the marble is in place, marble setters pack a special mixture between the

Education and Training
None

Salary Range
Average—$470 a week

Employment Outlook
Good

Tile setters apply tile to walls, floors, and ceilings in homes and businesses.

slabs and smooth and finish this mixture with a trowel. A trowel is a flat, pointed tool made of metal.

Tile setters apply a special cement to the walls, floors, and ceilings they are covering. Sometimes they put cement on the backs of the tiles, as well. Then they set each tile in place and tap it to make sure the cement will hold. To fit tiles in corners and around plumbing and electrical outlets, setters use chisels and other tools to crack the tiles to the proper shape and size. This requires a lot of skill and patience.

Terrazzo is an ornamental mixture of tinted concrete and marble chips. Terrazzo workers first lay a mortar base. Mortar is a mixture of cement or plaster used to hold the terrazzo in place. They level the mortar with a straight-edge. They put metal strips in the mortar wherever there is to be a joint or a change of color between the panels. Then they mix colored cement and marble chips to make the terrazzo. They put this mixture over the mortar base, and they roll and level it. In a few days, when it is dry, the terrazzo workers smooth and polish the surface with a grinding machine.

Education and Training Requirements

A high school diploma is preferred but not required. Many marble and tile setters and terrazzo workers learn their skill while working as helpers to skilled workers. The recommended way of learning these trades is through the formal apprenticeship programs. These are 3-year programs that combine on-the-job training with 144 hours of classroom instruction each year. To join an apprenticeship program, you should be in good health and have a certain degree of manual dexterity. A sense of color harmony is very helpful. On the job, apprentices learn how to use materials and perform the various operations of the trade. In the classroom, they are taught blueprint reading, basic mathematics, and layout work.

Getting the Job

The best method of entering these trades is to apply to the apprenticeship programs. You may find a position as a helper by contacting contractors in your area. Check the Yellow Pages or newspaper classifieds for job openings.

Advancement Possibilities and Employment Outlook

Marble and tile setters and terrazzo workers are already at the top of their craft. However, skilled and experienced workers in these crafts can become supervisors. Some start their own contracting businesses.

Currently more than 135,000 people are employed as marble and tile setters and terrazzo workers in the U.S. This number is expected to increase as fast as the average for all occupations through the year 2006. However, employment opportunities in these trades depend on the state of the general economy.

Working Conditions

The materials used in these trades are heavy and in some cases bulky. Helpers are responsible for moving materials and cleanup duties. The work requires extended periods of standing and squatting. Terrazzo workers and marble setters work both indoors and out. Their work can be affected by bad weather. Tile setters work mostly indoors, so their work is unaffected by weather. Marble, tile, and terrazzo workers generally work 40 hours a week. They earn extra wages for overtime hours. A large number of tile and marble setters are union members.

Earnings and Benefits

Apprentices earn 50 to 60 percent of the experienced worker's wage. Wages are increased periodically until the apprentice becomes a qualified craft worker and earns the full salary. Today's average weekly earnings for union workers is $470. Experienced marble, tile, and terrazzo workers who are skilled in their craft often earn $40,000 or more each year. Union workers generally receive paid holidays, life insurance, and hospitalization and pension plans. The number of vacation days they receive depends on the number of days they work each year. Other benefits are negotiated separately for each union contract.

Where to Go for More Information

Mason Contractors Association of America
1910 Highland Avenue, Suite 101
Lombard, IL 60148-6147
(630) 705-4200

National Terrazzo and Mosaic Association
110 East Market Street, Suite 200-A
Leesburg, VA 20176-3122
(703) 779-1022

Tile, Marble, Terrazzo, Finishers, Shop
  Workers and Granite Cutters
  International Union
c/o United Brotherhood of Carpenters and
  Joiners of America
101 Constitution Avenue, NW
Washington, DC 20001
(202) 546-6206

Painter and Paperhanger

Definition and Nature of the Work

Painters and paperhangers apply finishes to walls, ceilings, and other surfaces. Although painting and paperhanging are two separate trades, many workers have mastered them both. Painters apply paint, varnish, and other finishes with brushes, rollers, and spray machines. These finishes decorate and protect surfaces both inside and out. Paperhangers apply wallpaper, vinyl, and fabric covering to preserve and decorate the indoor surfaces of older buildings as well as those under construction.

Painters and paperhangers put the finishing touches on new homes and buildings. Painting and paperhanging must be done after most other work has been completed so that the walls and other surfaces are clean when the building is ready to be occupied. Painters and paperhangers also work on old buildings and homes. They give homes a new look by hanging paper or putting fresh coats of paint on inside walls. Many painters also repaint the outside of homes and other buildings to add color and protect them from weathering and dirt.

Before painters and paperhangers put on the paint or paper, they clean the dirt, oil, and grease from the surfaces to be covered. Old paint and wall covering must be removed; they are heated or wetted down and then scraped off. Cracks and holes made by nails are filled with plaster and smoothed over. This process is called spackling.

Painters must apply the paint quickly and smoothly. They must know what materials were used to make the paint. Different materials, such as plaster, wood, brick, and metal, require different paints. Painters must have a good eye for color in order to mix and match paints.

Paperhangers first apply sizing, which is a mixture that makes the surface less porous and makes the paper stick well. They measure the surface and cut the

Education and Training
None

Salary Range
Average—$285
to $515 a week

Employment Outlook
Good

A paperhanger uses a putty knife to cut the wallpaper so that it fits perfectly on the wall.

paper to fit it. Then they mix the adhesive used to glue the paper to the wall. They brush the adhesive on the back of the paper strip and press the strip on the wall. They pay careful attention to match the pattern from strip to strip. When the paper is placed on the wall, the paperhangers cut the edges at the ceiling and baseboards. They smooth out any air bubbles or creases by pushing them toward the corners with a straightedge. Tools used by painters and paperhangers include brushes, spray guns, rollers, putty knives, scissors, and rulers.

Education and Training Requirements

A high school diploma is preferred but not required. Many painters and paperhangers learn their skills while working as helpers for experienced craft workers. In paperhanging, more than in any other field, it is easy for a helper to gain recognition as a qualified craft worker.

Another way to enter the field is by participating in a 3- or 4-year apprenticeship program. Some programs offer training in both painting and paperhanging. Others train for only one trade. Apprenticeship programs are directed by joint union-management committees. They combine on-the-job training with at least 144 hours of related classroom instruction a year. To become an apprentice, you must be at least 16 years of age. You should be able to work well with your hands. An ability to sense and judge colors is important. During the apprenticeship, you learn what colors go well together and how to mix paints. You learn what paints are made of so you know what kinds of paints can be mixed together. You are also taught how to figure out how much a job will cost before you begin to work. Figuring the cost is important because you or your employer must know if the job is worth doing. In short, you learn how to use all the tools and techniques of the trade.

Getting the Job

The best way to enter these crafts is through an apprenticeship program. You can also start by getting a job as a helper with a local contractor. Check your Yellow Pages and newspaper classifieds for job opportunities.

Advancement Possibilities and Employment Outlook

Fully qualified painters and paperhangers are already at the top of their craft. However, experienced painters and paperhangers can become supervisors. They can also become job estimators or superintendents. Many painters and paperhangers open their own businesses as painters or decorating contractors.

About 444,000 people are now employed as painters and paperhangers in the U.S. This number is expected to increase as fast as the average for all jobs through the year 2006. However, the number of painters and paperhangers employed in the construction industry varies with the general economy.

Working Conditions

Most painters and paperhangers work 40 hours a week. They earn higher wages for overtime work. Paperhangers work indoors, so the weather has little effect on their work. Painters work both indoors and outdoors. Some of their work time may be lost due to bad weather. Since painters and paperhangers often work in crews or with helpers, they must be able to work well with other people.

Painters and paperhangers should not be allergic to paint fumes or other materials used in their trade. They must have strong arms, since most of their work calls for their arms to be raised overhead for extended periods of time. Since their job requires them to work on ladders and scaffolds, they risk injury from falls.

Earnings and Benefits

Earnings vary widely, depending on where you work. Currently fully qualified painters who are not self-employed earn between $285 and $515 a week. The most experienced and skilled workers can earn over $690 a week. Paperhangers generally earn more than painters. Certain kinds of work, such as bridge painting, pay higher wages.

Apprentices begin at 40 to 50 percent of the qualified craft worker's wage; they receive periodic increases as they progress through their training. Union members generally receive paid holidays, life insurance, and hospitalization and pension plans. The number of vacation days they receive depends on the number of days they work each year. Other benefits are negotiated separately for each union contract.

Where to Go for More Information

International Brotherhood of Painters and
 Allied Trades
1750 New York Avenue, NW, Eighth Floor
Washington, DC 20006
(202) 637-0700

National Association of Women in
 Construction
327 South Adams Street
Fort Worth, TX 76104
(817) 877-5551
www.nawic.org

United States Department of Labor
Bureau of Apprenticeship and Training
200 Constitution Avenue, NW, Room
 North 4649
Washington, DC 20210
(202) 219-5921

Plasterer

Definition and Nature of the Work

Plasterers are skilled craft workers who finish the interior surfaces of homes and buildings with plaster coating to strengthen, soundproof, insulate, and fireproof them. On the outside of buildings, they use cement plasters or stucco because these materials are strong and weatherproof. Plasterers who cast decorative molding, cornices, and paneling are called ornamental plasterers.

Plasterers work with carpenters, bricklayers, lathers, painters, and other craft workers. The carpenters build the frame of the building. Then lathers install the lath, a backing of wire mesh or gypsum board to which plaster easily sticks.

Plasterers then apply three different coats of plaster. The first coat is applied to the lath. It is called the scratch coat because it is scratched or raked so that the second coat will stick. The second coat, or brown coat, is smoothed and finished in preparation for the final coat. For an inside wall the final coat is a white lime mixture. This thin final coat is applied rapidly and then smoothed with a trowel, brush, and water. A trowel is a flat, pointed metal tool. For an outside wall, the final coat is a much heavier mixture of white cement and sand.

Education and Training
None

Salary Range
Average—$355
to $760 a week

Employment Outlook
Good

A plasterer smooths the final coat of plaster, a mixture of white cement and sand.

Plasterers may add marble chips or stone to the final coat to give the walls a decorative textured surface. They often use sand to create an unusual finish on outside or inside walls. By moving the trowel across the plaster in certain ways, plasterers can create intricate patterns.

Plasterers use many kinds of tools. The plate that holds the plaster is called a hawk. Plasterers also work with trowels, straightedges, brushes, floats (flat tools), bevel edges, rods, and power applicators. Power machines apply both the finish and base coats.

Education and Training Requirements

A high school diploma is preferred but not required. Courses in mathematics and drafting are helpful. Most plasterers are trained while working on construction sites. They work as laborers or helpers for experienced plasterers, and learn the trade by observing and assisting craft workers.

You can also become a plasterer by participating in a formal apprenticeship program. This is a 2- or 3- year program combining on-the-job training with at least 144 hours a year of related classroom instruction. At work, apprentices are taught by experienced plasterers. They learn how to use different methods and materials. For instance, they learn how to prepare different mixtures of plaster. Classroom instruction includes drafting, blueprint reading, and mathematics for layout work. Generally, you must be at least 17 years old to enter apprenticeship programs.

Getting the Job

You can enter the trade through an apprenticeship program. Contact a local contractor to find out about openings in the program. Working for an experienced plasterer as a helper or laborer is another way of entering the trade. A local contractor may know of openings for helpers. You can also try the Yellow Pages or newspaper classifieds for job openings.

Advancement Possibilities and Employment Outlook

Fully qualified plasterers are already at the top of their field. However, an experienced plasterer may become a supervisor or an estimator. Many plasterers are self-employed and have their own contracting businesses.

There are about 32,000 plasterers in the United States. Job opportunities in the construction industry vary with the economy. However, the employment outlook for plasterers is good. In fact, this is projected to be the fastest growing occupation in the construction trades. Although employment declined in past years with the increased use of drywall construction, that trend has reversed as builders came to appreciate the durability and appeal of plastered finishes.

Working Conditions

Plasterers may work alone or with others in crews, depending on the size of the building. They work indoors and outdoors. The work is often tiring. Plasterers must do much stooping and standing. Their arms must be extended for much of their working day. Sometimes they do heavy lifting, although this is often done by helpers. Most plasterers work 40 hours a week and get paid higher wages for overtime. Work is seasonal, as it is for most construction workers. Many plasterers belong to labor unions.

Earnings and Benefits

Fully qualified plasterers who belong to a union receive wages between $355 and $760 a week, including benefits. Wages vary greatly, depending on the location of the work. In some parts of the country plasterers are paid much higher wages than in other parts of the country. Plasterers typically make higher wages in big cities. Union workers generally receive paid holidays, life insurance, and hospitalization and pension plans. The number of vacation days they receive depends on the number of days they work each year.

Where to Go for More Information

International Institute for Lath and Plaster
3127 Los Feliz Boulevard
Los Angeles, CA 90039
(213) 660-4411

National Association of the Remodeling
   Industry
4301 North Fairfax Drive, Suite 310
Arlington, VA 22203-3000
(703) 276-7600

Operative Plasterers and Cement Masons
   International Association of the United
   States and Canada
14405 Laurel Place
Laurel, MD 20707
(301) 470-4200

Plumber and Pipe Fitter

Definition and Nature of the Work

Plumbers and pipe fitters assemble, install, and make changes in pipe systems used to carry water, steam, air, and other liquids and gases. They install plumbing fixtures, such as bathtubs and toilets. They also install heating and refrigeration units. Plumbing and pipe fitting are generally considered to be separate trades, though many qualified craft workers are skilled in both fields.

Many plumbers and pipe fitters work for contractors on the construction of new buildings. Some make repairs and alterations. They can also do maintenance work. Generally, those who do maintenance work are steadily employed by plants and factories. Plumbers and pipe fitters may work on the construction of ships and airplanes. Plumbers may also connect the water, gas, and waste disposal pipes to the city or town supply.

Before installing plumbing, plumbers study blueprints to see what kind and size of pipes are needed. They install plumbing in a new building in three basic steps. The first step is to run pipes inside the foundation before the concrete is poured. These pipes are used for water and waste. The second step is to install the pipes for the kitchen and bathroom. This is done after the carpenters have built the frame of the building. The plumbers must drill holes through the framework to run the pipes. The pipes must be bent, cut, and then connected to each other by solder or glue. Copper piping, used for water and heat, is joined by soldering. Plastic pipe, used for waste lines and air venting, is joined by glue.

After the piping has been installed, plumbers must check for leakage. To do this, plumbers cap all the pipe outlets and then pump air through the system to check for loss of pressure.

After the walls have been installed, the plumbers complete the final step. They put in plumbing fixtures, such as bathtubs, sinks, and toilets. When these fixtures are in place, the plumbers check to see that they are operating correctly.

Education and Training
None

Salary Range
Average—$33,000 to $38,000

Employment Outlook
Fair

After installing the plumbing in a new home, a plumber bends, cuts, and then connects all the water and waste pipes by soldering them.

Pipe fitters work with very large pipes, such as those used in industry. These pipes can withstand high or low pressures. Pipe fitters work in industries such as oil refineries, chemical plants, and food processing plants. They install, maintain, and repair the pipes through which these products pass. Pipe fitters also install boilers, oil burners, furnaces, and air-conditioning and sprinkler systems.

Pipe fitters follow many of the same procedures that plumbers do. After checking the blueprints and work area to find out where they should lay the pipes, the pipe fitters cut and thread the piping. To thread piping, pipe fitters use a machine to make a spiral ridge in the pipe. Then they bend the piping by hand or machine. The pipes are connected with the pipe joints by means of welding, brazing, soldering, gluing, caulking, or threading, depending on how the pipes are to be used.

Plumbers and pipe fitters use many tools, including benders, wrenches, drills, reamers, chisels, hammers, and other hand tools. They also use gas or acetylene torches and welding and soldering equipment for their work.

Education and Training Requirements

The best way to become a plumber or pipe fitter is to go through a 4- to 5-year apprenticeship program. A high school diploma is recommended. The apprenticeship program's standards and operations are set by a local union-management committee. This committee decides on the necessary training. It also determines the number of apprentices needed for the geographical area. The apprenticeship program combines on-the-job training with at least 144 annual hours of classroom instruction. To be considered for the program, you must pass a test given by the state employment service. The results of the test and your qualifications must then be approved by the local joint union-management apprenticeship committee. High school courses in mathematics, shop, chemistry, and physics are helpful if you are planning a career in plumbing and pipe fitting.

At first, apprentices in the program work as assistants to experienced craft workers. They learn to use the tools and materials of the trade. As they gain experience, their duties on the job become more complex. In the classroom, apprentices learn welding, soldering, applied mathematics, physics, and chemistry. They are taught how to read blueprints, and they learn the local and county building codes and regulations. In most states, a worker must have a license to work as a qualified plumber or pipe fitter. To get the license the qualified craft worker must pass a written test to demonstrate knowledge of the trade and of the local and county building codes.

Many plumbers and pipe fitters have learned their trade informally. They have gained experience by working with and observing experienced workers. This method of learning the trade generally takes longer and is less complete than a formal apprenticeship program.

Getting the Job

The best method of entering the plumbing and pipe fitting trade is to apply for an apprenticeship program. Contact a local contractor or union representative and ask about openings in the apprenticeship program. If you are still in high school, you might get a summer job as a helper. This is a very good way to gain experience. You can get a job as a helper by applying to a local plumbing and heating contractor. Also check the Yellow Pages and newspaper classifieds for job openings.

Advancement Possibilities and Employment Outlook

Plumbers and pipe fitters are already at the top of their trade. However, experienced craft workers can become supervisors. Some plumbers are self-employed, doing mainly repair, alteration, and modernization work. Many plumbers and pipe fitters open contracting businesses and employ other workers. In most areas contractors are required to have a master plumber's license.

In the long run, the employment outlook for plumbers and pipe fitters is fair. Although a number of workers will be needed as building construction increases, advances (such as more efficient sprinkler systems and plastic pipes and fittings) may mean less need for maintenance in the future.

More than 389,000 plumbers and pipe fitters are employed in the United States. Although employment is expected to grow more slowly than the average for all occupations through the year 2006, there will be plenty of job opportunities for skilled plumbers and pipe fitters. Currently, the demand for well-trained workers far exceeds the supply. Those workers willing to undergo the intensive training programs available will find themselves at an advantage.

Working Conditions

Plumbers and pipe fitters do active and strenuous work. They must frequently stand for long periods of time. There is also a good deal of kneeling, squatting, stooping, and working in cramped quarters. Generally, they work 40 hours a week. Higher wages are paid for overtime hours. The amount of work time lost due to bad weather is not as great as in other construction trades because plumbers and pipe fitters spend a good deal of time indoors. The risk of injury among plumbers and pipe fitters is lower than in most construction trades. Many plumbers and pipe fitters belong to labor unions.

Earnings and Benefits

Currently the average weekly wage for plumbers and pipe fitters who are not self-employed is $590. Most workers earn between $33,000 and $38,000 a year. Apprentices start at about 50 percent of the qualified worker's wage and earn periodic increases until they finish the program. Union workers generally receive paid holidays, life insurance, and hospitalization and pension plans. The number of vacation days they receive depends on the number of days they work each year. Other benefits are negotiated separately for each union contract.

Where to Go for More Information

Plumbing-Heating-Cooling Contractors—
National Association
180 South Washington Street, Box 6808
Falls Church, VA 22040-1148
(703) 237-8100

Plumbing-Heating-Cooling Information
Bureau
200 East Randolph, Suite 5000
Chicago, IL 60601-6401
(312) 372-7331

United Association of Journeymen and
Apprentices of the Plumbing and Pipe
Fitting Industry of United States and
Canada
901 Massachusetts Avenue, NW
Washington, DC 20001
(202) 628-5823
www.ua.org

Power Tool Repairer

Definition and Nature of the Work

Tool repairers fix a wide range of equipment from power drills, saws, wrenches, and riveters to jack hammers and pile drivers. Repairers may work for power tool manufacturers, construction equipment dealers, construction contractors, equipment rental companies, or repair shops. They may work in small shops and repair many types of tools, or they may work in large shops and specialize in repairing one type of tool.

When power tools do not work, repairers look for sources of trouble, such as faulty electrical connections. They may disassemble the tools to examine the parts for damage or excessive wear. They repair, replace, clean, and lubricate the parts. Then they reassemble and test the tools to make sure they are operating.

Power tool repairers also perform routine maintenance to keep the equipment in operation. This includes keeping the tools greased and oiled in addition to periodically cleaning and replacing parts before they are worn. They may keep records that show how often the tools are used, serviced, and repaired.

Power tool repairers use pliers, wrenches, screwdrivers, and soldering guns. They also use welding equipment to weld parts or to make new parts. They may use micrometers and gauges to measure wear on parts and ohmmeters, ammeters, and voltmeters to test electrical systems. Tool repairers study service manuals, wiring diagrams, and troubleshooting guides. They use catalogs to order replacement parts.

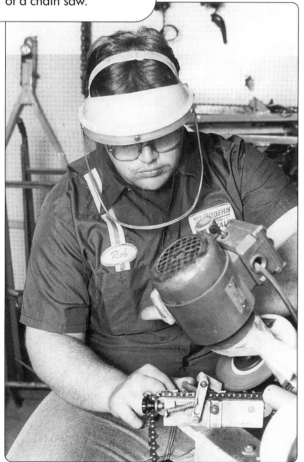

Power tool repairers often perform routine maintenance on tools to keep them functioning properly. This repairer is sharpening the blade of a chain saw.

Education and Training Requirements

You will most likely need a high school diploma to become a power tool repairer. While in high school, take courses in basic electricity and electronics. Some high schools offer 2-year applied physics courses that teach the principles of operating mechanical, fluid, electrical, and thermal devices. Vocational schools offer courses that are good for practical, hands-on experience in equipment operation and service.

Most employers provide additional on-the-job training. You may need up to three years of on-the-job training to become skilled in the repair of the more complex power tools. Some large companies, such as power tool manufacturers, have formal training programs that include home-study courses and shop classes. Power tool manufacturers also conduct seminars that last one or two weeks and deal with the repair of a specific tool.

Getting the Job

To enter into this field, contact potential employers listed in the Yellow Pages of your phone book. Check such headings as "Tools—Power," "Tools—Repairing and Parts," "Contractors' Equipment and Supplies—Dealers and Services," and "Contractors—General." Listed under these and other related headings are companies to contact.

Be sure to check the newspaper classifieds, Internet job banks, and the state and local employment offices. If you are a vocational school graduate, you should check the placement office. Local union offices may also have information about power tool repairing jobs.

Advancement Possibilities and Employment Outlook

Power tool repairers are already at the top of their craft. Repairers in large shops or service centers may be promoted to assistant service manager, service manager, and then supervisor. Some may advance to regional service manager or parts manager for tool manufacturers. Experienced repairers may open their own shops.

Employment of power tool repairers is expected to increase slower than the average for all occupations through the year 2006. Although the number and variety of power tools are increasing, the use of solid-state circuits, microprocessors, sensing devices, and self-diagnostic tests make the tools more reliable.

Working Conditions

Power tool repairers normally work a 40-hour week. Repair shops are generally well lighted, ventilated, and heated. Most repairers work indoors in the shop. Some repairers work in the field repairing tools that cannot be brought to the shop. In either case, repairers usually work with little or no supervision.

Repairers handle greasy, dirty parts. They may have to lift heavy tools and parts, and they may work in cramped positions. They may suffer burns, bruises, and cuts from handling hot motors and equipment with sharp edges. Serious accidents can be avoided if the repairers wear protective gear and follow safety procedures.

Earnings and Benefits

The earnings of power tool repairers vary according to skill level, location, and the type of equipment they service. Currently, annual salaries range from $22,000 to $39,500. Power tool repairers may also receive such benefits as paid vacations, health and life insurance, and pensions.

Where to Go for More Information

Associated Contractors Equipment
    and Sales
P.O. Box 302
Plymouth, IN 46563
(219) 936-7426

Associated Equipment Distributors
615 West 22nd Street
Oak Brook, IL 60523
(630) 574-0650
www.aednet.org

International Union of Electronic, Electrical,
    Salaried, Machine, and Furniture
    Workers
1126 Sixteenth Street, NW
Washington, DC 20036
(202) 785-7200

Production, Planning, and Expediting Clerk

Definition and Nature of the Work

Production, planning, and expediting clerks perform a variety of communication and record-keeping tasks. They use production schedules to coordinate and facilitate the flow of work, materials, and personnel.

These clerks have several duties. In the production and planning phase of their work, they compile and record production data, calculate such factors as materials used and worker production rates, and maintain files. They also prepare work schedules, detailed production sheets, and chart production using wall charts or graphs. In the expediting phase of their work, clerks compile and maintain a parts and materials inventory. They determine the type, quantity, and availability of materials required. They also distribute materials to specific production areas.

Education and Training
High school

Salary Range
Average—$16,300
to $30,600

Employment Outlook
Fair

Education and Training Requirements

Most employers prefer to hire high school graduates as production, planning, and expediting clerks. Good reading and writing skills are essential, and computer literacy is very important. Clerical skills such as typing and record keeping are highly desirable, and a strong background in business math is helpful. Newly hired clerks develop specific skills through on-the-job training, which can last from several days to several months.

Production, planning, and expediting clerks must possess strength, good eyesight, and an ability to concentrate on repetitive tasks. They must also be able to work well under pressure and deadlines.

Getting the Job

Job information can be obtained from your high school job center or placement office or from classified ads in the newspaper. You can also contact the local office of the state employment service. Some applicants apply in person to a particular business. You might try searching job banks on the Internet as well.

Advancement Possibilities and Employment Outlook

Advancement opportunities vary according to the type of business or industry. Production, planning, and expediting clerks can be promoted to head clerks or enter a related field such as industrial traffic management. They may become warehouse managers or purchasing agents after receiving additional training.

The job outlook for production, planning, and expediting clerks is only fair through the year 2006. Due to automation and productivity improvements, clerks will be able to handle materials and data more efficiently, thus reducing the need for new clerks.

Working Conditions

Most production, planning, and expediting clerks work for manufacturing or wholesale and retail firms. They work in a variety of locations such as warehouses, stockrooms, loading platforms, storage rooms, and shipping and receiving rooms. Sometimes they work outside, exposed to the weather. Other times they may work inside rooms that are not temperature controlled. The work requires frequent standing, lifting, and carrying. Production, planning, and expediting clerks usually work a 40-hour week, although some extra hours may be required when inventory is taken or large shipments arrive.

Earnings and Benefits

Earnings for production, planning, and expediting clerks vary somewhat according to the type of business or industry. The average salary range is $16,300 to $30,600 a year. Experienced clerks can earn more.

Benefits for full-time clerks generally include paid vacations and sick days, health insurance, and pension plans. Employers usually provide any uniforms required or give the employee an allowance to purchase them.

Where to Go for More Information

For more information, contact the nearest office of the state employment service.

Rigger

Definition and Nature of the Work

Riggers help operate machines that move heavy objects including steel plates, bundles of steel rods, drilling towers, platforms, and the heavy construction equipment used to build and take down steel structures.

Riggers have many responsibilities. They decide which pulleys, booms, braces, and cables are strong enough for each job. They also must know where to attach the hooks, chains, and cables to lift a load safely. In some cases, riggers build equipment around the object to be moved, such as a tower or boom. While the object is being lifted, riggers use hand signals and other means to direct crane operators and help guide the objects into place.

Education and Training Requirements

A high school education is recommended. Courses in mathematics, plan reading, and shop are especially valuable. Communication courses such as English are also important, since riggers give directions to others.

After high school, riggers can begin their training by working on the job as riggers' helpers. The trade can usually be learned in several years. However, the best training is offered by formal apprenticeships. Apprenticeships are supervised by union contract or committees. These programs involve both on-the-job training and classroom instruction. Apprenticeships for riggers last 3 years in every field of the construction industry except shipbuilding, which requires 4 years. Riggers who complete apprenticeship programs have a thorough background in their trade.

Getting the Job

To enter an apprenticeship, your first step should be to contact the appropriate union. Check the Yellow Pages of your phone book under "Labor Organizations." If an apprenticeship is not a possibility, contact companies that employ riggers. Construction companies, trucking and hauling firms, steel mills, chemical companies, oil refineries, and heavy equipment manufacturers all employ riggers. Also check for job openings at your state employment office, job banks on the Internet, and in the newspaper classifieds.

Advancement Possibilities and Employment Outlook

Riggers advance mainly by receiving increases in pay. Wages frequently depend on the company's location and the worker's skill and experience. Wages also vary with the particular job.

Opportunities depend, to some extent, on the condition of the economy. However, the employment outlook for riggers is generally poor. Employment is expected to decline due to the use of more structural steel in construction.

Education and Training
None

Salary Range
Average—$380 a week

Employment Outlook
Poor

Riggers use pulleys, cables, and hooks attached to cranes to lift heavy objects such as steel plates, bundles of steel rods, and drilling towers.

Working Conditions

Working conditions for riggers depend on the specific job. Some riggers work mainly in industrial plants, where it can be noisy and dirty. Others work outdoors on construction job sites. They may lose work time because of bad weather. Riggers also work around shipyards and docks, where it can be cold and damp. A 40-hour, 5-day workweek is normal. When overtime is necessary, a higher wage is paid.

The demand for riggers varies in different areas. As a result, some riggers, especially those working for contractors, must travel long distances or even move to find employment. Riggers who work for industrial plants and similar organizations usually do not have this problem.

The rigger's work is physically demanding. The workers must be in good physical condition. Good eyesight and an ability to judge distances are important. Riggers must also be able to give and take instructions, solve problems, and work well with others.

Earnings and Benefits

Earnings vary, depending on the location of the work. Experienced riggers in large urban areas earn approximately $380 a week. Very experienced riggers might earn as much as $650 a week. Apprentices normally earn 60 to 70 percent of the qualified craft worker's wage. During their training period, apprentices receive regular increases. Nonunion workers generally earn less than union workers. Union contracts provide health benefits, life insurance, paid vacations, and pension plans.

Where to Go for More Information

International Association of Bridge, Structural, Ornamental, and Reinforcing Iron Workers
1750 New York Avenue, NW, Suite 400
Washington, DC 20006
(202) 383-4800

National Association of Women in Construction
327 South Adams Street
Fort Worth, TX 76104
(817) 877-5551
www.nawic.org

United States Department of Labor
Bureau of Apprenticeship and Training
200 Constitution Avenue, NW, Room North 4649
Washington, DC 20210
(202) 219-5921

Roofer

Education and Training
None

Salary Range
Average—$20,000 to $26,700

Employment Outlook
Fair

Definition and Nature of the Work

Roofers install and repair roofs on buildings that are made of metal, slate, tile, and other materials. Some roofers also waterproof surfaces, such as the insides of new swimming pools.

One kind of roofing material is composition (synthetic) roofing. When roofers put a composition roof on a building, they first cover the whole surface with strips of asphalt or with felt coated with tar. Then the roofers spread a coat of asphalt or other tar-like material on the surface. After they alternate layers of felt and asphalt at least three times, the roofers cover the surface with asphalt or with a gravel and tar mixture. This last layer protects the roofing materials from the weather.

Roll, or prepared, roofing and asphalt shingles are other types of roofing. These materials are put on in overlapping rows so that water can run off quickly. After overlapping the rows of shingles, the roofers fasten the roofing with nails or asphalt cement. The roofing material is cut to fit around corners, pipes, and chimneys. Where two surfaces of a roof meet at a corner, the roofers seal the joint by nailing flashing (metal strips) or by applying roofers' cement.

When roofers build a metal roof, they solder metal sheets together. Then they nail these sheets to the wood covering of the house or building. In tile and slate

There are several different types of roofing material and several methods of installation. This roofer fastens asphalt shingles to a roof with nails.

roofing, the roofers cover the area with roofing felt. Then they punch holes in the slate or drill holes in the tiles and nail them into place. The rows overlap each other. Cement is put on the heads of the nails to protect them from rust and to keep water from leaking in.

Roofers protect stone and concrete walls, swimming pools, and tanks from the effects of water damage. First, they prepare the surface by removing rough spots. Then they put on waterproofing compound with a brush or by spraying. They also damp-proof the surface to protect it from moisture. To damp-proof a surface, roofers apply a coating of asphalt or tar on both the outside and inside.

Roofers use hand tools including hammers, knives, mops, power fastening machines, brushes, and caulking guns. They generally work for roofing contractors who build new buildings. Roofers also do repair work on homes and other buildings. A few roofers are self-employed and have their own contracting businesses.

Education and Training Requirements

The best way to become a fully qualified roofer is through an apprenticeship program. High school graduates are preferred, but you can sometimes enter into an apprenticeship program without a diploma. The apprenticeship lasts 3 years. It combines at least 2,000 hours of on-the-job training with 144 hours of classroom instruction. On the job, apprentices learn to use the tools and materials of the trade. They also learn how to apply different types of roofs.

In the classroom, apprentices learn to read blueprints and do the basic mathematics used in layout work. They also learn about safety procedures. Apprentices should be at least 18 years old. In addition, they must be in good health and have a good sense of balance. Many roofers learn their trade on the job by working as helpers for experienced craft workers.

Getting the Job

Contact a local union or contractor and ask about openings in the apprenticeship program. You can also contact contractors for a job as a roofer's helper. If you are still in high school, you might get a summer job as a helper. This is a very good way to get experience in this field.

Advancement Possibilities and Employment Outlook

Roofers are already at the top of their craft. However, experienced roofers specialize in certain types of roofing such as composition roofing, slate and tile roofing, or aluminum and metal shingle roofing. Some have their own contracting businesses or are supervisors for roofing contractors. Roofers can also become estimators for contractors or salespeople for building supply companies.

Currently, there are about 138,000 roofers in the U.S. Employment is expected to grow more slowly than the average for all occupations through the year 2006. However, turnover is high, and jobs will be available because of the need to replace roofers who leave the field. Most roofing work is repair and replacement, so employment is less susceptible to changes in economic conditions than are other construction trades.

Working Conditions

Roofing is active and strenuous work. A 40-hour workweek is usual in the roofing trade. Higher wages are paid for overtime hours. Roofers work outdoors, sometimes in harsh weather. Roofers risk injuries from slips or falls from steep roofs, ladders, and scaffolding. Their work involves much standing, bending, squatting, and climbing. The work is usually seasonal. Many roofers belong to labor unions.

Earnings and Benefits

Apprentice roofers start at 40 percent of the qualified craft worker's salary. Every few months throughout the training period, the pay increases until the apprentice becomes a fully qualified roofer. Most roofers earn between $20,000 and $26,700 each year. Union workers generally receive paid holidays, life insurance, and hospitalization and pension plans. The number of vacation days they receive depends on the number of days they work each year. Other benefits are negotiated separately for each union contract.

Where to Go for More Information

National Roofing Contractors Association
O'Hare International Center
10255 West Higgins Road, Suite 600
Rosemont, IL 60018-5607
(708) 299-9070
www.roofonline.org

Roofers International
1125 Seventeenth Street, NW
Washington, DC 20036
(202) 638-3228

United States Department of Labor
Bureau of Apprenticeship and Training
200 Constitution Avenue, NW,
    Room North 4649
Washington, DC 20210
(202) 219-5921

Sheet Metal Worker

Education and Training
High school

Salary Range
Average—$32
an hour

Employment Outlook
Good

Definition and Nature of the Work

Sheet metal workers make, install, and repair heating and air-conditioning ducts and many other building parts made of sheet metal. They also make and install roofing, siding, stainless steel kitchen equipment, gutters, and light metal partitions. These workers are different than production-line sheet metal workers, who are semiskilled factory workers.

A duct is a long, hollow pipe or tube through which air or other substances pass. When installing heating and air-conditioning ducts, sheet metal workers first decide on the size and type of sheet metal to be used. Then they use construction plans to figure out the measurements and angles for the ducts. They mark patterns for the shapes and sizes of the ducts on the sheet metal and cut out the ducts by hand or with power shears. Then they bend the metal to form the shape

Sheet metal workers cut sheet metal by hand or with power shears to form the shapes and sizes needed to make heating and air-conditioning ducts and other building parts.

they need, and drill or punch holes in it so they will be able to bolt the pieces together. Workers put the ducts together by bolting, welding, soldering, or riveting the metal edges, and they smooth the rough edges with a file or grindstone. They nail, screw, bolt, or weld the ducts into place and use hangers and braces for support. Although ready-made ducts are often used, they need to be altered to fit certain structures.

Some workers specialize in shopwork, which is the layout and manufacture of sheet metal parts. Others work on the construction site installing the ducts. Skilled sheet metal workers know how to do a variety of tasks. They also work on jobs not directly related to the construction of buildings. Some work in railroad, aircraft, and shipbuilding factories. Others work for shops that make kitchen equipment, electrical equipment, and machinery.

Education and Training Requirements

A 4-year apprenticeship is the best way to learn the trade. You must have a high school diploma to enter a formal apprenticeship program. Some workers learn their trade by working as helpers for experienced sheet metal workers.

To enter the 4-year apprenticeship program, you must be at least 17 years of age and in good physical condition. This program includes on-the-job training and classroom instruction. On the job, apprentices learn to use tools and materials. In the classroom, apprentices are taught blueprint reading, drafting, and mathematics relating to layout work. Apprentices also learn the relationship of sheet metal work to the other building trades.

On-the-job training usually takes longer than an apprenticeship. The trainee starts as a helper and develops the skill and experience needed for more difficult work. Sometimes a trainee combines this work experience with trade school courses.

Getting the Job

The best way to enter the sheet metal trade is to contact a local union or contractor and apply for the apprenticeship program. Your local state employment agency can also tell you about apprenticeship opportunities. You can ask a local contractor about on-the-job training.

Advancement Possibilities and Employment Outlook

Sheet metal workers are already at the top of their trade. However, experienced workers can become specialists in design or layout work, supervisors or job superintendents, and estimators. Estimators calculate the potential total cost of materials and labor. Some sheet metal workers open their own contracting businesses.

There are about 110,000 sheet metal workers employed today in the U.S. This number is expected to increase about as fast as the average for all occupations through the year 2006. Employment opportunities for sheet metal workers in the construction industry depend on the state of the general economy. However, the growing demand for energy-efficient central air-conditioning and heating should create many jobs for sheet metal workers.

Working Conditions

Although some jobs are indoors, sheet metal workers are often subject to bad weather and noisy construction sites. The work on ladders can be dangerous, and the sharp edges of sheet metal can cause injuries. Sheet metal workers stand most of the time, and repair work often involves working in awkward, cramped, or stooped positions. Sheet metal workers generally work 40 hours a week. Higher wages are paid for overtime hours. Many sheet metal workers belong to labor unions.

Earnings and Benefits

The average hourly wage, including benefits, for union sheet metal workers is $32. Wages vary from one part of the country to another. Apprentices earn 40 percent of the fully qualified worker's salary at the start of the training period. The pay increases periodically until the apprentice becomes a fully qualified sheet metal worker.

Union members generally receive paid holidays, life and medical insurance, and pension plans. The number of vacation days they receive depends on the number of days they work each year. Other benefits are negotiated separately for each union contract.

Stonemason

Education and Training
None

Salary Range
Average—$23,300 to $32,500

Employment Outlook
Good

Definition and Nature of the Work

Stonemasons build stone constructions such as churches, hotels, piers, and arches. They also make stone sills, steps, hearths, and floors. Stonemasons often put stone facing on private homes and small buildings. Because stone is very costly, stonemasons are usually needed to work on expensive and large-scale projects.

Stonemasons work with both natural and artificial stone. The natural stones they use are marble, granite, sandstone, and limestone. The artificial stones are made of cement and cement mixed with marble chips or other masonry materials. Stonemasons use tools such as hammers, chisels, trowels, mallets, wedges, pneumatic (compressed air) drills, and brushes. They generally work with helpers who bring them the stones.

Stonemasons are building a granite floor outside the Library of Congress building.

Stonemasons sometimes work from plans that number each piece of stone. Helpers find and bring them each piece of stone. Then the masons spread a cementlike material called mortar, which is used to set the stones. The masons work with derrick operators, who run hoists that lift and lower the large stones into place onto the mortar. When the stones are in the proper position, the stonemasons check their placement with a plumb line to make sure they are aligned. The stonemasons then smooth the mortar between the stones with a trowel. A trowel is a flat, pointed tool made of metal.

The stone facing that stonemasons put on the surfaces of buildings is called veneer. It is generally 2 inches thick, and it is fastened on and supported by the building's steel frame.

Sometimes stonemasons must cut stone to exact size. They determine the grain of the stone for easy cutting and mark a line along it. They use a stonemason's hammer to strike the stone along this line. Sometimes they use an abrasive saw to cut valuable stones.

Some stonemasons specialize in soapstone or Alberene stone setting. Alberene stone is resistant to acid and is used to contain dangerous acidic substances. Masons set Alberene linings in tanks, vats, and on floors.

Education and Training Requirements

A high school diploma is preferred but not required. The best way to learn this trade is through a 3-year apprenticeship program. However, many masons learn their trade while working as helpers for experienced craft workers. To join an apprenticeship program, applicants should be at least 17 years of age and in good physical condition. The apprenticeship program consists of 3 years of on-the-job training combined with more than 400 hours of classroom instruction. On the job, apprentices are helpers. They learn to use the tools and materials. In the classroom, they are taught blueprint reading, mathematics, and other subjects relating to the craft.

Getting the Job

The best way to enter the craft is to join an apprenticeship program. To do so, you should contact a local union about training opportunities. You can also learn a craft by getting a job as a stonemason's helper. You should contact a contractor and ask about openings if you want to enter the field in this way.

Advancement Possibilities and Employment Outlook

Stonemasons are already at the top of their craft. However, experienced stonemasons can become supervisors. They can also become cost and material estimators for stonemason contractors. Some stonemasons start their own contracting businesses.

The employment outlook for stonemasons is good. Some openings occur every year as experienced workers retire or transfer to other fields. Over 142,000 stonemasons are currently employed in the United States. Employment is expected to experience the most growth in the New York City area, where extensive remodeling is being done.

Working Conditions

Since most stonemasons work outdoors, they can expect to lose work time in bad weather. Generally, they work 40 hours a week and earn extra pay for overtime and weekend work. The work is physically strenuous and involves much heavy lifting. Stonemasons must climb ladders and scaffolding. They also spend much time stooping, standing, and kneeling. Many stonemasons belong to labor unions.

Earnings and Benefits

Stonemasons generally earn salaries of about $23,300 to $32,500 a year. More experienced workers often earn up to $40,000 a year.

Union members generally receive paid holidays, life and medical insurance, and pension plans. The number of vacation days they receive depends on the number of days they work each year. Other benefits are negotiated separately for each union contract.

Where to Go for More Information

Mason Contractors Association of America
1910 Highland Avenue, Suite 101
Lombard, IL 60148-6147
(630) 705-4200

National Association of Women in
  Construction
327 South Adams Street
Fort Worth, TX 76104
(817) 877-5551
www.nawic.org

United States Department of Labor
Bureau of Apprenticeship and Training
200 Constitution Avenue, NW,
  Room North 4649
Washington, DC 20210
(202) 219-5921

Surveyor's Helper

Education and Training
None

Salary Range
Average—$13,400
to $16,400

Employment Outlook
Fair

Definition and Nature of the Work

Surveyors measure and write descriptions about land where highways, airports, and other buildings are to be constructed. Instrument workers, rod workers, and chain workers help surveyors with the surveying equipment.

Instrument workers set up, adjust, and operate surveying instruments such as the theodolite and electronic distance measuring equipment. A theodolite looks like a telescope and measures horizontal and vertical angles, distances, and elevations. The theodolite operator sights on vertical rods that are held by *rod workers*. The rods look like large rulers and have markers or targets that can be moved up or down. The theodolite operator signals for the rod worker to adjust the marker on the rod. Then a reading is taken and recorded.

Chain workers work in pairs. They measure distances with steel tapes or surveyors' chains. When they are finished measuring, they mark the points on the ground with chalk or with a wooden or metal stake.

Together the surveyors, instrument workers, rod workers, and chain workers measure all the important distances and heights on a piece of land. They keep notes and use mathematical calculations to locate land boundaries, help prepare maps, and compute the total acreage of a piece of property.

New technology is changing the nature of surveying. For large projects, more and more surveyors use the Global Positioning System (GPS). This is a satellite system that locates the points on the earth using radio signals transmitted by satellites.

Education and Training Requirements

Most training is given on the job. A high school education with mathematics courses such as geometry, algebra, and trigonometry is recommended. Usually, high school graduates start as apprentices or rod workers. After several years of on-the-job training and more education, they become chain workers and instrument workers. It is possible to start as an instrument worker with the additional training offered by night schools, technical schools, or junior colleges. As technology advances and more surveyors use the GPS, more formal training may be required to enter this field.

To succeed as a surveyor's helper, you must be in good physical condition and must pay close attention to detail. You should also work well with others.

Getting the Job

During the summer, high school and college students fill many surveyor's helper jobs. Summer experience can be very helpful in getting a permanent job in this field. Gas, electric, water, and telephone companies almost always need surveying teams. Contact them and check with local contractors and construction firms.

Check the Yellow Pages of your phone book and call professional surveyors to see if they need helpers. Register with your state employment office and check with civil service. Keep your eye on newspaper classifieds and Internet job banks, and contact real estate developers about openings.

Advancement Possibilities and Employment Outlook

The key to advancement is education. After several years of on-the-job experience and some courses in surveying, a person can move from rod worker to chain worker to instrument worker. With more training and experience, an instrument worker can become a licensed surveyor. To do this, a worker must pass two written tests, one prepared by the state and one given by the National Council of Examiners for Engineering and Surveying.

The job outlook for surveyor's helpers is fair through the year 2006. The use of GPS will increase the accuracy and productivity of surveyors, which will negatively affect the employment of surveyor's helpers. However, job openings will result from the need to replace workers who retire or transfer to other occupations. In addition, growth in construction through the year 2006 should require the surveying of land for roads, shopping centers, housing developments, and other buildings.

Working Conditions

Surveyor's helpers must be able to work in all kinds of weather. Often they must carry equipment long distances, climb hills, and stand for long periods of time. Because surveying teams are often the first people to work at construction sites, conditions can be difficult. Teams also work in cities near construction equipment and heavy traffic.

A 5-day, 40-hour workweek is normal. Some overtime and weekend work may be required during the warm months, when conditions are best for surveying. Higher wages are paid for extra hours. Some surveyor's helpers belong to labor unions.

Earnings and Benefits

Earnings vary, depending on experience and location of the work. Union workers generally earn more than nonunion workers. Surveyor's helpers who work for the federal government with little or no training or experience earn salaries that range between $13,400 and $14,600 a year. Those with an associate degree who start as instrument assistants earn about $16,400 a year. Union members generally receive paid holidays, life and medical insurance, and pension plans. Vacation days are based on the number of days worked each year. Other benefits are negotiated separately for each union contract.

Welder

Education and Training
None

Salary Range
Average—$18,300
to $31,500

Employment Outlook
Fair

Definition and Nature of the Work

Welding is the process of heating and melting metal parts to join them together permanently. It is used to construct and repair parts of cars, airplanes, ships, and sheet metal products. Welding is also used to join beams when constructing bridges and buildings. Some welders work at steel mills, railroad shops, and highway departments.

Welders are classified as either skilled or unskilled, depending on their training and the kind of welding they do. Skilled welders work from blueprints and written specifications. They know the welding properties of various kinds of metal. Unskilled and semiskilled welders work on projects in home construction, industry, shipbuilding, and other fields. They often work on assembly lines and do repetitive work that requires no special knowledge of welding properties.

There are more than 40 methods of welding, which are divided into three basic types: arc welding, gas welding, and resistance welding. Arc and gas welding are done either by hand or by machine. Resistance welding is usually done on machines that are operated by unskilled welders.

In arc welding, the welder uses a tool called an electrode. First, he or she adjusts the electric current running through it. Then an arc, or electric current, is produced by touching the metal with the electrode. The welder runs the electrode down the seams of the edges and melts and joins the metal. The melted metal of the electrode tip mixes with the melted metal edges. Then the melted metal solidifies to make a strong connection. The type of electrode used depends on the properties of the metals to be joined and the strength needed for the weld.

This welder is using gas welding to melt the disconnected edges of a railroad track and the rod that joins them.

In gas welding, the welder applies a hot flame from an acetylene and oxygen torch to join metal edges. When the edges are melted, the welder melts a rod into the joint. The rod supplies the extra metal needed to make the weld. Gas welding is used more than other types of welding because the size of the flame and type of welding rod can be adjusted according to the particular job.

Resistance welding is done by machine and is used for mass production. In this type of welding, metal pieces resist the flow of electricity applied to the edges. The edges are fused together by the pressure of the contacting electrode. The machine operator must adjust the flow of electricity and the pressure of the electrode. The operator feeds the metal pieces into the machine, aligns them, and removes the welded metal. The different types of resistance welding are spot, flash, projection, and upset welding.

Some welders work with aluminum, magnesium, and titanium. To weld these materials, they use an atomic welding process that uses hydrogen gas with an arc.

Other welders specialize in arc cutting and oxygen cutting. In these processes, the area to be cut is superheated. Then a stream of oxygen is released to cut through the metal. This technique is used to cut metal into pieces according to patterns. The finished pieces are used as parts of manufactured products, such as cars.

Education and Training Requirements

A high school diploma is preferred but not required. You should take high school courses in mathematics, physics, and mechanical drawing. Shop courses that include welding and principles of electricity are also helpful. A knowledge of computers is gaining importance, as some welders are responsible for the programming of computer-controlled machines, including robots.

The unskilled jobs in welding can be learned in a relatively short time. For instance, workers can learn resistance welding in a few days. On the other hand, skilled welding techniques take several years to master. Some vocational and trade schools offer training programs for welders. A few companies have apprenticeship programs. However, most training is done on the job, where trainees can gain experience in different types of welding. Trainees should have manual dexterity, good eyesight, good hand-eye coordination, and be in good health. Trainees must often pass tests before they are allowed to work on projects where the strength of the weld is very important or where the work must be very precise.

Getting the Job

You can contact local manufacturing plants that employ welders and ask about job opportunities. You can also contact a local union or state employment service about training and job openings. Check the classified ads of local newspapers and Internet job banks.

Advancement Possibilities and Employment Outlook

Skilled welders are already at the top of their craft. However, experienced welders can become supervisors. With additional training they can also become welding technicians or inspectors. Some experienced welders open their own welding and repair shops. Others specialize in working with certain metals or techniques.

Over 453,000 welders are employed today in the U.S. This number is expected to grow more slowly than the average for all jobs through the year 2006. Although the overall number of welders employed is expected to change little, fewer resistance welders and arc and gas cutters will be needed because of automation and robotics. However, automation is not expected to affect highly skilled welders. Some job openings occur each year as workers retire or change fields.

Working Conditions

Welders must wear protective clothing, goggles, helmets with protective lenses, and other safety equipment to prevent burns and eye injury. Proper ventilation of the work area is important since welders must sometimes work with toxic gases. Resistance welders need only goggles because their work is less dangerous. Welders who work in construction do a good deal of standing, stooping, reaching, and climbing. Welders often come into contact with dust, dirt, grease, and paint on metal surfaces.

Earnings and Benefits

Welders' earnings vary greatly and depend on the level of skill. The average salary for welders is between $18,300 to $31,500 a year. Many experienced welders work independently and earn higher wages than salaried workers. However, there are many expenses for independent workers, such as equipment and trucks. Self-employed welders also must provide their own benefits. Benefits for salaried workers usually include paid vacations and holidays, pension plans, and health insurance.

Where to Go for More Information

American Welding Society
550 Northwest Le Jeune Road
Miami, FL 33126
(305) 443-9353
www.amweld.org

International Brotherhood of Boilermakers,
   Iron Ship Builders, Blacksmiths, Forgers,
   and Helpers
753 State Avenue, Suite 570,
   New Brotherhood Building
Kansas City, KS 66101
(913) 371-2640

Welding Research Council
345 East 47th Street, 14th Floor
New York, NY 10017
(212) 705-7956

Air-Conditioning and Heating Technician

Definition and Nature of the Work

Air-conditioning and heating technicians install, repair, and maintain service equipment. They also help engineers to design and manufacture equipment. Air-conditioning and heating equipment controls the temperature and humidity of the air. It also filters and regulates the circulation of air. Commercial offices, residential homes, and industrial buildings depend on air-conditioning and heating systems to regulate their room and office temperatures. For example, without air-conditioning, an industry's vital chemical processes and data processing equipment would not function.

Some employers of technicians include manufacturers of environmental control equipment; dealers who sell, install, and service the equipment; and heavy users of the equipment, such as utilities or building contractors. Research and development divisions of manufacturing companies also employ technicians to help them plan new ways to use air-conditioning equipment. Technicians test new machines and build experimental equipment and models under the guidance of engineers. Frequently, technicians write descriptions of tests or research.

Some technicians work with equipment suppliers, dealers, and installers to design fairly standard systems. They may also supervise the mechanics and work crews that install the compressors, fans, evaporators, duct work, and other parts. Technicians may be involved in connecting the important pipes and meters and in running a complete systems check on a unit. Technicians should be able to read blueprints, plans, and layouts.

Once an air-conditioning system is installed, the technician needs to maintain and service the unit. A mechanic often handles the routine task of changing the filters and lubricating the machine. Then technicians read the meters and run periodic tests on the system. When a problem occurs, the technician must be able to take the unit apart, find the broken component, and make the repair or install a replacement.

Technicians working for dealers may help customers decide which type of air-conditioning and heating systems they need and may prepare estimates and designs. Building contractors may hire technicians to estimate costs, select fittings, supervise building workers, and check the completed system.

Education and Training Requirements

You need a high school diploma to become an air-conditioning and heating technician. During high school, concentrate on courses in mathematics, physics, drafting, mechanical drawing, English, chemistry, and machine and electrical shop. Working for an equipment supplier or similar company during the summer will also give you valuable background experience.

Technical schools and junior or community colleges offer 2-year programs in air-conditioning and heating. Although most employers prefer to hire those with formal training, some still have on-the-job training programs you can enter after high school. Technical schools or junior and community colleges provide

Education and Training
High school plus training

Salary Range
Starting—$15,000
to $18,500
Average—$30,000
to $34,000

Employment Outlook
Very good

the necessary training in laboratory and drafting skills, as well as classes in algebra, trigonometry, and technical writing.

Getting the Job

Because so many different areas of the air-conditioning and heating industry need technicians, finding a job is not hard. Check with manufacturers, dealers, and distributors of air-conditioning and related equipment. Call or write architects, contractors, and building consultants. Contact the state employment service about job openings, check Internet job banks, and keep an eye on the classified ads in your newspaper.

Also, determine which companies operate and maintain large buildings in your area, and see if they need a technician to oversee their system. If you go to a trade, technical school, or junior college, check its placement service. Many employers contact these schools to find qualified people. Some employers offer jobs to students with 2-year degrees who have worked for them in the summer or part-time.

Advancement Possibilities and Employment Outlook

Technicians usually begin as trainees, performing simple tasks under the supervision of fully trained technicians or engineers. As they progress, they help engineers with design work, help run experiments, help supervise the installation of equipment, and help monitor and service existing systems.

There will continue to be a need for technicians. As the population grows, so will the demand for residential, commercial, and industrial air-conditioning and heating systems . In addition, as manufacturing processes become more complex and automated, there is a corresponding rise in the need for closely controlled environmental conditions.

Concern for energy conservation will also continue to spur the development of new technologies for energy-saving and chlorofluorocarbon-reducing heating and air-conditioning systems. Demand for technicians to install and maintain these new systems should increase as they become more common.

Working Conditions

Technicians involved in production, design, and research normally work in offices or laboratories. Those who help install equipment work at job sites. They may work outside, in high places, or in awkward positions. Maintenance and service technicians work near their machines, which are usually found in the basements of buildings. Training in safety aspects has minimized the dangers to technicians.

A 5-day, 40-hour workweek is normal in this industry. But occasional overtime or weekend work may be necessary to make repairs, complete installations, or meet deadlines.

Earnings and Benefits

Earnings for air-conditioning and heating technicians depend on educational background, experience, and geographical location, as well the area of the industry in which an employee works. Beginning technicians earn approximately $15,000 to $18,500 a year. Highly trained and experienced technicians earn average annual salaries of $30,000 to $34,000. Employment benefits vary with the employer, but most include paid vacations, legal holidays, life and health insurance, and pension funds.

Architectural Drafter

Definition and Nature of the Work

Architectural drafters make detailed scale drawings used in construction. They draw building plans for office buildings, private homes, theaters, factories, and school buildings. Since buildings are constructed exactly as shown on these drawings, the work must be clear, complete, and accurate. Architects, engineers, and designers give sketches, notes, and other information to drafters who use it to make drawings. Drafters often work in the engineering, research, or development departments of large companies. They also work for architects and construction companies.

Drafters are classified by the type of work they do and by the amount of responsibility they have. *Senior drafters* take the initial information and ideas and develop the final construction drawings. These drawings include both the plans of the building and the details of construction. *Junior drafters,* who work under senior drafters, draw up plans and details that senior drafters have developed. *Tracers* make minor corrections to finished drawings and trace details onto final sheets. In the final stages of a project, some drafters act as *checkers,* who carefully examine the detailed drawings for mistakes.

Traditionally, drafters use pencil and ink, protractors, compasses, scale rulers, triangles, curves, lettering guides, and electric erasers. They use calculators, slide rules, and engineering handbooks and tables to figure out technical problems. Most drafters now use computer-aided drafting (CAD) systems to prepare drawings. These systems allow the drafter to create a drawing on a video screen.

Despite advances in computer technology, architectural drafters still must rely on traditional skills and abilities such as doing detailed work with great accuracy.

Education and Training
High school plus training

Salary Range
Starting—$18,600
to $22,400
Average—$23,000
to $41,500

Employment Outlook
Fair

Although drafters use computer-aided drafting (CAD) systems to prepare drawings, they still must be able to check the drawings for mistakes and make corrections by hand.

They should also be able to visualize objects in two and three dimensions. Drafters must have good eyesight, hand-eye coordination, and form perception. Form perception is the ability to see the fine difference between shapes, lines, shadings, and forms.

Education and Training Requirements

Employers prefer those who have completed post-high school training in drafting, which is offered by junior colleges, extension divisions of universities, and vocational and trade schools that offer 2-year programs of study. You should take high school courses in science and mathematics, and if available, any design or computer graphics and drafting courses. Once you learn the basic skills in high school, you can go on to get specialized training. Prospective drafters should be able to draw freehand, and some artistic ability is helpful.

Getting the Job

If you attend a training school or junior college, you can get help from the school's placement service. Federal, state, and local governments also have jobs for architectural drafters. To get a job with the government, you will have to take a civil service examination. You can call or write to local architects about job openings and check job banks on the Internet.

Advancement Possibilities and Employment Outlook

Usually drafters start as tracers and then advance to junior drafters. After demonstrating skill and ability as junior drafters, they can advance to senior drafters within 3 to 5 years. If drafters show leadership abilities and do outstanding work, they can become supervisors of other drafters. Some drafters become independent designers. Those who take engineering courses sometimes transfer to engineering jobs.

The employment outlook in this field is fair. Employment is sensitive to local industrial growth, so there is a demand for drafters when and where the economy is growing. Eventually, almost all drafters will use CAD systems, which simplify many traditional drafting tasks and reduce the demand for drafters.

Working Conditions

Architectural drafters work in clean, well-lighted, and well-ventilated offices. Drafters must sometimes work closely with architects or as part of a team of other drafters. Drafters draw on slanted desks while sitting on stools or use computers. Tracing and alterations are done on a light table. This is a glass table with a light built into it. The light shines from underneath the paper or chart, making it easy to trace. Drafters who work on design layouts may have to visit construction sites to get firsthand information.

Earnings and Benefits

The pay for architectural drafters varies according to their experience and the type of work they are doing. In private industry, drafters start at about $18,600 to $22,400 a year. Experienced workers earn about $23,000 to $41,500 a year. Employee benefits may include paid holidays and vacations, health insurance and pension plans, and in some cases, retirement plans and profit sharing.

Where to Go for More Information

American Design Drafting Association
P.O. Box 799
Rockville, MD 20848-0799
(301) 460-6875
www.adda.org

American Institute of Architecture Students
1735 New York Avenue, NW
Washington, DC 20006
(202) 626-7472
e-mail: aiasnatl@aol.com

International Federation of Professional and
    Technical Engineers
8630 Fenton Street, Suite 400
Silver Spring, MD 20910-3803
(301) 565-9016
www.itpte.org

Architectural Model Maker

Definition and Nature of the Work

Architectural model makers create scale models of proposed construction projects. These projects include schools, shopping centers, housing developments, hospitals, bridges, and office buildings. Models are useful because, unlike blueprints or plans, they show exactly what the building will look like. They are essential in presentations, since they can help to convince a committee or governmental board to raise funds for a building or project.

Architectural models vary in complexity from an arrangement of painted boxes to a layout that includes scaled-down trees, grass, human figures, and electric lights. The architect decides on the amount of detail that is necessary, and then the model maker creates either a simple or complex model, or both.

Model makers begin with the architect's detailed blueprints and drawings. Then they plan the construction stages of the model so that everything is done in the proper order. For example, the windows of a building must be designed and cut at a certain stage of the model's construction.

Model makers must decide which materials to use during the planning stage. They use materials such as wood, Plexiglas, Lucite, and Styrofoam to make different parts of the models. However, in some cases, model makers order specially designed materials and miniature building parts from supply houses. Some models, for instance, may need specific lighting fixtures, or they may need to be assembled in different sections that come apart to show the inside of the building. Model makers use glue, paste, and paint to construct the models. They use special drills for plastic, glue guns, miniature screwdrivers, and other precision cutting and measuring tools. They must be careful and neat.

Education and Training Requirements

For entry-level positions in this field, there is no specific training available. However, high school classes in drafting, mechanical drawing, shop (especially wood shop), and fine arts will help to prepare for a career in this field.

College courses in the fine arts and drafting will also help to develop the skills you will need. Working for an architectural or model-making firm during the summer provides good experience. You can also practice by using plastic and wooden model kits and plans that hobby and craft stores sell.

Getting the Job

The two major employers of model makers are model-making companies and architectural firms . Most architectural firms do not hire model makers permanently, mainly because models are not needed for every project. However, some large architectural firms in major cities have one or more full-time model makers.

Most architectural model makers work for companies that specialize in making models and creating the films, drawings, and charts used in presentations for builders or owners. Some model makers may work for architects on a freelance basis, which means they work on a job-to-job basis for different clients.

Many model-making firms are based in or near large cities. To find the names and addresses of the companies near you, check the Yellow Pages of your phone book under the listing "Model Makers." Also, check phone books from other cities. You will usually be able to find these phone books at your public library.

Architectural model makers create scale models of proposed construction projects that, unlike blueprints or plans, show exactly what the building will look like.

Another good approach is to phone several of the architects in your area and ask them for the names of model-making firms they use. Also check newspaper classifieds, Internet job banks, placement offices at art schools, and your local state employment office.

Advancement Possibilities and Employment Outlook

Advancement for fully qualified model makers is usually in the form of higher earnings. A few highly skilled model makers may open their own firms. The employment outlook is poor partly due to an increased demand for computer-aided designers (CAD). However, in general, when the economy is good, more buildings are constructed and more models are needed. When the economy is poor, there is no demand for models, and many model makers work for individual clients creating models of boats and private homes. The competition for jobs in model making can be stiff. People with the greatest skill, talent, and desire usually have the best chance of finding a job.

Working Conditions

Model makers do most of their work in clean, well-lighted offices. They may have their own offices or they may work in large rooms with several others. A steady hand and a good eye for detail, proportion, and color are important qualities for a model maker. Since some models are divided into sections, each made by a different person, an ability to work well with others is also important.

Earnings and Benefits

Earnings in this field almost always depend on skill. Model makers generally start at $17,500 to $19,000 a year. A skilled model maker earns between $24,000 and $35,000 a year. A 40-hour workweek is normal, but some overtime may be required to meet important deadlines. Benefits generally include life and health insurance, pension plans, and paid vacations.

Where to Go for More Information

American Design Drafting Association
P.O. Box 799
Rockville, MD 20848-0799
(301) 460-6875
www.adda.org

American Institute of Architecture Students
1735 New York Avenue, NW
Washington, DC 20006
(202) 626-7472
e-mail: aiasnatl@aol.com

International Federation of Professional and
   Technical Engineers
8630 Fenton Street, Suite 400
Silver Spring, MD 20910
(301) 565-9016
www.itpte.org

Civil Engineering Technician

Definition and Nature of the Work

Civil engineering technicians help civil engineers plan and design roads, bridges, tunnels, water and sewerage systems, airfields, and harbors. Technicians sometimes work in urban renewal and community planning to improve the living conditions of cities or towns. They help plan the construction of new buildings and the destruction of old ones. Civil engineering technicians may work for city governments or large corporations.

The first stage of the technician's job is planning the project. The technicians help the engineers decide on the types and amounts of materials needed. They often help to estimate the costs of projects. They go to the work site and help the engineers to survey the area or lay out the position of the structure's foundation. The technicians also help the engineers in drafting, or making a scale drawing of the object to be built.

During the construction of the project, the technicians work with the building contractor or site supervisor. They help schedule the work to be done by the different building trades. They also check the construction to see that it is being done according to the building plans. Technicians make sure that the workers complete each stage of construction before the next stage begins.

Civil engineering technicians must have good eyesight and manual dexterity. They must be able to pay strict attention to detail and be able to work closely with others.

Education and Training Requirements

To become a civil engineering technician, you should have a high school diploma. You should be able to use algebra, geometry, trigonometry, and logarithms.

There are several ways to get the additional training you will need. Many junior and community colleges offer 2-year programs that lead to associate degrees in civil engineering. Some large companies offer training programs in which the trainee works during the day and then attends evening classes. Such a program allows the beginner to learn while simultaneously gaining practical experience. The armed services train thousands of technicians each year.

Getting the Job

If you go to a 2-year college, the placement office at your school will help you look for a job. These offices are usually in touch with agencies and businesses that need civil engineering technicians. Another method of entering the field is to apply directly to civil engineering firms or large companies for on-the-job training.

Advancement Possibilities and Employment Outlook

Most civil engineering technicians begin as trainees under experienced technicians or civil engineers. As the trainees gain experience, they are given more responsibility. Some technicians move on to supervisory positions. Those with the ability sometimes get additional education and become civil engineers.

National economic conditions influence employment. When the economy is good, there will be a greater demand for technicians, and when the economy is poor, there will be little demand. The use of computer-aided design and

Education and Training
High school plus training

Salary Range
Starting—$18,900
to $22,800
Average—$26,800
to $32,700

Employment Outlook
Good

drafting (CADD) will increase productivity, which will limit employment growth. Despite these factors, the employment outlook for civil engineering technicians is good through the year 2006. In addition to the projected growth, technicians are needed every year to replace those who retire or leave their jobs.

Working Conditions

Technicians work in offices or on construction sites. Their offices are modern, well-lighted, and well-ventilated. On construction sites, the work is cleaner than the work in most other construction trades. Civil engineering technicians usually work 40 hours a week with extra pay for weekends and overtime work.

Earnings and Benefits

The earnings of civil engineering technicians vary depending on their training and the location of their employer. Beginning workers generally start at about $18,900 to $22,800 a year. Experienced workers often earn between $26,800 and $32,700 a year. Benefits vary, but most companies include paid vacations and holidays, health insurance plans, and sometimes profit sharing.

Where to Go for More Information

American Society for Engineering
  Education
1818 N Street, NW, Suite 600
Washington, DC 20036
(202) 331-3500
www.asee.org

American Society of Civil Engineers
1801 Alexander Graham Bell Drive
Reston, VA 20191-4400
(703) 295-6000
www.asce.org

Society of Women Engineers
120 Wall Street, 11th Floor
New York, NY 10005-3902
(212) 509-9577
www.swe.org

Construction Equipment Dealer

Education and Training
Varies—see profile

Salary Range
Varies—see profile

Employment Outlook
Varies—see profile

Definition and Nature of the Work

Construction equipment dealers sell or rent the trucks, cranes, bulldozers, cement mixers, pile drivers, and other equipment to the contractors of construction jobs. They help contractors find the right machines for the job as well as help manufacturers sell their machines. Dealers must be very familiar with the different machines and methods of construction.

Some dealers may specialize in a particular brand or type of equipment, such as road-building machinery. Others may handle the products of several companies and sell whole ranges of equipment, including hand tools, air compressors, power lifts, and asphalt rollers. Most dealers have some form of service department.

Many dealers are independent and have their own sales agencies or dealerships. Dealers usually have a franchise agreement with one or more manufacturers. In a franchise agreement, the dealers own the equipment, the building, and the surrounding property, all of which are supplied by the manufacturer. This is a considerable financial investment, so dealers must be capable salespeople as well as good business managers. They manage the company's finances including items such as inventory, overhead, and advertising or marketing. Dealers also must manage a sales force to make sure that their machines continue to sell.

Education and Training Requirements

There are no specific educational requirements for becoming a construction equipment dealer. However, a high school diploma is recommended. Courses in business, mathematics, accounting, public speaking, and English will develop your financial and communication skills. Other courses, such as shop, mechanical drawing, and the sciences, may be helpful in understanding how construction equipment works.

Technical schools and community or junior colleges offer courses in business law, construction methods, engineering, psychology, sales methods, and business and sales management. These courses will develop your skills and increase your chances of success.

After you have completed your education, one of the best ways to further prepare for your career as an equipment dealer is to become a salesperson. Whether you work in a store or on a sales route, it will be a valuable experience. When you work for a dealership, you will receive additional on-the-job training. You will learn different selling techniques and about the different types of equipment. Equipment manufacturers may offer training sessions to salespeople to introduce new machinery.

Getting the Job

There are a number of ways to enter this field. You might work directly for an equipment manufacturer, or you might begin in the service and parts department of an established dealership. Many future dealers begin as equipment salespeople. They learn about the machines, about organizing and managing a dealership, and about the entire construction industry. It is possible to advance from salesperson to assistant sales manager, to sales manager, and to general manager.

Construction equipment dealers must be very familiar with different types of machines and methods of construction.

Your first step in getting a job in this field should be to contact the dealerships in your area. You may find them listed in the Yellow Pages of your phone book under "Contractors' Equipment—Rented" or "Contractors' Equipment and Supplies." Contact the sales manager and ask about job openings.

Sales managers usually prefer those who are well-rounded, sociable, and able to communicate knowledgeably. A potential salesperson should also be well-groomed, confident, and determined.

Check with equipment manufacturers in your area about sales jobs. Also, contact your local state employment service, scan newspaper classifieds, and search Internet job banks. If there are no sales jobs in the construction equipment industry, try to find a sales position in a related area, such as automobiles, hardware, or construction materials.

Advancement Possibilities and Employment Outlook

Dealers own their businesses, so advancement is usually in the form of increased sales and higher profits. They may also expand their businesses. Generally, when the economy is strong and construction is in demand, there are more opportunities. When the economy is weak, there are fewer opportunities. Also, the type of equipment a dealer sells makes a difference. There is almost always a market for power saws and drills, for example, but not for the heavier equipment, such as bulldozers or cement mixing trucks.

Working Conditions

Dealers spend most of their time at the dealership supervising salespeople and office staff and meeting with customers and suppliers. Since they are independent businesspeople, dealers often work more than a 40-hour week.

Earnings and Benefits

It is not uncommon for a talented salesperson to earn up to $30,000 in the first year. However, it is difficult to describe the average earnings of a dealer, since earnings depend on many different factors. As mentioned above, the amount earned varies depending on the product the dealer sells and the state of the economy. Most dealers earn commissions, which are percentages of the selling prices of the equipment. They usually buy their buildings and equipment, and they need to pay their employees and other overhead costs. Dealers must be able to build up a list of satisfied customers and motivate their salespeople. In general, those who have the most knowledge of the machinery, the best management, and the best selling techniques will be the most successful. Dealers must provide their own life and health insurance, pension plan, and other benefits.

Energy Conservation Technician

Education and Training
Varies—see profile

Salary Range
Starting—$18,000
to $20,000
Average—$35,000

Employment Outlook
Good

Definition and Nature of the Work

Energy conservation technicians work in businesses, factories, and residential homes to reduce utility expenses by lowering energy consumption. They offer different services, including energy audits, in which they inspect structures and provide energy-saving measures and advice to implement them. Some technicians do the actual renovation work. They install faucets that save water and insulate areas where heat escapes.

A few firms specialize in cutting energy costs for large buildings. They install and operate remote-controlled computers that lower the heat and control the lights during off hours.

Some conservation specialists are employed by utility companies and state agencies. Other technicians have their own businesses. Energy technicians must have a good grasp of the workings of energy-related equipment. Such equipment may incorporate the use of electric motors, heaters, lamps, electronic controls, thermal systems, and pneumatic and hydraulic drives.

Education and Training Requirements

An energy conservation technician must have a clear understanding of operational manuals, blueprints, and computational formulas. Technical colleges offer

An energy conservation technician conducts an energy audit, in which he inspects a home and provides suggestions on energy-saving measures and advice on how to implement them.

2-year training programs that cover these areas as well as provide a background in energy economics, electricity and electromechanical devices, and computer technology. In some training-program courses, students work in laboratories and learn about the integrated systems of machines by assembling and disassembling, adjusting, and operating them. More and more technical and community colleges are offering courses in energy management and conservation.

Getting the Job

College professors and placement offices can help graduates of technical programs to find jobs. Local energy consultants sometimes schedule recruiting visits to colleges.

Advancement Possibilities and Employment Outlook

Those who begin as staff technicians may eventually start their own businesses. Self-employed technicians may advance by expanding their services or by selling weather stripping, door sweeps, and other energy-saving products. They may teach energy conservation seminars offered by local schools or suppliers on such subjects as building insulation, heat pumps, and solar heating. They may report on energy conservation matters for a newspaper.

The employment outlook is good because many residential, industrial, and commercial programs are being started to reduce energy consumption. In addition, as natural resources continue to be depleted, their costs will continue to rise, as will the demand for energy conservation technicians.

Working Conditions

Conditions vary according to the type of services provided. Those who are involved strictly in consulting work must inspect structures and perform a series of tests. Other jobs require more physical labor, such as weatherization, which involves caulking windows, insulating water heaters, and installing ceiling fans. Remote-controlled energy conservation requires installing and monitoring equipment as well as some computer work. In all cases, evening and weekend work may be involved. The work is somewhat seasonal because consumers tend to be more energy-conscious during cold weather.

Earnings and Benefits

Technicians who work for public utility companies earn starting salaries of $18,000 to $20,000 a year. Technicians with several years of experience can earn up to $35,000 a year. Those with engineering degrees can earn up to $50,000 a year in conservation work.

Self-employed technicians often charge according to the size of the area inspected or renovated, but a few entrepreneurs earn profits commensurate with the amount of energy they save for the client. Those in the second group have enormous earning potential if their client companies are large, since the cost savings can register in the millions.

Benefits for technicians who are employed by public utility companies include paid vacations and holidays, health insurance, and pension plans. Self-employed technicians must provide their own benefits.

Where to Go for More Information

National Association of Energy
  Service Companies
1615 M Street, NW, Suite 800
Washington, DC 20036
(202) 822-0950

Estimator

Education and Training
High school plus training

Salary Range
Starting—$20,000
to $30,000

Employment Outlook
Good

Definition and Nature of the Work

Estimators predict the costs of future construction projects. The cost of a project is important because several contractors often submit bids or price quotes on a construction job. Usually the contractor who submits the lowest bid is asked to do the work. Without a good estimate, a contractor could either bid too high and lose a potential project, or bid too low and lose money after the work is completed.

Estimators usually make several cost estimates as a bid is being prepared. They begin with a general figure even before the architect completes the drawings of the proposed project. When all the plans and details are complete, a final estimate is made.

Estimators consider many things when preparing an estimate. They take into account previous projects that are similar, the costs and quantities of almost every material to be used, whether special machinery will be needed, and the productivity and pay of the various workers involved. After these and other details have been added together, estimators add a certain amount to cover unforeseen or emergency expenses, overhead, and a percentage of the total to make a profit.

Estimators have a very important job. Once a bid or price quote is submitted and accepted, a contractor must build the project for that set amount. If the contractor spends more than was estimated, he loses money or does not make a profit. On the other hand, if the estimate is originally too high, the contractor may not be awarded the job. In many cases, the success or failure of the contractor depends on the estimator.

Education and Training Requirements

Future estimators need a high school education with courses in mathematics and accounting. Courses in plan reading, drafting, mechanical drawing, and shop may also be helpful. If available, a program in business mathematics or business management is recommended.

After high school, attend a technical school or 4-year college if possible. Here you will learn about architecture, engineering, design, construction management, specification writing, and estimating. Knowledge of the various building trades and the different stages of construction is also important. Working as a laborer or in some other construction activity during the summer also provides valuable experience.

Many estimators begin in a trainee position in a contractor's office. As a trainee you may help the people involved in drafting, designing, engineering, purchasing, managing, and other areas of the business. Eventually you may advance to junior estimator.

Getting the Job

Although there are some firms that do nothing but estimating, most construction companies rely on someone within their own organization to handle this job. Large firms may have a staff that does nothing but estimating. Smaller companies usually have someone who does the estimating in addition to another job. In general, the more jobs you are able to do, the greater your chances of being hired.

Contact the contractors in your area about job opportunities. You may find the names and addresses you need in the Yellow Pages of your phone book. Look under "Construction Estimates," "Building Contractors," "Contractors—General," and similar headings. Also check with your state employment service, search Internet job banks, and scan the newspaper classifieds.

Advancement Possibilities and Employment Outlook

A fully qualified estimator can advance to become an engineer, a business solicitor, a vice president, or even a partner in a firm. The outlook for estimators is good through the year 2006. The number of estimator jobs available is somewhat linked to the growth of the construction industry. However, even when construction and manufacturing activity decline, there should still be a demand for cost estimators.

Working Conditions

Estimators normally work indoors. They usually have offices where their technical manuals, material catalogs, calculators, and other necessary materials are close at hand. The job usually does not require a great deal of physical exertion. Estimators should be well-organized people who enjoy technical work.

Estimators normally work a 40-hour week. However, they may have to work nights and weekends to meet a deadline. In many cases employees may be paid extra or given time off to compensate for overtime work.

Earnings and Benefits

Starting salaries for contractor trainees average between $20,000 and $30,000 a year. The size of the firm and the area of the country, however, are important factors. Those with a bachelor's degree in construction science may start at $30,000 or more a year. Highly experienced cost estimators earn up to $75,000 a year. Many companies provide benefits, such as life and health insurance, retirement plans, and paid vacations.

Where to Go for More Information

American Society of Professional Estimators
11141 Georgia Avenue, Suite 412
Wheaton, MD 20902
(301) 929-8848
www.cmpi.com/aspe

National Association of Women
   in Construction
327 South Adams Street
Fort Worth, TX 76104-1002
(817) 877-5551
www.nawic.org

Expediter

Definition and Nature of the Work

The expediter buys building materials and makes sure that the right materials arrive at the job site at the right time. There are many reasons why all the materials used in a construction project are not delivered at once. Usually there is not enough room to store all the materials until they are needed. The materials may also be damaged by weather or broken at building sites. For example, if the glass windows are delivered at the same time as the bricks and mortar, many windows might be broken before they are installed.

The expediter's job is extremely important to the success of any construction project. If the expediter does not buy the correct materials, or if the materials are not at the job site at the right time, the work cannot continue. Delays in a building project can be very costly to the contractor.

While a job is in progress, expediters constantly check to make sure that the materials are ready for their scheduled delivery. If there is difficulty buying materials, or if the workers do not have enough of a particular material, the expediters must be able to solve the problem quickly to keep the work flowing smoothly.

Expediters are responsible for many things, and they frequently use filing systems to keep everything organized. Some expediters even work on several jobs at once, and many of them are responsible for returning unused materials.

Education and Training Requirements

Expediters should have a high school education that includes courses in mathematics, accounting, and business management. Classes in drafting and mechanical drawing are helpful, as well as shop courses that will help you understand tools and materials. Summer work as a construction laborer or a part-time job with a contractor offers valuable experience.

While a job is in progress, expediters constantly make sure that the materials are ready for their scheduled delivery.

After high school it is a good idea to go to a technical school. It is possible to become an expediter by entering a building trade and working your way up. However, as construction materials and methods become more complex, the person with the most technical training will have the best job opportunities.

In technical school, you will learn about various building materials, architecture, engineering, plan reading, business management, estimating, and expediting. You should also look for ways to improve your communication skills. As an expediter, you must have good written and verbal communication skills. For example, a misunderstanding about the time or place of delivery of a certain material can cause serious problems.

As a technical school graduate, you may begin with a construction firm as an engineering aide or in some other trainee position. At a construction firm, you will learn the different aspects of construction, including specifications, scheduling, and purchasing. It is possible to advance from an aide or trainee to an assistant expediter.

Getting the Job

All construction companies have an expediter. In large companies, there may be a group of people who do nothing but expediting. In small companies, the job may be handled by someone who has other duties as well.

To enter this field, you should first contact the construction firms in your area. Tell them of your interest in becoming an expediter. Be sure to mention your training and other capabilities. You may find the names and addresses you need in the Yellow Pages of your phone book under "Contractors."

If it is not possible to work for a contractor, contact firms that make and distribute building materials. Lumberyards, supply houses, stores that sell aluminum products, paint companies, and many other related businesses offer opportunities. Many expediters start out in material distribution. A background in supplying materials to expediters can be very useful. Also, check your local state employment office, Internet job banks, and the classifieds in local newspapers.

Advancement Possibilities and Employment Outlook

Fully qualified expediters can advance to purchasing agent or a similar position. Some expediters even become vice presidents of the firm.

The employment outlook for expediters is related to the economy. When the economy is strong, there is more construction and more expediters are needed. When business is slow, there are fewer opportunities. Generally the person with the most experience and broadest background has the best chance of finding a job.

Working Conditions

Some expediters have offices. During construction, they spend much of the day at the job site checking on materials and visiting materials suppliers to schedule shipments.

Expediters do not always work 40-hour weeks. They may work late nights or very early mornings at job sites. An expediter is normally paid to complete the job, whether it takes 40 or 70 hours a week.

Because of the great amount of activity required, expediters should be in good physical condition. They should be able to get along well with people. Expediters should be able to keep track of details and enjoy solving problems.

Earnings and Benefits

Because they work in the contractor's office, many expediters are paid a salary instead of an hourly wage. Starting salaries for college-educated expediters working for the federal government range from $17,000 to $19,000 a year. However, the size of the firm and its location, as well as the amount of activity in the construction industry, all have a bearing on salaries. A fully qualified senior expediter working in the private sector may earn between $30,000 and $42,000 a year. Many contractors offer some form of benefits. Life and health insurance, paid vacations, sick leave, and other benefits may vary with the employer.

Where to Go for More Information

Associated General Contractors of America
1957 E Street, NW
Washington, DC 20006-5199
(202) 393-2040

National Association of Home Builders of
the United States
1201 Fifteenth Street, NW
Washington, DC 20005-2800
(202) 822-0200
www.nahb.com

National Association of Women
in Construction
327 South Adams Street
Fort Worth, TX 76104-1002
(817) 877-5551
www.nawic.org

Maintenance Electrician

Definition and Nature of the Work

Maintenance electricians work in factories, hospitals, and other large businesses. They keep the generators, lighting, and electrical systems in working order. Electricians find out the cause of the trouble and then repair or replace the defective part.

Maintenance electricians spend a large portion of their time on preventive maintenance. They make periodic inspections of equipment to find defects before costly breakdowns occur. The specific nature of their work depends on the size of the building and the kind of industry in which they work. Electricians who work in factories maintain the machines that make the company's products. Maintenance electricians who work in hospitals and large office buildings keep lighting and air-conditioning systems in working order. Those who are employed by public utilities and mines must ensure a constant and reliable flow of electricity from generators.

Maintenance electricians test equipment and replace fuses, circuit breakers, and switches. Sometimes they must repair wiring by splicing or by bending and cutting conduit. Conduit is a type of metal tubing that protects the wire. Maintenance electricians use wiring diagrams, blueprints, and other building specifications to plan their repair work. They use tools such as screwdrivers, pliers, wire cutters, conduit benders, knives, drills, and meters to test voltage, ohms, and amps.

Maintenance electricians need to act quickly when a breakdown occurs. They must be able to tell management whether the problem can be corrected and whether business can continue as usual. If regular activities must be stopped, the management must know how long a shutdown will last.

Education and Training Requirements

The best way to become a maintenance electrician is to complete a 4-year apprenticeship program. A high school diploma is desirable, especially if you want to enter the apprenticeship program. While in high school you should take courses in algebra, trigonometry, physics, and shop. You must be in good health, have a certain degree of manual dexterity, and be able to do simple mathematics. You must also have accurate color perception. Wires are often color-coded according to function.

The apprenticeship program combines on-the-job training with at least 144 hours of classroom instruction each year. Apprentices learn electrical theory, mathematics, motor repair, wire splicing, welding, and the repair of electrical controls and circuits. On the job, apprentices learn to use the materials and tools of the trade. They also get experience deciding how to solve electrical problems.

Many electricians learn their trade by working as helpers for experienced electricians, but employers usually prefer formal apprenticeship training. Most cities and counties require electricians to hold a master electrician's license. In order to obtain a license, you must pass an exam that tests your knowledge of the trade, of the National Electric Code, and of the building regulations in your area.

Getting the Job

The best way to become a maintenance electrician is to apply for an apprenticeship. For information about openings in the program, contact a reliable electrical contractor or your local union office. Another way of getting into the trade is to start in the maintenance department of a factory or an establishment such as a hospital, public utility company, or office building. There you can begin as a helper and work your way up.

Advancement Possibilities and Employment Outlook

Maintenance electricians are already at the top of their craft. However, experienced maintenance electricians in factories can become supervisors or even plant maintenance superintendents. They can move into related jobs in purchasing and sales, estimating, contracting, and inspecting. Maintenance electricians can also become construction electricians.

The employment outlook for maintenance electricians is good. There has been a steady growth in job opportunities related to building development. Openings are expected to occur each year as the result of expansion in the field. Openings also occur as workers retire or change fields. Maintenance electricians service computers, which are being used more in industry. The increased use of all types of communication devices will create more work for maintenance electricians.

Working Conditions

Maintenance electricians work indoors, in both clean and dirty settings. They generally work a standard 40-hour week, although serious breakdowns may require overtime. Higher wages are paid for extra hours. They may work from ladders or catwalks. They work with high-voltage equipment. To avoid serious injury, they must be alert and precise. Protective clothing and equipment are used. Even with protection, electricians must be aware of the dangers of electricity. The safety and comfort of the people who work in the buildings often depend on maintenance electricians. Maintenance electricians must be able to diagnose and solve problems quickly.

Earnings and Benefits

The average salary for experienced electricians is $15.25 to $21.75 an hour. Beginning apprentices earn 30 to 50 percent of this salary. The pay increases periodically as the apprentices progress through their training. Union members generally receive paid holidays, life insurance, and hospitalization and pension plans. Vacation days vary depending on the number of days they work each year. Other benefits are negotiated separately for each union contract.

Where to Go for More Information

Electrical Apparatus Service Association
1331 Baur Boulevard
St. Louis, MO 63132
(314) 993-2220
www.easa.com

International Brotherhood of
 Electrical Workers
1125 Fifteenth Street, NW
Washington, DC 20005
(202) 833-7000

International Union of Electronic, Electrical,
 Salaried, Machine, and Furniture Workers
1126 Sixteenth Street, NW
Washington, DC 20036
(202) 785-7200

Real Estate Developer

Definition and Nature of the Work

Real estate developers work in one of the most challenging areas of the real estate field—land development. They purchase large tracts of land on which they build residential communities, industrial complexes, and shopping malls or other commercial structures. Sometimes they buy neglected properties and turn them into modern apartment complexes or commercial centers.

Developers must be able to recognize the potential of a particular property. Once they select the site for a prospective development, they must secure enough "seed" money to purchase the land. Real estate developers collaborate with architects to design the proposed development. The developer is also responsible for hiring a

Education and Training
Varies—see profile

Salary Range
Varies—see profile

Employment Outlook
Good

contractor for the building. Upon completion of the construction, either a real estate broker or the developer's own real estate organization puts the houses or other buildings up for sale or lease.

Education and Training Requirements

Real estate developers must have broad knowledge of the different aspects and phases of real estate. To acquire this knowledge, most prospective developers take postsecondary school courses offered by local real estate boards, community colleges, technical schools, or universities.

In addition, most people interested in becoming developers gain experience in the real estate field as salespeople, leasing agents, or brokers. Real estate developers must possess strong communication skills, since they need to sell their ideas to succeed.

Getting the Job

Most real estate developers begin with an entry-level position in real estate. The classified sections of newspapers and Internet job banks list openings for entry-level positions. You can also apply directly to real estate firms. Some real estate developers gain experience by working in the construction industry. The placement offices of colleges and technical schools have lists of available positions.

Advancement Possibilities and Employment Outlook

Real estate developers may work for large real estate agencies or land development firms. They advance by taking on increasingly larger and more complex projects. Some eventually specialize in certain types of land development, such as industrial

After a building site is chosen, real estate developers design the proposed development with architects and oversee its construction.

complexes or even entire communities. Successful developers sometimes start their own development and construction firms or real estate organizations.

The real estate industry as a whole is greatly affected by economic trends. Overall, however, the job growth for real estate developers is expected to be good through the year 2006. Job opportunities will vary in different areas of the country depending on a region's specific needs and economic health.

Working Conditions

Real estate developers work in offices but may spend a lot of time searching for sites, overseeing construction, and meeting with bankers, architects, contractors, and others involved in the development project. The work can be exciting and challenging but also stressful and financially risky.

Earnings and Benefits

Earnings for real estate developers vary widely depending on many factors, including geographic location, the size and success of projects, and the condition of the economy. Real estate development is very risky, but those who are successful can be substantially rewarded. Some experienced real estate developers who own their own firms often earn $1 million or more a year. However, those developers who invest a great deal of money in an unsuccessful project may lose their entire investment.

Developers employed by real estate firms or development companies may have some benefits provided for them. Self-employed developers must provide their own benefits.

Septic Tank Installer

Definition and Nature of the Work

Septic systems dispose of sewage and gray water (wastewater from showers, sinks, and washing machines) from houses that are not connected to a public sewer line. A septic system consists of a sewer line, a septic tank, distribution boxes, and a drain system. Sewage and gray water flow through the sewer line from the house to the septic tank. Bacterial action inside the septic tank dissolves some of the waste. The solid waste flows through lines from the septic tank to the distribution boxes and from the distribution boxes to the drain system, where it disperses into the surrounding gravel and soil. Septic tank installers put all the parts of the septic system in place, except for the plumbing inside the house.

Septic tank installers install septic systems according to local building codes and plans developed by the local health departments. A plan specifies the construction details of the septic system. It states whether to use a drain field or seepage pit (dry well) for drainage. It also shows the location of the septic system in relation to the house, to the well water supply, and to the adjoining properties.

There are two groups of septic tank installers: backhoe operators and laborers. Backhoe operators oversee laborers. Usually, one backhoe operator and two laborers work on one job.

Education and Training
Varies—see profile

Salary Range
Average—$20,000 to $25,000

Employment Outlook
Varies—see profile

Septic tank installers use backhoes to dig the pits and ditches where they install the parts of the septic system.

The installers use the backhoe to dig the pits for the septic tanks and the distribution boxes. They also use the backhoe to dig the ditches to the drain fields or the seepage pits. They may use shovels and picks to level and trim the ditches and pits. Then they use a level to check the final results.

Generally, the supplier brings the septic tank and the distribution boxes to the site and puts them into place. The installers may use the backhoe to put the pieces into place. After the septic tank and the distribution boxes are in place, the septic tank installers put in the sewer lines from the house to the tank and from the tank to the distribution boxes. These lines may be made of cast-iron pipe, solvent-welded plastic pipe (PVC), self-sealing vitrified (turned to glass) clay tile, tapered-joint fiber pipe, or self-sealing cement asbestos pipe. The lines must be watertight to prevent the seepage of liquid waste.

Next, the installers put in drain lines from the distribution boxes to the drain field or seepage pits. These lines may be made of concrete, clay tiles, perforated plastic, or fiber pipe. They are not watertight. The tile or pipe slopes away from the distribution boxes. Waste travels along the line and seeps into the surrounding gravel. If a seepage pit is required, the installers may use cement blocks to build it. Since the liquid in the pit seeps through the blocks into the surrounding gravel, the blocks do not have to be cemented.

Before the septic tank installers backfill the excavation, an inspector checks to see that the septic system complies with the local codes and the health department plan. If the system complies, the installers use the backhoe to put five inches of gravel over the drain lines. They place a layer of building, or resin, paper on top of the gravel to prevent soil from clogging the drain lines. Then the installers backfill the trenches, the seepage pits, and the pits containing the septic tank and the distribution boxes. They grade the land and may plant grass.

Education and Training Requirements

You do not need to be a high school graduate to enter this field, but a diploma is preferred. While in high school you should take courses in mechanics, blueprint reading, engine repair, and shop. Similar courses are available at technical schools, along with courses in concrete work and the use of surveying tools and levels.

Training companies offer instruction for heavy equipment operators. This training covers the operation, maintenance, and repair of backhoes, bulldozers, graders, and scrapers. It may also cover surveying and how to set grading stakes.

Getting the Job

Your first step in getting a job in this field should be to contact potential employers listed in your phone book's Yellow Pages under "Sewage Disposal Systems," "Sewer Contractors," "Septic Tanks and Systems, Cleaning—Residential," and "Septic Tanks and Systems—Contractors and Dealers." You should check the newspaper classifieds, Internet job banks, and the state employment offices. City and local governments employ workers to dig trenches and connect buildings to public sewer lines. Local union offices may also have information about septic tank installation jobs.

Advancement Possibilities and Employment Outlook

Septic tank installers are already at the top of their trade. After some years of experience, some open their own installation businesses. A septic tank installer may also serve an apprenticeship under a licensed plumber. At the end of the apprenticeship, he or she may apply for a plumber's license and become a sewage disposal contractor.

Employment of septic tank installers depends on the state of the housing industry, which is affected by general economic conditions. When the economy is good and housing construction is in demand, there are many opportunities for septic tank installers. When the economy is poor, there are few opportunities.

Working Conditions

Septic tank installers perform hard physical labor outside in all climates. They lift, bend, stoop, and kneel to do their work. They may suffer muscle strains, bruises, and cuts from handling the material and equipment associated with the job.

Normally installers work a 40-hour week. However, the number of working hours in a week depends on the weather, completion dates, and the number of jobs under contract. They may work fewer than 40 hours a week in severe cold or rainy weather. They earn extra pay for overtime.

Earnings and Benefits

Currently the average salary earned by septic tank installers is $20,000 to $25,000. They may not receive some benefits, such as holidays, vacations, sick leave, or pensions.

Where to Go for More Information

Associated General Contractors of America
1957 E Street, NW
Washington, DC 20006-5199
(202) 393-2040

Laborers International Union of
   North America
905 Sixteenth Street, NW
Washington, DC 20006-1765
(202) 737-8320

National Association of Women
   in Construction
327 South Adams Street
Fort Worth, TX 76104-1002
(817) 877-5551
www.nawic.org

Solar Energy Technician

Definition and Nature of the Work

In what is known as the photovoltaic process, radiation from the sun is converted into electricity. Although understood by scientists for many years, this process did not receive attention until the 1950s, when the first silicon solar cell was invented. Since the energy crises of the 1970s, there has been an increasing demand for solar energy technicians. These technicians install, maintain, operate, and test equipment and energy systems that use solar energy.

Each solar energy project, from conception to installation, requires the services of many technicians with various skills. Some technicians are construction craft workers, such as plumbers, carpenters, roofers, and sheet metal workers, who install or repair solar energy systems. Others work for architects or engineers, assisting them in the design of solar energy equipment and buildings. Sometimes systems are integrated into new buildings as they are constructed. Older buildings are also renovated to use solar energy equipment.

A solar energy technician may help construct and install active systems, which require solar collectors, concentrators, pumps, and fans. A technician may also help install passive systems, which rely on the best use of windows and insulation to absorb and reflect solar radiation for heating and cooling. Another type of solar energy system uses mirrors to absorb and concentrate the sun's radiation and convert it to heat. A fluid circulates among the mirrors collecting the heat and then transfers it to a central boiler or steam turbine, which generates the electricity.

Education and Training Requirements

Many workers in the solar energy field are experienced construction trade workers who have completed an apprenticeship training program. They have received special training in solar energy technology through programs offered by trade associations and by vocational schools and community colleges. Such programs, which last from several weeks to a year, usually offer a certificate of completion. Courses include hands-on system installation, system maintenance, and retrofitting (converting old buildings to solar energy). High school graduates who want to install or repair solar systems take these training courses to get started in the field. They may also have to apprentice in one of the construction trades. On-the-job training is another possibility.

Those who are interested in the design, planning, or research aspects of solar energy should enter a community college or 2-year vocational school program leading to an associate degree. Such programs provide practical and theoretical courses, including math, science, photovoltaics, solar-thermal systems, and solar architecture. Students who want professional engineering training can transfer some of the credits.

Getting the Job

To get a job, you can apply directly to solar contractors. If you are enrolled in a degree or certificate program, you can ask the school placement office for assistance in finding a job. If you are a graduate of a degree program, you may be able to find a job with an architectural or engineering firm. Solar research and development firms and solar equipment manufacturers may also have openings. Job seekers may find it helpful to talk to company representatives at convention exhibits that demonstrate the latest developments in solar technology.

A solar energy technician makes adjustments to a solar energy system, which uses mirrors to absorb and concentrate the sun's radiation.

Advancement Possibilities and Employment Outlook

Those who have strong credentials and an ability to keep pace with continual changes in solar technology should be able to advance, possibly to project supervisor or manager. Some solar energy technicians become owners of consulting or installation businesses.

The expansion of solar technology depends heavily on several factors, such as the amount of support offered by the government and the price of oil and other fuels. Job and career opportunities in this branch of solar energy are strongest in the warm southwestern region of the United States and in rural and remote areas. There are opportunities in solar power generator design, construction, and operation. Other opportunities exist in the researching and developing of system generators that are not harmful to the environment.

Working Conditions

Solar energy technicians work under a variety of conditions and in various settings, depending on the type of job and employer. They work in the offices of large corporations, in research laboratories, or with outdoor crews. The work can be either physically demanding or fairly sedentary. The hours for installing solar equipment may be long when the weather is good. Layoffs can occur when the economy is bad or when the weather does not permit outside work.

Earnings and Benefits

Salaries vary widely. Solar energy technicians earn anywhere from $18,000 to $39,000, depending on education, geographical location, and type of position. Technicians who are employed by large companies usually receive benefits, including health insurance and paid vacations and holidays.

Where to Go for More Information

American Solar Energy Society
2400 Central Avenue, #G-1
Boulder, CO 80301-2843
(303) 443-3130
www.ases.org/solar

Specification Writer

Definition and Nature of the Work

Specification writers describe to builders the different types of materials used in construction projects. They also instruct builders on how to use the materials. These descriptions or specifications cover everything from the type of concrete used in the foundation to the type of paint used on the front door.

Specifications are important because they provide legal protection for the owner, the architect, the contractor, and any other people involved in a construction project. In the bidding process, the architect presents the plans and specifications to construction firms and asks them to submit a bid, or price quote. Contractors from the construction firms then determine what they must charge to build the project. Usually, the contractor who submits the lowest bid is awarded the contract. The specifications then become a part of the legal contract that binds all parties concerned. Therefore, the specification writer is an essential member of the construction industry.

Education and Training Requirements

A high school education is usually needed to enter this field. While you are in school you should take courses in mathematics, plan reading, drafting, mechanical drawing, and shop. Courses in physics and other sciences will also help you to understand the qualities of various materials. Since specification writers must express themselves clearly, English and other communication courses are also helpful.

After high school, you should consider advanced training at either a technical school or a college program in architecture. In either institution, you will learn about engineering, architecture, design, building materials, drafting, estimating, and specification writing.

You can also gain valuable experience by working during the summer as a helper in an architectural firm, as a construction laborer, or in a building materials supply firm. Many things about construction can be learned only by working in the industry.

Getting the Job

Many specification writers are employed by architects or large architectural firms that hire people only for specification writing. In many cases, however, specification writers also have other duties. Frequently, the person who makes the drawings or someone in the design area of the firm writes the specifications. A few companies specialize in specification writing.

Because specification writing requires on-the-job training, you will probably start out as an assistant design technician, a junior drafter, or some other kind of trainee. Your first step in getting a job should be to contact the architectural firms in your area. You will find them listed under "Architects" in the Yellow Pages of your phone book. Also check with the civil service about a job as a government specification writer.

You can also contact your local state employment service, check job banks on the Internet, and scan newspaper classifieds. If you are attending a post-secondary school, check with the career placement office at your technical school or college.

For construction projects, specification writers describe everything from the type of concrete used in the foundation to the type of paint used on the front door.

Advancement Possibilities and Employment Outlook

Advancement in this field depends mostly on education, skill, and experience. Trainees can become fully qualified specification writers or senior drafters. They may also become purchasing agents with a construction firm. Specification writers may become architects after receiving more education. The need for specification writers almost always depends on the level of activity in the construction industry, which depends on general economic conditions.

Working Conditions

Many specification writers work in offices where they can easily research materials in catalogs, use specification files, and consult with other people involved with the project. Specification writers may have to visit job sites and materials manufacturers at times.

Specification writers normally work a 40-hour week, but overtime may be required to meet deadlines. In some cases, employees are paid extra for overtime work or given extra time off at a later date.

Earnings and Benefits

The starting salary for a trainee in an architectural firm is approximately $20,000 a year. However, the size of the firm and its location are always important factors. A fully qualified specification writer earns between $22,000 and $30,000 a year.

Benefits vary with different companies. Some specification writers receive health and life insurance, a pension plan, sick leave, and paid vacations.

Where to Go for More Information

American Institute of Architects
1735 New York Avenue, NW
Washington, DC 20006-5292
(202) 626-7300
www.aiaonline.com

Construction Specifications Institute
601 Madison Street
Alexandria, VA 22314-1791
(703) 684-0300

National Association of Women
    in Construction
327 South Adams Street
Fort Worth, TX 76104-1002
(817) 877-5551
www.nawic.org

Water Well Driller

Definition and Nature of the Work

Water well drillers sink wells into the earth to tap natural water supplies. They drill agricultural wells for irrigation, commercial or industrial wells, and wells for homes that are not served by municipal water systems.

Usually drillers hire a crew of six workers, consisting of well driller helpers, pump service rig operators, and pump service rig helpers. They set up a truck-mounted derrick or rig with the drill and other required equipment. Once the drilling rig is set up and working, the drillers continue to monitor the operation.

As the well shaft goes into the ground, the drillers line the shaft with steel or plastic pipe to prevent the ground from caving in and to keep out water that may be polluted. The drillers fill the shaft with fluid to keep the bit cool. They may adjust the pressure or impact of the drilling rig and change the bit as it penetrates different layers of the earth. The well drillers or their helpers may splice worn or broken cable and use welding and cutting equipment to do repairs. Sometimes they use special fishing or retrieval tools to recover broken or lost drill bits and pieces of pipe.

When the well is driven, the drillers install a pump designed for the depth, diameter, and capacity of the well. They sterilize the entire system to prevent the growth of bacteria. Finally, they start the pump to bring water up through the system.

Water well drillers do not always work on new wells. They may set up a rig to repair or restore wells that have stopped producing.

Education and Training Requirements

To enter this field you need a high school diploma. While in high school you should take shop courses to learn how to run and maintain machines and small tools. You should also take science courses such as geology, chemistry, and physics, to learn about rock formations, minerals, and the properties of water. Algebra, trigonometry, and English are also important.

After high school, you may join a union apprenticeship program. Apprenticeship programs usually last 3 to 4 years and include classroom study and on-the-job training. After completing your apprenticeship, you will become a qualified rig operator.

Several 2-year colleges offer well drilling technology programs. These programs give courses in geology, mathematics, and inorganic chemistry. You learn techniques for finding good-quality water, methods of drilling, and equipment operation. You learn about equipment maintenance and repair, setting specifications, inspection and quality control, and record keeping and accounting. When you graduate you are certified as a groundwater resource technician.

Getting the Job

The first step in getting a job in this field should be to contact potential employers listed in your phone book's Yellow Pages under "Water Well Drilling and Service" and "Drilling and Boring Contractors." You should contact drilling rig manufacturers and geological consulting firms. You can also check newspaper classifieds, Internet job banks, and state and local employment offices. If you are a technical school graduate, check the placement office. Local union offices may also have information about drilling jobs.

Advancement Possibilities and Employment Outlook

Water well drillers are already at the top of their craft. Most work for drilling contractors, and others may work as consultants, sales representatives, or service technicians for equipment manufacturers. They may also work for state or federal agencies concerned with the use and control of water resources. After some years of experience, they may set up their own drilling businesses.

As with most jobs in construction, employment mainly depends on general economic conditions. However, there will always be a demand for drillers because an increasing population always needs more water. Groundwater supplies must also be found to replace surface water supplies that are often polluted and too expensive to clean up.

Working Conditions

Water well drillers perform hard physical labor in all kinds of weather. They stoop, squat, and crawl to do their work. They often work on narrow, slippery surfaces. They lift heavy equipment. They may suffer muscle strains, bruises, and cuts from handling the material and equipment associated with the job. Noise and vibration may cause stress and possibly some hearing loss if ear plugs and other safety devices are not used.

The number of working hours in a week depends on the completion dates. Normally water well drillers work about 50 hours a week. The hours may be irregular because of emergencies.

Earnings and Benefits

Currently, water well drillers earn an average of $25,000 a year. Benefits may include health plans, pensions, and paid vacations.

Where to Go for More Information

Groundwater Management Districts
   Association
P.O. Box 795
Colby, KS 67701
(913) 462-3915

National Ground Water Association
601 Dempsey Road
Westerville, OH 43081-8978
(614) 898-7791
www.h2o-ngwa.org

Water Systems Council
800 Roosevelt Road, Building C, Suite 20
Glen Ellyn, IL 60137
(708) 545-1762

Architect

Definition and Nature of the Work

Architects design, plan, and supervise the construction of buildings. They are responsible for the safety, usefulness, and aesthetics of their buildings. They must design structures that satisfy their clients' needs while conforming to the laws and regulations of the areas in which the structures will be built.

Architects work with engineers, urban planners, contractors, and landscape architects. They may work for large architectural firms, or they may be self-employed. Some architects work for engineers or builders. Others work for federal, state, or local governments. They may work on a variety of projects. Some architects specialize in certain kinds of architecture, such as designing school campuses, health facilities, shopping centers, or dwellings for urban renewal projects.

When a client hires an architect to design a building, the client and architect discuss the type of building wanted and how much money is available. Then the architect inspects the building site to see what the land looks like. The architect has to consider what kind of design the building should have in relation to the site. The architect must also consider the climate, the surrounding buildings, and the slope of the site. Next the architect draws preliminary sketches. These first drawings suggest the general appearance of the building, the method of construction, where it will be placed on the site, and how the inside will look. The architect might have to revise the plans to go along with the client's ideas.

Once the client approves these preliminary plans, the architect prepares more detailed plans, called working drawings. These drawings show exactly how the building is to be built. They indicate the dimensions and placement of each wall and window. They also serve as diagrams for heating duct locations and indicate the paths for plumbing pipes and electrical wiring. The architect writes down technical information, such as the quality of materials to be used and the proper methods of installation. This information is called the specifications. At this point, the architect gives the plans and specifications to contractors. The contractors examine the plans and submit bids on labor and material costs. When the architect has received these bids, the client and the architect decide who will get the work. Considerations in selecting the contractor include the price submitted and the quality of past work. The contractor who is chosen uses the plans and specifications to direct the actual construction work.

Once construction begins, the architect visits the site often to check that the plans are being followed. The architect must also approve the materials being used. The architect checks the interior hardware and fixtures, and works with the landscape planner and other workers and engineers on the building site. The architect's final duty is to decide whether the contract between the client and the contractor has been satisfied.

The amount of detail that the architects handle themselves depends on the size of their firm. In large offices many of the smaller details are the responsibility of other staff members. Architects who work in small companies handle most of the details personally. Architects must be artists, businesspeople, organizers, planners, and coordinators. They must understand building codes. They should be aware of their clients' needs, as well as the needs of those who will use the buildings they design. Architects must consider the effect their buildings will have on the natural and artificial surroundings. An extensive knowledge of design and construction coupled with creative ability is the best combination of qualities for an architect.

Education and Training Requirements

Architects must have a degree from a college of architecture and must serve an apprenticeship. In addition, all 50 states require that architects be licensed. Each state has different requirements for admission to the licensing exam. Generally, in addition to a bachelor's degree, you must have 3 years of practical experience in an architect's office.

If you are interested in architecture as a career, you should start your studies in high school. Courses in mechanical drawing, art, physics, and mathematics are very helpful. You can get valuable experience by working part-time in an architectural firm. Many large companies recruit students from high school. These companies help pay the students' college tuition while the students work for them part-time.

You should apply to one of the approximately 100 architectural colleges accredited by the National Architectural Accrediting Board (NAAB). These schools offer 5-year programs that lead to a bachelor of architecture degree. Students attend classes in engineering, architectural design, building construction, structural theory, professional administration, and graphic representation. State architectural registration boards set their own standards, so you may be able to graduate from a non-NAAB-accredited program and still meet education requirements for licensure in some states.

In addition to preparing the sketches and final specifications of a building, architects oversee and approve the construction as it progresses.

After graduation students can begin their apprenticeships with architectural firms. They start as junior drafters. Their tasks include model making, lettering, and tracing. As they gain experience, their duties become more complex. They can become senior drafters, who are responsible for the details in working drawings. After working in architecture for about 3 years, the trainee may take the state licensing examination. This test includes the theory and history of architecture, construction, engineering, design, and professional practice.

Getting the Job

A good way to enter this field is to get a part-time job in an architectural firm while attending high school or college. You can also contact companies about their employment needs. Your college placement office can help you find a job with an architectural firm after you graduate. Another source of job openings is the classified section of your newspaper. You can also try job banks on the Internet.

Advancement Possibilities and Employment Outlook

Licensed architects can start their own businesses. Nearly one-third own their own companies. There are many possibilities for advancement in architectural firms. Architects can become supervisors and project managers. They can go into construction management and government service.

The employment outlook for architects is mixed. Currently there are about 91,000 licensed architects in the U.S. Although the growth for architects is expected to increase about as fast as the average through the year 2006, employment of architects depends on the level of activity in the construction industry. The amount of construction also depends on the economy as a whole. The increase in computer-aided design and drafting (CADD) systems for architectural drawings, specifications, and estimates will increase the need for architects who know how to use this technology. Employment growth will take place in urban centers seeking to renovate old buildings. Demand for schools and healthcare facilities is also expected to rise.

Working Conditions

Architects spend most of their time in modern office buildings that are well-lighted and well-ventilated. However, architects work outdoors when they visit construction sites. Many architects work a standard 40-hour week. Very often, however, they must change their schedules to meet deadlines. They may also work nights and weekends. Self-employed architects generally work longer hours and often meet clients during the evening. Despite these irregular hours, architectural work is challenging and offers a great deal of personal satisfaction.

Earnings and Benefits

Earnings for architects vary widely, depending on experience and talent. Intern-architects generally start at $24,700. Licensed architects with about 8 to 10 years of experience average an annual salary of $38,900. Principals or partners in architectural firms earn an average of $50,000, with those in management positions earning over $100,000. Architects who successfully run their own firms can make even more money.

Many architectural firms offer such benefits as life and health insurance plans, profit-sharing plans, and retirement funds. Most companies provide paid holidays and vacations.

Where to Go for More Information

American Institute of Architects
1735 New York Avenue, NW
Washington, DC 20006-5292
(202) 626-7300

American Institute of Architecture Students
1735 New York Avenue, NW
Washington, DC 20006
(202) 626-7472

Society of American Registered Architects
303 South Broadway
Tarrytown, NY 10591
(914) 631-3600

Building Inspector

Education and Training
High school plus training

Salary Range
Average—$25,200
to $43,800

Employment Outlook
Good

Definition and Nature of the Work

Building inspectors check to see that certain standards of safety and structural quality are being met in buildings. They inspect new buildings, old buildings, buildings under construction, and buildings undergoing renovation. Most building inspectors work for local governments.

Some inspectors specialize. *Electrical inspectors* check the safe functioning of electrical systems. They inspect wiring, lighting, and generating systems. *Elevator inspectors* examine escalators, elevators, hoists, and amusement rides. *Plumbing inspectors* examine water supply, distribution, and drainage systems. *Public works inspectors* ensure that highways, bridges, and dams comply with building code regulations.

When builders or land development companies want to build structures on land, they must apply to the city for a building permit. Once the city has issued the permit, an inspector, or group of inspectors, is assigned to oversee construction of the building. Usually the inspectors follow the construction process to its completion, visiting the site as each phase of construction is completed.

Before construction begins, inspectors look at the plans for the building and decide whether they meet local zoning regulations. They check that the building is an appropriate height and that the type of building is suitable to the area. They also decide whether the plans meet the engineering and environmental demands of the building site.

The inspectors check the building's foundation to make sure it is properly constructed for the type and condition of soil. They see that it is placed correctly in the ground. The site is also checked for proper drainage. As construction continues, the electrical and plumbing systems are inspected. Inspectors examine every aspect of the construction, including roofing, lathing and framing, installation of the stairways and chimneys, and the usage of structural steel and reinforced concrete.

Inspectors notify the supervisor if any part of the building code is being broken. Inspectors have to find problems quickly to avoid unnecessary costs and delays. In cases where the supervisor deliberately fails to conform to building regulations, inspectors can issue orders to stop construction. In older structures, inspectors check to see that buildings are being maintained safely. They may condemn, or declare a building unsafe for occupancy. This situation can occur after a major fire, for example.

Building inspectors examine every aspect of the construction including the roofing, the lathing and framing, and the installation of stairways and chimneys. They must decide if the building meets safety regulations.

A person who wants to remodel a building must apply for a building permit. Then the local government sends out a building inspector, who will conduct regular inspections to make sure local safety standards are being met.

Education and Training Requirements

To become a building inspector you must have a high school diploma. In most places an apprenticeship and several years of experience in one of the construction trades are required for the job. College courses in engineering or architecture are often required as well. These courses include construction technology, blueprint reading, mathematics, stress analysis, physics, and building inspection. Many specialized inspectors may have experience as electricians or plumbers.

Building inspectors get most of their training on the job. By working with an experienced inspector, you learn about inspection techniques, codes, ordinances, regulations, record keeping, and reporting duties. You must be able to communicate your ideas clearly and accurately. Federal, state, and local governments require that inspectors pass a civil service examination. At least 3 years of experience in a construction trade is required before taking these examinations.

Getting the Job

After you pass the civil service examinations, you should check the government job listings available at many public libraries and state employment offices. The classifieds in local newspapers or job banks on the Internet will also inform you of openings for building inspectors.

Advancement Possibilities and Employment Outlook

In public agencies, advancement depends on passing the civil service examinations for higher positions. A building inspector can become a construction inspector. The construction inspector's job requires additional knowledge and involves greater responsibility. Inspectors are assigned to large construction projects as resident inspectors. They work with the architects, engineers, and contractors to make sure the project conforms to building codes. They also assist in enforcing the plans, specifications, and technical requirements.

The number of jobs for building inspectors varies with the amount of construction taking place in an area. In areas where construction is limited, the job prospects are also limited. Currently about 64,000 construction inspectors are employed by the government. Most work for county or municipal agencies.

Employment of inspectors is not always directly affected by changes in the level of building activity. Unlike some construction workers, inspectors do not usually experience layoffs, as maintenance and renovation work continues to require regular inspection. However, engineers and construction supervisors now perform many functions previously performed by building inspectors. Therefore, employment should reflect the average growth of all occupations through the year 2006.

Working Conditions

Building inspectors must travel daily from site to site, checking on construction. They generally work 40 hours a week on a steady, year-round schedule. Usually automobiles are furnished by their employers, or mileage is paid if they use their own car. They must be able to walk through construction sites in all stages of completion and be prepared to climb ladders, ride on platform hoists, and work many stories above the ground. Since much of their work is spent outdoors, they are subject to all kinds of weather. They also spend time in the office reviewing blueprints and writing reports.

Earnings and Benefits

Salaries for building inspectors vary widely depending on where they work. Currently, building inspectors earn between $25,200 and $43,800 a year. The most experienced building inspectors can earn over $57,000 a year. Benefits vary from area to area, but most government jobs offer paid holidays and vacations along with health and life insurance and retirement plans.

Civil Engineer

Definition and Nature of the Work

Civil engineers plan and design bridges and tunnels, as well as highways, airfields, harbors, water and sewerage systems, and buildings. They also supervise the construction of such projects to ensure that they are built according to the carefully drafted plans. Civil engineers are employed by all levels of government, by construction companies, and by engineering and architectural firms. Some civil engineers do independent consulting work. Others work for public utility companies or in such industries as the iron and steel industry. Still other civil engineers teach at colleges and universities.

Civil engineering is such a broad and varied field that most engineers specialize in one area. Some of the main specializations are structural, construction, hydraulics, sanitary, environmental, transportation, and soil mechanics engineering.

Structural engineers are experts in building structures safely and efficiently. They work with architects to design large buildings, bridges, and tunnels. *Construction engineers* supervise the actual construction of projects once they are designed. They decide on the best materials and methods to use in building such structures as skyscrapers. Civil engineers who work in hydraulics design canals, flood-control systems, and irrigation systems. They study water sources and try to develop ways of using water that will benefit the community. For example, a *hydraulic engineer* builds a dam in a river in order to construct a reservoir to safeguard the water supply of an area.

Sanitary engineers design systems to purify water and treat wastes in order to provide a safe and economical supply of water. They work with *environmental*

Education and Training
College plus training

Salary Range
Starting—$29,400
Average—$43,400

Employment Outlook
Good

Civil engineers work with architects, other engineers, and construction personnel to design and oversee the construction of bridges, tunnels, highways, large buildings, and other such projects.

engineers to control water and air pollution. *Transportation engineers* plan and build highways, subways, airports, and railroads. *Soil mechanics engineers* develop ways to use soil so that building foundations can be improved.

Civil engineers work with architects, other engineers, and construction personnel. These professionals often bring their specialized talents together to work on urban planning projects. Civil engineers must be accurate and consider the safety of the thousands of people who will use the structures they design and build.

Education and Training Requirements

Civil engineering is an intellectually demanding field that requires a high aptitude for mathematics and the physical sciences. You will need the ability to think logically and creatively to work successfully in this field.

You must have a bachelor's degree in civil engineering to enter the field. Many colleges offer 4- or 5-year engineering programs that include courses in thermodynamics, fluid mechanics, circuitry, stress analysis, and structural design. Some colleges offer cooperative programs in which you can divide your time between classes and work experience. If you want a career in research, development, or teaching, a graduate degree is required. Some companies help pay students' tuitions.

Once you have a degree, you must get field training. A state license is also needed before you can be a civil engineer in private practice. Most states require you to have about 4 years of work experience before taking a licensing examination. Even after licensing, civil engineers must be willing to continue their education in order to keep up with their field.

Getting the Job

Many civil engineers work for the government on the state, federal, or municipal level. A good way to start looking for a job is to take the civil service examination, which is required for government work, and then check the specific openings listed at your local state employment office.

Some engineers work for consulting architectural and engineering firms and in the major manufacturing industries. The placement services of your college may know of some job openings. Contact construction and engineering companies directly. Check professional journals and local newspapers about job opportunities. Job banks on the Internet may also provide some leads.

Advancement Possibilities and Employment Outlook

There are many opportunities for advancement. Civil engineers who work in civil service can advance from junior engineer to assistant engineer to associate engineer, and then become the head of a department.

Promotion of this type also occurs in large firms. Engineers can advance from project management to an administrative position as a consulting engineer, department head, or chief engineer of a large construction firm. In smaller companies advancement takes the form of specialization. Self-employment or partnership in a company is possible for those with exceptional ability and capital.

The employment outlook for civil engineers is good. Approximately 184,000 civil engineers are now working in the United States. Urban renewal, growth in rapid transit and industry, and an expanding economy will create an increasing demand for civil engineers. The increased use of computers should help civil engineers by freeing them from the more mechanical aspects of the work, such as mathematical computation.

Working Conditions

Civil engineers work in many different places, depending on their specialization and their employer. They can work in offices as well as at construction sites. Civil engineers doing research may work in laboratories.

In most fields of engineering, there is steady employment. However, engineers working in construction may experience periodic layoffs. Those who work for government agencies enjoy a job security not found in other types of engineering. Regardless of where they work, civil engineers must face the strain of deadlines and tight schedules. Their work is exacting. They must be very accurate because their work involves costly projects. They must work as part of a team and be able to communicate their ideas to the other specialists with whom they work. Problem solving sometimes requires innovation and the ability to make decisions. The personal satisfaction in this work usually outweighs the pressures.

Earnings and Benefits

Currently, beginning government civil engineers earn starting salaries of about $29,400 a year. Experienced engineers earn average annual salaries of about $43,400. Engineers with master's degrees earn about $53,200, and those with doctoral degrees may earn $62,300. Civil engineers who work as executives for large engineering firms often earn $80,000 or more a year. Federal government employees in nonsupervisory, supervisory, and managerial positions earn approximately $58,100. Government-employed engineers receive the same benefits offered to other civil service workers. Private firms generally offer retirement plans, life and health insurance, and paid vacations and holidays to their engineers.

Where to Go for More Information

American Association of Engineering
  Societies
1111 Nineteenth Street, NW, Suite 608
Washington, DC 20036-3690
(202) 296-2237

American Society of Civil Engineers
345 East 47th Street
New York, NY 10017
(212) 705-7496

National Society of Professional Engineers
1420 King Street
Alexandria, VA 22314-2794
(703) 684-2800

Construction Supervisor

Definition and Nature of the Work

Construction supervisors manage crews of skilled and unskilled workers at construction sites. Supervisors, also known as foremen or forewomen, are usually experienced construction workers. An experienced bricklayer might supervise a crew of bricklayers. Supervisors are responsible for the efficient use of labor, machines, and materials within their crew. Supervisors report to *site superintendents,* who are responsible for the efficiency of all the crews on a construction job.

Supervisors plan and schedule work and keep records on the materials used and the progress made on a job. These records are included in the supervisor's reports to the superintendent. Supervisors also report on such things as personnel, costs, and safety. Supervisors must see that safety rules are followed. They also communicate company rules and policies to the workers. When the workers have grievances or complaints about their jobs, the construction supervisor meets with union representatives to work out solutions. Supervisors must be familiar with union contracts and procedures.

In some cases, especially on small jobs, supervisors work alongside their crew. These supervisors are called *working supervisors.* On large jobs they spend their

Education and Training
High school

Salary Range
Average—$35,000
to $110,000

Employment Outlook
Very good

A construction supervisor discusses blue-prints and plans with a contractor.

time in management activities. Supervisors must be able to read blueprints and plans. Supervisors advise qualified craft workers on the best way to handle certain tasks. Sometimes supervisors oversee the training of newly hired laborers.

Supervisors must be experts in their craft. They must be able to give clear directions and see that they are followed. They must also be able to communicate well with their bosses, who may be superintendents or contractors. Supervisors are very important to the efficient completion of all construction jobs, large and small. They are more familiar with their particular trade than are the superintendents. Superintendents and contractors rely on supervisors to maintain high standards of workmanship and efficiency in their craft.

Education and Training Requirements

The majority of construction supervisors are former union members who have worked their way up through the construction trade. A high school diploma is necessary to enter many of these trades and is desirable for those who want to become supervisors. Few supervisors are college graduates, although a growing number of employers are hiring supervisors with college training.

Supervisors should have a thorough knowledge of construction. They learn from experience how a job should be done, what problems to anticipate, and how to fix these problems. Supervisors who begin as apprentices and work to become experienced craft workers know what to expect from their workers. They are aware of management policies and are sensitive to workers' attitudes toward these policies. Experience with union negotiations and grievance procedures helps supervisors avoid problems with workers. Employers look for experience and skill in construction trades, as well as leadership ability.

Getting the Job

Most contractors hire supervisors in each of the building trades and employ them on a steady basis. Experienced trade workers can apply to contractors for positions.

Advancement Possibilities and Employment Outlook

Supervisors are already at the top of their trade. Some supervisors become site superintendents or contractors. Others become inspectors for city or county governments.

Employment is expected to increase faster than the average through the year 2006 as construction activity continues to grow. Increased government spending on the national infrastructure will also create more job opportunities. Construction jobs, however, are often short-term. Both supervisors and workers may be laid off temporarily or experience lulls in employment.

Working Conditions

Construction supervisors are among the first to arrive at a job site and the last to leave. This work demands participation in many activities and communication with many workers and managers on the job site. Supervisors spend a lot of time going through the construction site, checking the production and efficiency of the workers. Supervisors, like other construction workers, are unable to work in bad weather. But since they are salaried employees, they are paid whether or not they work.

Earnings and Benefits

Earnings vary widely depending on the nature and location of the work. Companies pay their supervisors anywhere from $35,000 to $110,000 a year, depending on supervisory experience, location, and size of job and crew. Most employers provide health insurance plans and paid holidays and vacations.

Heavy Construction Contractor

Definition and Nature of the Work

Heavy construction contractors specialize in building large-scale projects, such as bridges, dams, tunnels, and sewerage systems. Other heavy construction projects include railroads and subways, oil and water pipelines, docks, harbors, hydroelectric systems, and industrial sites. Some contractors specialize in one of these areas, while others can handle many kinds of heavy construction projects.

Before contractors begin a project, they must submit a bid or price quote to the company or government agency sponsoring the project. To make an accurate bid, contractors study the building plans and specifications while keeping in mind material, labor, and safety considerations. The lowest bid is usually accepted.

Heavy construction contractors either own or rent the equipment needed for the job. They contact companies that supply concrete, steel, electrical equipment, lumber, and other building materials to arrange shipments. Contractors are also responsible for hiring workers and subcontractors and for working out a timetable that will get the job completed on time.

Education and Training
Varies—see profile

Salary Range
Average—$600
to $675 a week

Employment Outlook
Varies—see profile

Contractors supervise the work as it progresses, making sure that the specifications are met and that the work flows smoothly. They must be able to solve unforeseen problems quickly and correctly.

Depending on the job, the contractor may have several people to help with management details. There may be an estimator to help prepare bids, an expediter to oversee material shipments, various job supervisors, an office staff, and others. However, the responsibility and the risk involved in every heavy construction project are almost always the contractor's alone.

Education and Training Requirements

Although there are no educational requirements for becoming a heavy construction contractor, it is usually best to get as much education as you can. In high school it is good to take mathematics and science courses. Accounting, business mathematics, drafting, plan reading, and English are especially useful subjects in this field. If possible, you should go to technical school or college. Although becoming an engineer would be very useful, it is not essential. However, courses in engineering, surveying, estimating, business administration, and building methods and materials would be assets.

Practical training in the construction field is essential to gain the necessary experience. One of the best ways to get experience is to work in an established contractor's office. Depending on your qualifications, you may enter the industry as an engineering aide, assistant estimator or expediter, or in some other position. You can also work for a company that supplies heavy equipment or building materials. Some contractors start as apprentices in one of the construction trades and work their way up.

Getting the Job

For a list of places to contact, look under the headings "Contractors—General" and "Contractors' Equipment and Supplies" in the Yellow Pages of your phone book. If there are no heavy construction contractors listed, ask those contractors who are listed for advice on where to look. You may have to broaden your search to include several geographical areas.

Newspaper classifieds and your local state employment office may also be good sources of jobs. So might job banks on the Internet. Also, check with the placement or career office at your technical school or college. Any job that will teach you about the heavy construction business is worth considering.

Advancement Possibilities and Employment Outlook

Heavy construction contractors are usually independent businesspeople who advance by expanding their businesses. Increased business usually depends on the contractor's knowledge, skill, and determination. However, the economy can also affect business.

Opportunities for contractors specializing in dams, harbors, tunnels, and similar projects can be limited. However, there will always be some heavy construction going on, particularly smaller projects. Those contractors who are able to handle the greatest variety of jobs generally have the best chances of continuous employment.

Working Conditions

A contractor's job can be very strenuous. Contractors usually work at the job site, which can be anywhere from a waterfront to a wilderness area. The job sites are usually dirty and noisy. Since the contractors work outdoors at times, they must sometimes work in bad weather.

Tension, pressure, and almost constant problem solving and decision making are part of many heavy construction jobs. A contractor must be able to handle these problems and enjoy the challenge of hard work.

Earnings and Benefits

Earnings depend on the size of the firm and the number of jobs performed. Average earnings for heavy construction contractors are $600 to $675 a week. Some contractors find that they are unable to make money in the field and decide to move into another kind of work. Because contractors usually own their own companies, they must provide their own life and health insurance, pensions, and other benefits.

Where to Go for More Information

Associated General Contractors of America
1957 E Street, NW
Washington, DC 20006-5199
(202) 393-2040

National Association of Women
   in Construction
327 South Adams Street
Fort Worth, TX 76104
(817) 877-5551
www.nawic.org

Highway Contractor

Definition and Nature of the Work

Highway contractors are in charge of all phases of the construction of highways, airport runways, and similar projects. They hire workers and gather the materials needed to complete the job. As with many construction projects, highway and road-building jobs are assigned to contractors through the competitive bidding system. Federal, state, or local governments usually assign contracts. The government agency responsible for building a particular road draws up the plans and writes the specifications. Highway contractors then submit bids or price quotes for the job. Usually the contractor offering the lowest bid is awarded the job.

Highway contractors arrange either to buy or rent the needed machinery. They buy material such as gravel, cement, and asphalt from suppliers. They hire the subcontractors and workers and plan the work schedule. Contractors may also have to arrange large loans from financial institutions to begin construction.

As the job progresses, the contractor must be sure that the government's specifications are met, that the building materials continue to arrive on time, and that the job is completed on schedule. The contractor may also have to spend some time planning for the next job.

Depending on the size of the business, contractors hire a variety of people to help them with their work. They may employ job superintendents, office managers, estimators, expediters, machinery specialists, and many other workers. Highway contractors must be able to supervise and manage all the people who work for them. Ultimately it is the highway contractor who is responsible for getting the job done.

Education and Training Requirements

There are no educational requirements for becoming a highway contractor. However, the more education you have, the greater your chances are for success.

In high school you should take courses in accounting, business mathematics, the sciences, English, and shop. After high school you should consider technical school or college. You do not have to be an engineer to become a highway contractor, but you will find an engineering background helpful. In technical school or college you should take courses in civil and industrial engineering, business, economics, contract law, cost estimating, and construction management. If possible, you

Education and Training
Varies—see profile

Salary Range
Average—$35,000

Employment Outlook
Good

should take courses in construction planning, equipment, and methods. Summer work in some area of the road building industry will also be helpful.

Getting the Job

A good way to get started in this field is to work for a highway contractor. Depending on your education and experience, you can enter as an engineering aide, an assistant expediter or estimator, an assistant accountant, or in some other position. You may work your way up and become a partner in a contracting firm. You may also buy a firm or start your own. Another way to gain experience is to start with an equipment or materials supplier. Some contractors start as apprentices in one of the construction trades. After years of experience they open their own businesses.

Contact the highway contractors in your area. You may find their names listed under "Road Building Contractors" or "Concrete Contractors" in the Yellow Pages of your phone book. Also check the heading "Contractors' Equipment and Supplies" for other companies in the industry. Ask for information at your school's placement or career office. Scan newspaper classifieds and check with your local state employment office. If no job is available at the time in a contractor's office, try for a job in a related business until there is an opening. Your goal should be to learn as much as you can about road building and highway contracting.

Advancement Possibilities and Employment Outlook

Highway contractors are independent businesspeople. Advancement usually means expanding the company by offering more services or taking on more projects.

The outlook for highway contractors is generally good. Contractors will always be needed, but the number needed will usually depend on the state of the economy. Many highway contractors also build sidewalks, parking areas, athletic fields, and other projects requiring grading or paving. Generally the contractor who can handle the greatest variety of jobs is the one most certain of employment.

Working Conditions

Highway construction contracting can be physically strenuous. During the peak construction season, a contractor may be busy 7 days a week. Many contractors spend most of their time at the job site. They may work out of construction trailers, and they may have to drive to several job sites to check the work. Because of the financial risks involved and the many pressures and problems that come with almost any project, highway contractors should be the type of people who enjoy the challenge of hard work and problem solving.

Earnings and Benefits

Earnings for highway contractors depend on education, experience, type of job, and geographical location. The size of the firm also affects the amount that a highway contractor earns. Highway contractors earn average salaries of $35,000, but experienced workers can earn more. Some contractors make much more. Others find that they make no money, and they move into another kind of work. As independent businesspeople, many highway contractors must provide their own insurance and pensions.

Where to Go for More Information

American Road and Transportation
  Builders Association
1010 Massachusetts Avenue, NW
Washington, DC 20001
(202) 289-4434
www.artba.org

Associated General Contractors of America
1957 E Street, NW
Washington, DC 20006-5199
(202) 393-2040

National Association of Women
  in Construction
327 South Adams Street
Fort Worth, TX 76104
(817) 877-5551
www.nawic.org

Highway Engineer

Definition and Nature of the Work

Highway engineers are civil engineers who plan and help build the thousands of miles of roads built across the country every year. There are three major branches of highway engineering: planning, research, and construction. Most highway engineers specialize in one of these areas.

Planning engineers work with city and regional planners. They try to figure out ways to relieve the traffic congestion in overcrowded areas. They analyze traffic patterns and keep abreast of the construction of new buildings that might cause more traffic problems in the future. Highway engineers must also consider the effect new roads will have on the environment. These workers are usually employed by city, state, and federal governments, and by consulting firms used by government agencies. Highway planners may also work for transportation departments that control the transit systems of large cities.

Highway engineers who specialize in research are concerned with finding new ways and means for building highways. They investigate new machines and technology, new pavement designs, and improved maintenance operations. This research is the basis for well-planned and well-built highways. Research is usually conducted by federal agencies and by engineering colleges that employ highway engineers.

In construction, state-employed highway engineers supervise the contractors who have been chosen to build the new road. Highway engineers work on the site to check on the quality of the work. They make sure the cost of the project is not greater than the amount of money that has been budgeted for it. Contractors sometimes employ highway engineers for the same purpose.

Highway engineers work with building materials such as concrete, earth, steel, and asphalt. They work with tools range from earth-moving equipment to computers.

A highway engineer works on-site to supervise the contractors who are building the new road and to check the quality of their work.

Education and Training Requirements

You must have a bachelor's degree in civil engineering to enter this field. In highway engineering, the more education you have, the better your job opportunities and the higher the pay. To prepare for a career in this field, you should take high school courses in physics, mathematics, mechanical drawing, and art. In civil engineering programs, college courses include stress analysis, engineering dynamics, and the mechanics of fluids and materials. Specialized courses in highway engineering include structural design, traffic control, surveying, and highway pavement design.

Summer jobs relating to highway construction provide valuable experience and possible contacts for future job opportunities. Part-time jobs in surveying or traffic study are excellent ways for a college student to gain experience. A highway engineer must have an aptitude for mathematics and estimating, as well as a strong sense of imagination and responsibility. An engineer must also have the ability to work with others.

Getting the Job

Many highway engineers work for federal, state, and local governments. To work for the government, you must take a civil service examination. Contact the civil service directly. Another source of jobs is the placement service of your college or engineering school. You can also apply directly to engineering firms. Check the Yellow Pages of your phone book under "Engineers—Civil," "Engineers—Consulting," and "Engineers—Highway." You might also try newspaper classifieds for job openings.

Advancement Possibilities and Employment Outlook

In most cases, advancement in this field depends on the ability of the worker. In state and municipal jobs, seniority is also a basis for advancement. Experienced highway engineers can become construction supervisors. They can supervise technical workers in engineering. Some engineers become project engineers or consulting engineers, while others become heads of construction firms.

The employment outlook for highway engineers is good. More roads will be built to accommodate the increased traffic. Commercial and private motorists will continue to demand larger and better highways and transit systems on which to travel.

Working Conditions

Highway engineers can work either outdoors or indoors. Where they work depends on the branch of highway engineering they pursue. Engineers who work outdoors can expect some discomfort due to the weather. Most highway work continues through the winter so that no work time is lost. The highway engineer works a 40-hour week with extra pay for overtime. Engineers often put in extra hours when deadlines have to be met.

Earnings and Benefits

Highway engineers with bachelor's degrees start at about $28,000 a year. Experienced engineers earn an average of $35,000 a year. Most highway engineers work for state or municipal governments and receive benefits, such as paid holidays and vacations and health and life insurance plans.

Where to Go for More Information

American Road and Transportation
    Builders Association
1010 Massachusetts Avenue, NW
Washington, DC 20001
(202) 289-4434
www.artba.org

American Society of Civil Engineers
345 East 47th Street
New York, NY 10017
(212) 705-7496

National Association of Women
    in Construction
327 South Adams Street
Fort Worth, TX 76104
(817) 877-5551
www.nawic.org

Highway Inspector

Definition and Nature of the Work

Highway inspectors check the materials used during road construction and oversee the contractor's work to make sure the road meets the established specifications. Roads and highways are built by federal, state, and local governments. Highway inspectors work for the government and perform an important function in the road-building process. They protect the public in at least two ways. First, they make certain that the taxpayers are getting their money's worth and are not being cheated through the use of inferior materials. Second, they help reduce accidents by making sure highways are built properly.

Highway inspectors check every phase of road construction. They inspect the excavation of the roadbed and the use of landfill. They supervise the placement of wooden forms into which concrete is poured. Inspectors may test the concrete to make sure the proper amount of water has been used in the mix. Highway inspectors may also specialize in a certain phase of road construction, such as bridges, drainage structures, or concrete or asphalt paving.

After the concrete has been poured and allowed to set, inspectors often look for bulges, rough spots, or other faults. When defects are found, they are chipped out, patched, and reinspected. Asphalt roads are handled in a similar manner. Highway inspectors test building materials, such as reinforced concrete beams, metal pipe, and aluminum bridge rails.

Highway inspectors are also important to the contractor. Part of the inspector's job is to record the amount of work that has been done and the materials that have been used. Inspectors use these records to calculate periodic payments to the contractor as the work progresses.

Often highway construction plans just estimate the distance of the road. After a road has been finished, the highway inspector is usually responsible for measuring and recording the exact distances. These measurements are called builts, and they are often used to determine the contractor's final payment.

Education and Training Requirements

In most cases you must have a high school diploma to become a highway inspector. While in school, take courses in mathematics, plan reading, chemistry, physics, and other technical subjects. Shop courses and communication courses such as English may also be helpful.

After high school there are several ways to receive the needed training. You may enter an apprenticeship program in one of the building trades. You may go to technical school for training in blueprint reading, construction technology, technical mathematics, and inspection methods. Or you may attend an engineering school and study civil engineering. In any case, a thorough knowledge of road-building materials and methods is essential to become a highway inspector. Summer work as a laborer on a road-building project is an excellent way to get experience.

When you become a highway inspector, you will receive on-the-job training. You will learn about inspection techniques, regulations, specifications, record keeping, and report writing. At first you will work under an experienced inspector. Later, as your skills increase, you will be given more responsibilities.

Getting the Job

Usually only people with engineering degrees go into inspecting immediately. Many highway inspectors start as craft workers, engineering aides, or trainees in a contractor's office. If you have an engineering degree, you should contact the appropriate federal, state, or local government agencies. If you want to work in a contractor's office to get experience, contact the companies in your area listed under "Road Building Contractors" in the Yellow Pages of your phone book. To apply for an apprenticeship program in a building trade, check with the appropriate local labor union. Also, be sure to check with your local state employment service and look for classifieds in the newspaper.

To work for the state or federal government, you must take a civil service examination. Many government agencies also require that you pass the inspector's test to work as a highway inspector.

Advancement Possibilities and Employment Outlook

Fully qualified highway inspectors can become senior inspectors or principal inspectors. Some inspectors become contractors. In any case, the key to advancement is education and experience.

For some advanced positions a person must have a certain number of school credits. These can be earned at technical school, college, or through correspondence courses. Many government agencies conduct special programs to give inspectors advanced training.

The number of opportunities in this field is closely related to the economy. Roads are usually paid for with tax money. When the economy is slow, there is less tax money available for highway building. However, the public will always need roads. Usually those inspectors who are best qualified through experience and education will have the most opportunities.

Working Conditions

Some road-building projects are required by law to have an inspector on the job site whenever any construction is going on. In these and many other cases, the highway inspector works out of a field office. The office may be a nearby hotel room or a trailer on the job site.

Much of an inspector's time is spent outdoors observing the work and the use of building materials. Depending on the job's location, this can mean working in mud, dust, rain, or other uncomfortable conditions. Some inspectors also do a lot of driving as they go from one job site to another.

Inspectors work in both urban and rural areas. Their workweek normally parallels that of the construction crews. When the weather is good or a schedule must be met, an inspector may work more than 40 hours a week. Schedules may, however, be restricted during the winter months. Extra pay or vacation is frequently given for overtime work.

Earnings and Benefits

The amount highway inspectors earn depends on their education, experience, and qualifications. It can also depend on the particular government agency for whom they work and the geographical area. Currently salaries for highway inspectors average $31,200 a year. Experienced inspectors earn more.

Benefits often include vacation and sick pay, pension plans, health and life insurance, and sometimes tuition assistance. Many government agencies pay the inspector for job-related mileage.

Where to Go for More Information

American Association of State Highway
    and Transportation Officials
444 North Capitol Street, NW, Suite 249
Washington, DC 20001
(202) 624-5800

American Road and Transportation
    Builders Association
1010 Massachusetts Avenue, NW
Washington, DC 20001
(202) 289-4434
www.artba.org

International Conference of
    Building Officials
5360 Workman Mill Road
Whittier, CA 90601-2298
(310) 699-0541

Landscape Architect

Definition and Nature of the Work

Architects design buildings to provide useful and attractive indoor spaces. The job of landscape architects, on the other hand, is to create useful and attractive outdoor environments. They use natural elements, such as land, trees, and shrubs, to create attractive settings for buildings, highways, and parks.

Landscape architects work on small residential projects, as well as large public ones. For example, landscape architects might be asked to design a pond on a private estate. They might also design a public park. Some landscape architects work on industrial projects. They might design an attractive surrounding for a factory. They work on highways and freeways as well. There is a great deal of diversity in their profession.

One out of five landscape architects is self-employed. The rest work in private architectural firms or businesses that provide landscaping services. Others are employed by local and federal governments. These landscape architects plan landscaping for highways, parks, and public buildings. Some landscape architects work for engineering firms. Landscape architects often work with other specialists on a project. These specialists might include engineers, nursery managers, and zoning experts. Landscape architects may supervise trainees and drafters.

Landscape architects begin their job by talking with their clients about what is to be done. Then the landscape architects visit the sites. They make maps of the area and chart the positions of existing buildings and trees. They make topographic surveys. These surveys show the height of the land at various points on the site. They check such details as the makeup of the soil and its exposure to the sun and wind. They find out the value of the property and how much traffic crosses the land. They chart the placement of utility lines. With all these things in mind, landscape architects make recommendations on the proper use of land. They submit these recommendations, along with maps, photographs, reports, and sketches of what the areas should look like. If their clients decide to change these recommendations, the landscape architects modify the plans.

Once their plans are accepted, landscape architects can begin work. First, they make detailed drawings of the entire site. These drawings include all existing as well as new features. They show structures, buildings, shrubs, walkways, roads, and the new grading of the area. Next, landscape architects make detailed drawings of specific features of the plans, such as walks, terraces, benches, and curbs. They also indicate where trees and shrubbery are to be planted, and make lists of all the plans and materials needed for the project. The working drawings and lists are submitted to contractors for bids. Once a bid is accepted, construction can begin. The landscape architects help order the materials that will be needed and, on larger projects, work closely with the other specialists involved in the project. On small projects, landscape architects may be the only ones involved in the entire project. Often, several landscape architects work together on a project.

Education and Training Requirements

A good landscape architect is knowledgeable in many areas. These areas include design, horticulture, social science, engineering, and business.

A high school diploma is required to enter this field. Courses in biology, history, mathematics, and mechanical drawing will be useful. A 4- or 5-year college degree in landscape architecture is usually necessary as well. Relevant college courses include architecture, surveying, plant ecology, landscape construction,

Education and Training
College

Salary Range
Average—$30,200
to $53,900

Employment Outlook
Good

Landscape architects use natural elements, such as land, trees, and shrubs, to create attractive settings for homes, buildings, highways, and parks.

structural design, and city planning. About 55 colleges and universities offer accredited undergraduate and graduate programs in landscape architecture.

Some landscape architects have gained experience by working as apprentices to experienced landscape architects. It takes 6 to 8 years to become a landscape architect with this method. However, public agencies only hire landscape architects with college degrees. More than half the states require landscape architects to have a license. To take the licensing exam, candidates should have a college degree from an accredited school and 1 to 4 years of experience.

Getting the Job

You can become an apprentice in this field after you graduate from high school. The best way to get into this profession, however, is to complete college and then contact landscape firms about employment opportunities. The placement office of your college can help you find a job. You can also try searching job banks on the Internet.

Many jobs are also available in government service. To get one of these jobs, you have to take a civil service examination. To find out more about this method of entering the field, contact your local, state, or federal civil service commission.

Advancement Possibilities and Employment Outlook

Trainees starting in architectural firms begin as junior drafters. Their duties include simple drafting, lettering, and tracing. After 2 or 3 years of experience, they can advance to jobs as senior drafters. Senior drafters work on projects from the beginning sketches to the final drawings. Advancement in this field depends both on ability and on how much responsibility the worker is willing to accept.

The employment outlook for landscape architects is good, despite keen competition. Approximately 14,000 people work in this field today in the U.S. The number of landscape architects is expected to increase about as fast as the average for all occupations through the year 2006. As construction increases, the need for landscape architects will also increase. Builders and land developers use landscape architects more and more to create pleasing surroundings for the structures they build. Training in landscape architecture will also provide job opportunities in related fields such as landscape design, drafting, consulting, and environmental planning.

Working Conditions

The work of landscape architects is stimulating, challenging, and satisfying. Landscape architects work both indoors and outdoors. They usually work a regular 40-hour week, although self-employed landscape architects may work longer hours.

There are few disadvantages to working as a landscape architect. However, while gaining experience, beginning landscape architects may spend most of their time doing routine tasks. In addition, drafting work is exacting and can become tedious.

Earnings and Benefits

Architects in this field with several years of experience earn between $30,200 and $53,900 or more each year. Those working in the public sector earn slightly higher salaries. Landscape architects working for the federal government in non-supervisory, supervisory, and managerial positions earn an average annual salary of $53,300.

The benefits in this field vary widely with individual companies. Most firms offer health plans, paid vacations, and holidays. Landscape architects who are self-employed usually provide their own health and life insurance.

Where to Go for More Information

American Society of Landscape Architects
4401 Connecticut Avenue, NW, Fifth Floor
Washington, DC 20008
(202) 686-2752

National Institute on Park and
 Grounds Management
P.O. Box 1936
Appleton, WI 54913-1936
(414) 733-2301

National Landscape Association
1250 I Street, NW, Suite 500
Washington, DC 20005
(202) 789-2900

Surveyor

Definition and Nature of the Work

Surveyors are among the first workers on a construction site. Even before a site is designated for construction, surveyors are on the job. They collect information about the size and characteristics of pieces of land. They determine the exact boundaries of the land so that the buyer knows how much land is included in the purchase price. To determine the value of the property, the buyer must know what kind of construction is suitable for the land. Surveyors also measure elevations (heights), contours (curves), points, and lines on the land's surface. After collecting the necessary information and checking it for accuracy, surveyors prepare charts, maps, and reports. Based on the surveyors' findings, architects, engineers, and drafters decide on the most economical use of the land.

The surveyors continue to work with the builder once the construction plans have been drawn up. Surveyors measure the ground and mark it with wooden stakes to show where the corners of the building should be. The surveyor's report shows the different elevations of the land in various places. This information helps the builder determine how much leveling needs to be done to make a smooth building surface. In highway construction, surveyors work closely with civil engineers to determine how the land can be made suitable for roads and heavy traffic.

Surveyors are fully qualified professional workers. They usually lead crews of about five people. The crew members are technicians who specialize in using measuring instruments and electronic devices. *Instrument workers* operate instruments, such as the transit theodolite, which is used to measure horizontal and vertical angles. They use altimeters to measure altitudes. Electronic meters are used to measure land distances quickly and accurately. Pairs of *chain workers* use a steel tape to measure distances between surveying points. *Rod workers* help the instrument workers mark the exact point of an elevation. The rod worker holds a "range pole" and adjusts it according to signals from the instrument workers. Other crew members mark the ground with stakes, chalk, or tacks to show boundaries and starting points for construction.

Education and Training
2- or 4-year college;
license

Salary Range
Average—$28,400
to $44,100

Employment Outlook
Fair

Surveyors work with technicians to determine the land's boundaries, elevations, contours, points, and lines. This information is used in construction projects, for maps, and for mining surveys.

There are many types of surveying besides construction surveying. Some surveyors specialize in doing land surveys to establish boundaries. They make maps for legal documents, such as deeds and leases. Before any piece of land can be sold, its legal boundaries must be set down and recorded.

Other surveyors work on geodetic surveys. This type of surveying involves the measurement of large areas of land and water. These areas are so large that the roundness of the Earth must be taken into account to get accurate measurements.

Cartographic surveys are used to develop maps. There are two kinds of cartographic surveys: topographic and hydrographic. Topographic surveys indicate the elevations of mountains and the depth of valleys, as well as the location of rivers, lakes, and other landmarks. Hydrographic surveys, used to make nautical maps and charts, provide information about the depth of harbors, bays, and other large bodies of water.

Surveys are done in the air and underground, too. Aerial photography is used to survey rough areas where walking or car travel is difficult. Surveys based only on photographs are called photogrammetric surveys. Under the ground, mining surveys are done to show what raw materials are available and where they are located. Mining surveys also show underground passages. Pipeline surveys establish the right-of-way, or path, for pipelines of all kinds, such as natural gas lines. Other surveyors specialize in doing gravity surveys, magnetic surveys, and oil well directional surveys. Surveyors work at the construction sites of houses, shopping centers, highways, and skyscrapers. Surveyors are employed by construction companies and federal, state, and local governments, as well as by engineering and architectural firms.

Education and Training Requirements

You must have a high school education to enter this field, but many surveyors have some college education as well. A combination of relevant postsecondary courses and extensive on-the-job training provides a strong foundation for those interested in a career in surveying. Many junior colleges and vocational schools offer 2- or 3-year programs in surveying. Some colleges offer 4-year programs in surveying. College programs in engineering and physical sciences can give you a good background for technical surveying specialties, such as geodetic surveying. In high school you should take all the mathematics courses offered, as well as mechanical drawing and physics.

Those who enter the field right after high school usually start as rod and chain workers or apprentices. However, those with college experience start as instrument assistants or technicians and are likely to advance more rapidly. Surveyors who chart land boundaries must pass an examination on surveying techniques and be licensed by their state. License requirements vary from state to state but standards have increased due to advancing technology. In general, high school graduates must have 10 to 12 years of experience before they can take the test. College graduates usually need 2 to 4 years of experience to qualify. They also have to pass a licensing exam.

Surveyors must be accurate in their work. They must also be able to manage a crew and check its accuracy. Surveying demands physical strength, since surveyors stand a great deal and carry heavy equipment over long distances. Good eyesight and hearing are also necessary. Surveyors must have enough drawing ability to prepare charts, maps, and sketches of their findings.

Getting the Job

In order to work in federal and state government jobs, you must pass a civil service exam. State employment agencies list jobs in surveying. You can contact construction companies about a job as a rod, stake, or chain worker. Your college or technical school placement office can help you find a job as an instrument worker or surveyor's assistant. Check the classifieds in your local newspaper or search job banks on the Internet.

Advancement Possibilities and Employment Outlook

Surveyors start as surveyor's helpers or technicians and work up to the job of fully qualified surveyor after several years of experience. Professional surveyors who manage crews are called party chiefs. Party chiefs might begin by leading crews of three technicians on small jobs. They gradually assume the responsibility of bigger jobs, such as a survey for a large housing development. Some surveyors set up their own surveying businesses.

The employment outlook for surveyors is fair. Employment is expected to decline slightly through the year 2006. Of course, as in all construction occupations, demand for surveyors fluctuates with the general economy. When the economy is good, job opportunities increase. Opportunities will be more plentiful for college graduates because of upgraded licensing requirements, technological advances, and the demand for more specialized surveying services. The continued use of electronic equipment will make the surveyor's work more efficient, but it is unlikely that machines will take over the surveyor's job.

Working Conditions

Most of the surveyor's work is done outdoors. However, they do their charting, drafting, and report writing in the office. Time can be lost due to bad weather.

Sometimes surveyors work long hours in good weather to make up for lost time or to meet deadlines. Most surveyors work 40 hours a week. Some projects require traveling over rough terrain, which can be hazardous. On some projects, surveyors are away from home for several weeks. The surveyor's work is varied and rarely routine.

Earnings and Benefits

Earnings vary widely, depending on the nature of the work, the location of the business, and the surveyor's training. Currently surveyors earn an average salary ranging from $28,400 to $44,100 a year. The average annual salary of surveyors working for the federal government is $47,900. The government and most surveying companies provide paid vacations and holidays. Many employers also offer health and life insurance plans.

Resources — General Career Information

Books

Exploring the Working World

The Adams Job Almanac. Holbrook, MA: Adams Media Corp., annual.

American Almanac of Jobs and Salaries, John W. Wright. New York: Avon Books, biennial.

American Salaries and Wages, 4th ed., Helen S. Fisher. Detroit, MI: Gale Research, Inc., 1997.

America's Top Jobs for College Graduates, J. Michael Farr. Indianapolis, IN: JIST Works, 1997.

America's Top Jobs for People Without College Degrees, J. Michael Farr. Indianapolis, IN: JIST Works, 1997.

America's Top Technical and Trade Jobs, J. Michael Farr. Indianapolis, IN: JIST Works, 1997.

The Big Book of Jobs. Lincolnwood, IL: VGM Career Horizons, 1997.

Career Discovery Encyclopedia, Holli Cosgrove, ed., 6 vols. Chicago: Ferguson, 1997.

CareerSmarts: Jobs with a Future, Martin Yate. New York: Ballantine Books, 1997.

The Complete Guide for Occupational Exploration, J. Michael Farr. Indianapolis, IN: JIST Works, 1993.

The Complete Guide to Public Employment, 3rd ed., Ronald Krannich and Caryl Rae Krannich. Manassas Park, VA: Impact Publications, 1995.

The Harvard Guide to Careers, 5th ed., Martha P. Leape and Susan M. Vacca. Cambridge, MA: Harvard University Press, 1995.

Job Hunter's Sourcebook. Detroit, MI: Gale Research, Inc., biennial.

Jobs '98 (title changes annually), Kathryn Petras, Ross Petras, and George Petras. New York: Simon & Schuster, annual.

Jobs Rated Almanac, Les Krantz. New York: World Almanac, 1995.

Joyce Lain Kennedy's Career Book, Joyce Lain Kennedy and Darryl Laramore. Lincolnwood, IL: VGM Career Horizons, 1997.

The National JobBank, 1998 (title changes annually). Holbrook, MA: Adams Media Corp., annual. (The *JobBank* series also includes editions for several major U.S. cities and regions.)

Occupational Outlook series. Washington, DC: United States Government Printing Office. Briefs, separately published.

Occupational Outlook Quarterly. Washington, DC: Occupational Outlook Service, Bureau of Labor Statistics. Quarterly publication.

Recommended

Occupational Outlook Handbook, United States Department of Labor. Washington, DC: United States Government Printing Office, revised biennially. Expands on the *Dictionary of Occupational Titles.* Groups jobs into similar categories. Discusses the nature of the work, the employment outlook, and earnings.

VGM's Careers Encyclopedia, 4th ed. Lincolnwood, IL: VGM Career Horizons, 1997. A one-volume guide to 180 careers.

Professional Careers Sourcebook, 4th ed. Detroit, MI: Gale Research, Inc., 1996.

The Quick Internet Guide to Career and College Information, Anne Wolfinger. Indianapolis, IN: JIST Works, 1997.

A Student's Guide to Career Exploration on the Internet, Elizabeth H. Oakes. Chicago: Ferguson, 1998.

Vocational Careers Sourcebook, 2nd ed. Detroit, MI: Gale Research, Inc., 1996.

Education and Training Opportunities

American Universities and Colleges, 15th ed. Hawthorne, NY: De Groyter, 1997.

America's Lowest Cost Colleges, Nicholas A. Roes. Barryville, NY: NAR Publications, biennial.

America's Top Internships, Mark Oldman and Samer Hamadeh. New York: Random House, annual.

Barron's Guide to Graduate Business Schools, Eugene Miller, ed. Hauppauge, NY: Barron's Educational Series, revised regularly.

Barron's Guide to Law Schools. Hauppauge, NY: Barron's Educational Series, revised regularly.

Barron's Guide to Medical and Dental Schools, Saul Wischnitzer and Edith Wischnitzer, eds. Hauppauge, NY: Barron's Educational Series, revised regularly.

Bear's Guide to Earning College Degrees Non-Traditionally, 11th ed., John Bear. Benicia, CA: C&B Publishing, 1994.

Chronicle Vocational School Manual. Moravia, NY: Chronicle Guidance Publications, annual.

College Applications and Essays, 3rd ed., Susan D. Van Raalte. New York: Macmillan, 1997.

The College Costs and Financial Aid Handbook, The College Board Staff. New York: The College Board, annual.

College Financial Aid for Dummies, Herm Davis and Joyce Lain Kennedy. Foster City, CA: IDG Books Worldwide, 1997.

College Financial Aid Made Easy, Patrick L. Bellatoni. Berkeley, CA: Ten Speed Press, annual.

The College Guide for Parents, 3rd ed., Charles J. Shields. New York: The College Board, 1995.

The College Handbook. New York: The College Board, annual.

College Planning for Gifted Students, 2nd ed., Sandra L. Berger. Reston, VA: Council for Exceptional Children, 1994.

The Complete Book of Colleges. New York: Random House, annual.

Ferguson's Guide to Apprenticeship Programs, 2 vols., C. J. Summerfield and Holli Cosgrove, eds. Chicago: Ferguson, 1994.

Free Money for College: A Guide to More Than 1000 Grants and Scholarships for Undergraduate Study, 4th ed., Laurie Blum. New York: Facts on File, 1996.

Recommended

The following four sources are basic directories of information on colleges and universities. They include general information on each school, its address, a list of the programs offered, the size of the institution, and costs for tuition.

Barron's Top 50: An Inside Look at America's Best Colleges, Tom Fischgrund, ed. Hauppauge, NY: Barron's Educational Series, revised regularly.

The College Blue Book. New York: Macmillan, revised regularly.

Lovejoy's College Guide, Charles T. Straughn II and Barbarasue Lovejoy Straughn, eds. New York: ARCO, revised regularly.

Petersons Guide to Four-Year Colleges. Princeton, NJ: Petersons Guides, revised regularly.

Getting into College, Pat Orovensky. Princeton, NJ: Petersons, 1995.

The Gourman Report: A Rating of Undergraduate Programs in American and International Universities, Jack Gourman. Los Angeles, CA: National Education Standards, revised regularly.

Help Yourself: Handbook for College-Bound Students with Learning Disabilities, Erica-Lee Lewis. New York: Random House, 1996.

Index of Majors and Graduate Degrees. New York: The College Board, annual.

Insider's Guide to the Colleges, Yale Daily News Staff, ed. New York: St. Martin's Press, annual.

The Internship Bible. New York: Random House, annual.

Internships for 2-Year College Students. West Hartford, CT: Graduate Group, annual.

Internships Leading to Careers. West Hartford, CT: Graduate Group, annual.

Lovejoy's College Guide for the Learning Disabled, Charles T. Straughn. New York: ARCO, revised regularly.

The National Guide to Educational Credit for Training Programs, American Council on Education. Phoenix, AZ: ACE/Oryx Press, annual.

The 100 Best Colleges for African-American Students, Erlene B. Wilson. New York: Plume, 1998.

Petersons College Money Handbook. Princeton, NJ: Petersons, annual.

Petersons Competitive Colleges. Princeton, NJ: Petersons, annual.

Petersons Guide to Graduate and Professional Programs: An Overview. Princeton, NJ: Petersons, annual.

Petersons Guide to Two-Year Colleges. Princeton, NJ: Petersons, annual.

Petersons Internships. Princeton, NJ: Petersons, annual.

A Student's Guide to College Admissions: Everything Your Guidance Counselor Has No Time to Tell You, 3rd ed., Harlow Unger. New York: Facts on File, 1995.

Vocational Education: Status in 2-Year Colleges and Early Signs of Change. Upland, PA: Diane Publishing Company, 1994.

Career Goals

Adventure Careers, Alex Hiam and Susan Angle. Franklin Lakes, NJ: Career Press, 1995.

Career Anchors: Discovering Your Real Values, Edgar H. Schein. San Diego, CA: Pfeiffer & Co., rev. 1993.

The Career Atlas, Gail Kuenstler. Franklin Lakes, NJ: Career Press, 1996.

The Career Guide for Creative and Unconventional People, Carol Eikleberry. Berkeley, CA: Ten Speed Press, 1995.

Careers for the Year 2000 and Beyond: Everything You Need to Know to Find the Right Career. Piscataway, NJ: Research and Education Association, 1997.

Recommended

What Color Is Your Parachute? Richard N. Bolles. Berkeley, CA: Ten Speed Press, revised annually. One of the best sources for career changers and job hunters. Workbook style with exercises to identify skills and interests. Provides comprehensive list of sources including books, agencies, and associations.

Choices for the High School Graduate: A Survival Guide for the Information Age, Bryna J. Fireside. Chicago: Ferguson, 1997.

Choosing a Career Made Easy, Patty Marler and Jan Bailey Mattia. Lincolnwood, IL: VGM Career Horizons, 1997.

Chronicle Career Index 1994–95, Harriet Scarry, ed. Moravia, NY: Chronicle Guidance Publications, 1994.

The College Board Guide to Jobs and Career Planning, 2nd ed., Joyce Slayton Mitchell. New York: The College Board, 1994.

College Majors and Careers: A Resource Guide for Effective Life Planning, 3rd ed., Phil Phifer. Chicago: Ferguson, 1997.

Dr. Job's Complete Career Guide, Sandra "Dr. Job" Pesmen. Lincolnwood, IL: VGM Career Horizons, 1996.

Finding Your Perfect Work: The New Career Guide to Making a Living, Creating a Life, Paul Edwards and Sarah Edwards. New York: Putnam, 1996.

Graduate to Your Perfect Job in Six Easy Steps, Jason R. Dorsey. Austin, TX: Golden Ladder Productions, 1997.

Green at Work: Finding a Business Career that Works for the Environment, Susan Cohn. Washington, DC: Island Press, 1995.

The Job Seeker's Guide to Socially Responsible Companies, Katherine Jankowski. Detroit, MI: Gale Research, Inc., 1995.

Jobs for People who Love Travel: Opportunities at Home and Abroad, Ronald L. Krannich and Caryl Rae Krannich. Manassas Park, VA: Impact Publications, 1995.

The Off-the-Beaten-Path Job Book: You Can Make a Living and Have a Life!, Sandra Gurvis. Secaucus, NJ: Carol Publishing Group, 1995.

The Parent's Crash Course in Career Planning: Helping Your College Student Succeed, Marcia B. Harris and Sharon L. Jones. Lincolnwood, IL: VGM Career Horizons, 1996.

The PIE Method for Career Success: A Unique Way to Find Your Ideal Job, Daniel Porot. Indianapolis, IN: JIST Works, 1996.

The Right Job for You: An Interactive Career Planning Guide, J. Michael Farr. Indianapolis, IN: JIST Works, 1997.

Success 2000: Moving into the Millennium with Purpose, Power, and Prosperity, Vicki Spina. New York: Wiley, 1997.

Getting the Job and Getting Ahead

The Adams Electronic Job Search Almanac. Holbrook, MA: Adams Media Corp., 1997.

Almanac of American Employers, Jack W. Plunkett. Galveston, TX: Plunkett Research, Ltd., biennial.

CareerXroads: The Directory to Jobs, Resumes, and Career Management on the World Wide Web. Kendall Park, NJ: MMC Group, 1996.

The Complete Idiot's Guide to Getting the Job You Want, Robert Bly. New York: Alpha Books, 1996.

Electronic Job Search Revolution: How to Win with the New Technology that's Reshaping Today's Job Market, Joyce Lain Kennedy and Thomas J. Morow. New York: Wiley, 1996.

Getting Hired: A Guide for Managers and Professionals, Richard J. Pinsker. Menlo Park, CA: Crisp Publications, 1994.

Getting the Job You Want . . . Now!, David H. Roper. New York: Warner Books, 1994.

Government Job Finder, 1997–2000, Daniel Lauber. River Forest, IL: Planning/Communications, 1997.

Great Jobs Abroad, Arthur H. Bell. New York, McGraw Hill, 1997.

The Guide to Internet Job Searching, Margaret Riley, Frances Roehm, Steve Oserman, and the Public Library Association. Lincolnwood, IL: VGM Career Horizons, 1996.

Hoover's Directory of Human Resources Executives. Austin, TX: The Reference Press, revised regularly.

How to Get a Job in . . . (series for major U.S. cities). Chicago: Surrey Books, Inc., annual.

How to Hit the Ground Running in Your New Job, Lynda Pritchard Clemens and Andrea Trulson Dolph. Lincolnwood, IL: VGM Career Horizons, 1995.

International Job Finder, 1997–2000, Daniel Lauber. River Forest, IL: Planning/Communications, 1997.

Job Hunter's Yellow Pages: The National Directory of Employment Services. Harleysville, PA: Career Communications Inc.

Job Search 101: Getting Started on Your Career Path, Monica R. Fox and Pat Morton, eds. Indianapolis, IN: JIST Works, 1997.

Job Search Organizer, Hal Weatherman. Lincolnwood, IL: VGM Career Horizons, 1997.

Job Seeker's Guide to Private-Public Companies, Charity A. Dorgan, ed. Detroit, MI: Gale Research, Inc., 1995.

Jobsmarts for Twentysomethings, Bradley G. Richardson. New York: Vintage Books, 1995.

National Job Hotline Directory, Sue A. Cubbage. River Forest, IL: Planning/Communications, annual.

Non-Profits & Education Job Finder, 1997–2000, Daniel Lauber. River Forest, IL: Planning/Communications, 1997.

Petersons Hidden Job Market. Princeton, NJ: Petersons, annual.

Professional's Job Finder, 1997–2000, Daniel Lauber. River Forest, IL: Planning/Communications, 1997.

Using the Internet and the World Wide Web in Your Job Search, Fred Edmund Jandt and Mary B. Nemnich. Indianapolis, IN: JIST Works, 1996.

The Very Quick Job Search: Get a Better Job in Half the Time, J. Michael Farr. Indianapolis, IN: JIST Works, 1996.

The Work-At-Home Sourcebook, 6th ed., Lynie Arden. Boulder, CO: Live Oak Publications, 1996.

Recommended

Knock 'Em Dead: The Ultimate Job Seeker's Handbook, Martin J. Yate. Holbrook, MA: Adams Media Corp., 1997. Helps job seekers identify their strengths and improve their interview techniques. Also gives practical advice on networking, handling tough interview questions, and negotiating salaries.

Resumes and Interviews

Better Resumes for Executives and Professionals, 3rd ed., Robert F. Wilson. Hauppauge, NY: Barron's Educational Series, 1996.

The Complete Idiot's Guide to the Perfect Resume, Susan Ireland. New York: Alpha Books, 1996.

The Complete Resume Guide, 5th ed., Marian Faux. New York: Macmillan USA, 1995.

Cover Letters for Dummies, Joyce Lain Kennedy. Foster City, CA: IDG Books Worldwide, 1996.

Cover Letters: Proven Techniques for Writing Letters that Will Help You Get the Job You Want, Taunee Besson and National Business Employment Weekly. New York: Wiley, 1995.

Developing a Professional Vita or Resume, 3rd ed., Carl McDaniels. Chicago: Ferguson, 1997.

Get Hired!: Winning Strategies to Ace the Interview, Paul C. Green. Austin, TX: Bard Books, 1996.

Information Interviewing, 2nd ed., Martha Stoodley. Chicago: Ferguson, 1997.

Interviewing, Arlene S. Hirsch and National Business Employment Weekly. New York: Wiley, 1994.

Job Interviews That Mean Business, 2nd ed., David R. Eyler. New York: Random House, 1996.

The Resume Handbook, 3rd ed., Arthur Rosenberg and David Hizer. Boston: Adams Media Corp., 1996.

The Resume Kit, 3rd ed., Richard H. Beatty. New York: John Wiley & Sons, 1995.

Resume Power: Selling Yourself on Paper, Tom Washington. Bellevue, WA: Mount Vernon Press, 1996.

Resume Writing Made Easy, 6th ed., Lola M. Coxford. Scottsdale, AZ: Gorsuch Scarisbrick, 1997.

Resumes for Better Jobs, 7th. ed., Lawrence D. Brennan. New York: ARCO, 1998.

Resumes for Dummies, Joyce Lain Kennedy. Foster City, CA: IDG Books Worldwide, 1996.

Resumes that Knock 'Em Dead, 3rd ed., Martin Yate. Holbrook, MA: Adams Media Corp., 1998.

Your Resume: Key to a Better Job, 6th ed., Leonard Corwen. New York: Macmillan, 1995.

Recommended

Damn Good Resume Guide, 3rd ed., Yana Parker. Berkeley, CA: Ten Speed Press, 1996. Describes how to write a functional resume.

The New Perfect Resume, Tom Jackson and Ellen Jackson. New York: Doubleday, 1996. A CD-ROM version is also available.

Mid-Career Options

Beat the Odds: Career Buoyancy Tactics for Today's Turbulent Job Market, Martin Yate. New York: Ballantine Books, 1995.

The Career Trap: Breaking Through the 10-Year Barrier to Get the Job You Really Want, Jeffrey G. Allen. New York: AMACOM, 1995.

The Complete Idiot's Guide to Changing Careers, William Charland. New York: Alpha Books, 1998.

The Complete Idiot's Guide to Freelancing, Laurie Rozakis. New York: Alpha Books, 1998.

How to Hold it All Together When You've Lost Your Job, Townsend Albright. Lincolnwood, IL: VGM Career Horizons, 1996.

Kiplinger's Survive and Profit from a Mid-Career Change, Daniel Moreau. Washington, DC: Kiplinger Books, 1994.

Out of Uniform: A Career Transition Guide for Ex-Military Personnel, Harry N. Drier. Lincolnwood, IL: VGM Career Horizons, 1995.

Second Careers: New Ways to Work After 50, Caroline Bird. Boston: Little, Brown, 1992.

Toxic Work: How to Overcome Stress, Overload, and Burnout and Revitalize Your Career, Barbara Bailey Reinhold. New York: Plume, 1997.

Equality of Opportunity

The Black Resource Guide, 10th ed. Washington, DC: Black Resource Guide, 1992.

Cracking the Corporate Closet, Daniel B. Baker, Sean O'Brien Strub, and Bill Henning. New York: HarperBusiness, 1995.

Equal Opportunity. Hauppauge, NY: Equal Opportunity Publications, published 3 times a year.

Financial Aid for the Disabled and Their Families, 6th ed., Gail A. Schlachter and R. David Weber. San Carlos, CA: Reference Services Press, 1996.

Financial Aid for Minorities. Garrett Park, MD: Garrett Park Press, 1994.

Successful Job Search Strategies for the Disabled: Understanding the ADA, Jeffrey G. Allen. New York: Wiley, 1994.

Women and Work, Susan Bullock. Atlantic Highlands, NJ: Humanities Press, 1994.

Recommended

Career Change: Everything You Need to Know to Meet New Challenges and Take Control of Your Career, David P. Helford. Lincolnwood, IL: VGM Career Horizons, 1995.

Change Your Job, Change Your Life: High Impact Strategies for Finding Great Jobs into the 21st Century, Ronald L. Krannich. Manassas Park, VA: Impact Publications, 1997.

Recommended

The Big Book of Minority Opportunities, 6th ed., Willis L. Johnson, ed. Chicago: Ferguson, 1995. Directory of organizations that have special programs to help minorities meet their educational and career goals.

The Big Book of Opportunities for Women, Elizabeth A. Olson, ed. Chicago: Ferguson, 1996. Directory of organizations that have special programs to help women meet their educational and career goals.

Coping with Sexual Harassment, Beryl Black, ed. New York: The Rosen Publishing Group, rev. 1992. Helpful in giving direct ways to respond to and prevent sexual harassment at work.

Lists and Indexes of Career and Vocational Information

The Career Guide: Dun's Employment Opportunities Directory. Parsippany, NJ: Dun and Bradstreet Information Services, annual.

Chronicle Career Index. Moravia, NY: Chronicle Guidance Publications, annual.

Dictionary of Holland Occupational Codes (DHOC), 3rd ed., Gary D. Gottfredson and John L. Holland. Lutz, FL: Psychological Assessment Resources, 1996.

Dictionary of Occupational Titles, 4th ed. United States Department of Labor. Washington, DC: United States Government Printing Office, 1991. Supplemented by *The Classification of Jobs According to Worker Trait Factors* (Elliott & Fitzpatrick, 1992) and *Selected Characteristics of Occupations Defined in the Revised Dictionary of Occupational Titles* (Claitors Pub. Div., 1993).

Where the Jobs Are: A Comprehensive Directory of 1200 Journals Listing Career Opportunities, S. Norman Feingold and Glenda Ann Hansard-Winkler. Garrett Park, MD: Garrett Park Press, 1989.

Internet Sites

Sites with Extensive Links

Career Resource Center
www.careers.org

Catapult
www.jobweb.org/catapult/catapult.htm

JIST Works
www.jist.com

Job Hunt: A Meta-List of On-Line Job-Search Resources and Services
www.job-hunt.org

Job Search and Employment Opportunities: Best Bets
asa.ugl.lib.umich.edu/chdocs/employment/

Online Career Center (OCC)
www.occ.com

The Riley Guide: Employment Opportunities and Job Resources on the Internet
www.dbm.com/jobguide

What Color Is Your Parachute Job Hunting Online
washingtonpost.com/parachute

Career Development Resources

Career Assistance from the Online Career Center
www.occ.com/occ/CareerAssist.html

Career Magazine
www.careermag.com

Kaplan's Career Center
www.kaplan.com/career

Online Information and References

AT&T Toll-Free Internet Directory
www.tollfree.att.net

Beatrice's Web Guide—Careers
www.bguide.com/webguide/careers

The Best Jobs in the USA Today
www.bestjobsusa.com

CareerMart
www.careermart.com

Federal Jobs Digest
www.jobsfed.com

GaleNet
galenet.gale.com

Infoseek Guide—Jobs & Careers
guide-p.infoseek.com/Careers

Job Finders Online
jobfindersonline.com

Occupational Outlook Handbook
stats.bls.gov/ocohome.htm

StudentCenter
www.studentcenter.com

U.S. Bureau of Labor Statistics Home Page
stats.bls.gov/blshome.htm

US News Online Colleges and Career Center
www4.usnews.com/usnews/edu/home.htm

Wall Street Journal Interactive Division
careers.wsj.com

Yahoo! Business and Economy
www.yahoo.com/business

Job Databases and Resume Posting

America's Job Bank
www.ajb.dni.is/index.html

CareerCity
www.careercity.com

CareerMosaic
www.careermosaic.com

CareerPath
www.careerpath.com

Career Site
www.careersite.com

CareerWeb
www.careerweb.com

e-span
www.espan.com

JobBank USA
www.jobbankusa.com

Job Trak
www.jobtrak.com

Job Web
www.jobweb.org

The Monster Board
www.monster.com

World Wide Web Employment Office
www.harbornet.com/biz/office/annex.html

Audiovisual Materials

The following titles include, where possible, the developer's name and location or else the name and location of a distributor. Audiovisual titles may be available through several distributors.

Exploring the Working World

The Career Builders series. Video. New York: Educational Design, Inc.

Career Cluster Decisions. Video; guide. Bloomington, IL: Meridian Education Corp.

Career Exploration: A Job Seeker's Guide to the OOH, DOT, and GOE. Video. Bloomington, IL: Meridian Education Corp.

Career Plan. Video; guide. Bloomington, IL: Meridian Education Corp.

Career Planning: Putting Your Skills to Work. Video; guide. Mt. Kisco, NY: Guidance Associates.

Career Planning Steps. Video. Charleston, WV: Cambridge Educational.

Career S.E.L.F. Assessment: Designing a Self-Directed Job Search. Video. Charleston, WV: Cambridge Educational.

Career Self-Assessment: Where Do You Fit? Video; guide. Mt. Kisco, NY: Guidance Associates.

Careers for the 21st Century series. Video; guide. Bloomington, IL: Meridian Education Corp.

Careers Without College. Video. Charleston, WV: Cambridge Educational.

Connect on the Net: Finding a Job on the Internet. Video. Charleston, WV: Cambridge Educational.

Educational Planning for Your Career. Video. Bloomington, IL: Meridian Education Corp.

The JIST Video Guide for Occupational Exploration series. Video. Indianapolis, IN: JIST Works.

Jobs for the 21st Century. Video; guide. Mt. Kisco, NY: Guidance Associates.

Learning for Earning. Video; guide. Bloomington, IL: Meridian Education Corp.

School-to-Work Transition. Video; guide. Bloomington, IL: Meridian Education Corp.

Skills Identification: Discovering Your Skills. Video. Indianapolis, IN: JIST Works.

Working Towards a Career. Video. Bloomington, IL: Meridian Education Corp.

Your Aptitudes: Related to Learning Job Skills. Video. Bloomington, IL: Meridian Education Corp.

Your First Cruise: A Beginner's Guide to the Internet. Video. Charleston, WV: Cambridge Educational.

Your Future: Planning Through Career Exploration. Video. Bloomington, IL: Meridian Education Corp.

Your Interests: Related to Work Activities. Video. Bloomington, IL: Meridian Education Corp.

Your Life's Work series. Video. Indianapolis, IN: JIST Works.

Your Temperaments: Related to Work Situations. Video. Bloomington, IL: Meridian Education Corp.

Your 21st Century Employability Skills series. Video. Calhoun, KY: NIMCO.

Getting the Job and Getting Ahead

Ace the Interview. Video. Columbus, OH: Career Paths/MarkED.

The Art of Effective Communication. Video; guide. Indianapolis, IN: JIST Works.

Career Change: Meeting the Challenge. Video. Arlington Heights, IL: Library Cable Network.

Common Mistakes People Make in Interviews. Video. Columbus, OH: Career Paths/MarkED.

Dialing for Jobs: Using the Phone in the Job Search. Video. Indianapolis, IN: JIST Works.

Directing Your Successful Job Search. Video; guide. Charleston, WV: Cambridge Educational.

Extraordinary Answers to Common Interview Questions. Video. Charleston, WV: Cambridge Educational.

From Pink Slip to Paycheck: The Road to Reemployment series. Video. Indianapolis, IN: Park Avenue/JIST Works.

Getting a Job series. Video. New York: Educational Design, Inc.

How to Be a Success at Work series. Video. Indianapolis, IN: JIST Works.

Interview Power. Video. Columbus, OH: Career Paths/MarkED.

Interview to Win Your First Job. Video. Indianapolis, IN: Park Avenue/JIST Works.

Job Search and Job Survival series. Video. New York: Educational Design, Inc.

JobSearch: The Right Track. Video. Bountiful, VT: ECLECON.

Job Survival Kit. Video. Charleston, WV: Cambridge Educational.

Job Survival Skills: Working with Others. Video. Mt. Kisco, NY: Guidance Associates.

Kennedy's Career Secrets. Video. Arlington Heights, IL: Library Cable Network.

Making It on Your First Job. Video or laserdisc; guide. Charleston, WV: Cambridge Educational.

Mastering Change: How to Be "Change Skilled" and Thrive in Turbulent Times series. Video; workbook. Harleysville, PA: Career Communications Inc.

Maximizing Your Public Image. Video. Hinesburg, VT: Image Vision.

The Resume Remedy. Video. Indianapolis, IN: JIST Works.

Shhh! I'm Finding a Job: The Library and Your Self-Directed Job Search. Video; workbook. Charleston, WV: Cambridge Educational.

Successful Job Hunting: The Inside Scoop on Finding the Best Jobs. Video. Charleston, WV: Cambridge Educational.

Survival Skills for the World of Work series. Video. New York: Educational Design, Inc.

Take This Job and Love It. Video. Bloomington, IL: Meridian Education Corp.

Ten Ways to Get a Great Job. Video. Charleston, WV: Cambridge Educational.

Tough Times: Finding the Jobs. Video. Bloomington, IL: Meridian Education Corp.

The Very Quick Job Search Video. Indianapolis, IN: JIST Works.

The Video Guide to JIST's Self-Directed Job Search series. Video. Indianapolis, IN: JIST Works.

Your Public Image: Conducting Yourself in the Business World. Video. Hinesburg, VT: Image Vision.

Computer Software

The following titles include, where possible, the developer's name and location or else the name and location of a distributor. Software titles may be available through several distributors.

Ace the Interview: The Multimedia Job Interview Guide. CD-ROM for Macintosh or Windows. Charleston, WV: Cambridge Educational.

Adams JobBank FastResume Suite. CD-ROM for Windows. Holbrook, MA: Adams Media Corp.

Barron's Profiles of American Colleges on CD-ROM. Windows or Macintosh. Hauppauge, NY: Barron's.

The Cambridge Career Counseling System. Diskettes for IBM. Charleston, WV: Cambridge Educational.

Career Area Interest Checklist. Diskettes for IBM or Apple. Bloomington, IL: Meridian Education Corp.

Career Compass. Diskettes for IBM or Apple II. Bloomington, IL: Meridian Education Corp.

Career CompuSearch. Diskettes for IBM or Apple. Bloomington, IL: Meridian Education Corp.

Career Counselor. CD-ROM for Windows. New York: Kaplan Educational Centers.

Career Directions (English and Spanish versions). Diskettes for Apple II. Charleston, WV: Cambridge Educational.

Career Finder. Diskettes for IBM DOS, Windows, or Macintosh. Bloomington, IL: Meridian Education Corp.

Career Match. Diskettes for IBM or Macintosh. Charleston, WV: Cambridge Educational.

Career Moves: The Best of the DOT (Dictionary of Occupational Titles). CD-ROM for Macintosh or Windows. Charleston, WV: Cambridge Educational.

Career Toolbox. CD-ROM for Windows. Orem, UT: Infobusiness, Inc.

CD-ROM Version of the Occupational Outlook Handbook. Charleston, WV: Cambridge Educational.

Create Your Dream Job. CD-ROM for Windows or Macintosh. Columbus, OH: Career Paths/MarkED.

Discovering Careers and Jobs. CD-ROM. Detroit, MI: Gale Research, Inc.

Encyclopedia of Careers and Vocational Guidance. CD-ROM for Windows or Macintosh. Chicago: Ferguson.

Getting into College (U.S. News and World Report). CD-ROM. Portland, OR: Creative Multimedia.

Hoover's Company and Industry Database on CD-ROM. Austin, TX: The Reference Press.

Interview Skills for the Future. CD-ROM for Windows or Macintosh. Charleston, WV: Cambridge Educational.

JIST's Electronic Enhanced Dictionary of Occupational Titles. CD-ROM for Windows. Indianapolis, IN: JIST Works.

JIST's Multimedia Occupational Outlook Handbook. CD-ROM for Windows. Indianapolis, IN: JIST Works.

Job Search Skills for the 21st Century. CD-ROM for Windows or Macintosh. Charleston, WV: Cambridge Educational.

MSPI: Exploring Career Goals and College Courses. Diskettes for IBM or Macintosh. Charleston, WV: Cambridge Educational.

Multimedia Career Center. CD-ROM for Windows or Macintosh. Charleston, WV: Cambridge Educational.

The Multimedia Career Path. CD-ROM for Windows or Macintosh. Charleston, WV: Cambridge Job Search.

The Multimedia Guide to Occupational Exploration. CD-ROM for Windows or Macintosh. Charleston, WV: Cambridge Educational.

Multimedia Take this Job and Love It. CD-ROM for Windows or Macintosh. Charleston, WV: Cambridge Educational.

The Perfect Resume. CD-ROM for Windows. Torrance, CA: Davidson.

Resume Express: The Multimedia Guide. CD-ROM for Windows or Macintosh. Charleston, WV: Cambridge Educational.

Resume Revolution: The Software Solution. Diskettes for Windows or Macintosh. Charleston, WV: Cambridge Educational.

The Ultimate Job Source, 2.0. CD-ROM for Windows. Orem, UT: Infobusiness, Inc.

What Color Is Your Parachute? CD-ROM for Windows. Boston: BumbleBee Technology.

General

Books

Careers Without College: Building, Brooke C. Stoddard and Peggy J. Schmidt. Princeton, NJ: Petersons, 1994.

Construction Trades Knowledge Base, Thomas G. Sticht and Barbara A. McDonald. Westerville, OH: Glencoe, 1993.

Exploring Careers in the Construction Industry, Elizabeth S. Lytle. New York: Rosen Publishing Group, 1994.

Exploring Construction, Richard M. Henak. South Holland, IL: Goodheart-Willcox Company, 1993.

Opportunities in Vocational and Technical Careers, 2nd ed., Adrian A. Paradis. Lincolnwood, IL: VGM Career Horizons, 1992.

Working in Construction, Paul M. Howey. Minneapolis, MN: Lerner Publications Company, 1998.

Internet Sites

American Institute of Architects Online
www.aia.org

American Public Works Association
www.pubworks.com

American Society of Landscape Architects
www.asla.org

ContractorNet
www.contractornet.com

eArchitect: Web Site of the American Institute of Architects
www.e-architect.com

The Electronic Blue Book of Building and Construction
www.thebluebook.com

Engineering News Record Career Opportunities
www.enr.com/find/jobsf.htm

Hardhats Online
www.hardhatsonline.com

Job Hunting in Planning, Architecture, and Landscape Architecture
www.lib.berkeley.edu/ENVI/jobs.html

Public Works Online
www.publicworks.com

Audiovisual Materials

African-American Role Models. Video series with segments on electrician and structural engineer. Bloomington, IL: Meridian Education Corp.

The Building Trades. Video series. Bloomington, IL: Meridian Education Corp.

Construction. Video. Bloomington, IL: Meridian Education Corp.

Construction (*School to Work* series). Video. Charleston, WV: Cambridge Educational.

Construction Cluster (*Vocational Visions* series). Video. Mount Kisco, NY: Guidance Associates.

The Construction Site. Video. Calhoun, KY: NIMCO.

Enter Here: Manufacturing Technology and Construction. Video series. Charleston, WV: Cambridge Educational.

Innerview: Construction. Video. Fresno, CA: Edgepoint Productions.

Innerview: Home Improvement. Video. Fresno, CA: Edgepoint Productions.

Success Stories in the World of Work: Multicultural Role Models. Video series with segments on carpenter, electrician, and structural engineer. Bloomington, IL: Meridian Education Corp.

Tech Prep and Industrial Technology Occupations. Video. Calhoun, KY: NIMCO.

Construction Planning, Architecture, and Management

Books

Architect: A Candid Guide to the Profession. Roger K. Lewis. Cambridge, MA: MIT Press, 1998.

Basic Construction Management: The Superintendent's Job, 3rd ed., Leon Rogers and Jerry Householder. Washington, DC: Home Builder Press, 1996.

The Career Connection for Technical Education: A Guide to Technical Training and Related Career Opportunities, Fred A. Rowe, ed. Indianapolis, IN: JIST Works, 1994.

Civil Engineering for the Community, Dennis Randolph. New York: American Society of Civil Engineers, 1993.

Opportunities in Architectural Careers, Robert J. Piper and Richard D. Rush. Lincolnwood, IL: VGM Career Horizons, 1992.

Opportunities in Drafting Careers, Mark Rowh. Lincolnwood, IL: VGM Career Horizons, 1994.

The Professional Practice of Landscape Architecture: A Complete Guide to Starting and Running Your Own Firm, Walter Rogers. New York: John Wiley & Sons, 1997.

Ready, Set, Practice: Elements of Landscape Architecture Professional Practice, Bruce G. Sharkey. New York: John Wiley & Sons, 1994.

You Can Be a Woman Architect, Judith Cohen and Valerie Thompson. Lake Oswego, OR: Cascade Press, 1992.

Audiovisual Materials

Architecture. (*Career Encounters* series). Video. Charleston, WV: Cambridge Educational.

The Hispanic Experience. Video series with segment on structural engineer. Bloomington, IL: Meridian Education Corp.

Innerview: Architectural. Video. Fresno, CA: Edgepoint Productions.

Innerview: Drafting. Video. Fresno, CA: Edgepoint Productions.

Women of Achievement. Video series with segment on structural engineer. Bloomington, IL: Meridian Education Corp.

Mechanical, Structural, and Finishing Trades

Books

Careers in Plumbing, Heating, and Cooling, Elizabeth S. Lytle. New York: Rosen Publishing Group, 1995.

Careers Inside the World of the Trades, Peggy Santamaria. New York: Rosen Publishing Group, 1995.

Careers Without College: Heating and Air Conditioning Servicer, Susan Clinton. Mankato, MN: Capstone Press, 1997.

Exploring Careers as an Electrician, Elizabeth S. Lytle. New York: Rosen Publishing Group, 1996.

Exploring Metalworking, John R. Walker. South Holland, IL: Goodheart-Willcox, 1994.

Opportunities in Heating, Ventilation, Air Conditioning, and Refrigeration Careers, Richard Budzik. Lincolnwood, IL: VGM Career Horizons, 1995.

Opportunities in Plumbing and Pipefitting Careers, Patrick Galvin. Lincolnwood, IL: VGM Career Horizons, 1995.

The Plumbing Apprentice Handbook. New York: McGraw-Hill Text, 1993.

Audiovisual Materials

Electrician (*Career Connections* series). Video. Charleston, WV: Cambridge Educational.

HVAC (*Career Connections* series). Video. Charleston, WV: Cambridge Educational.

Opportunities and Challenges: The Vocational Series. Video series with segments on carpenter, electrician, iron worker, and plumber. Bloomington, IL: Meridian Education Corp.

Pipefitter (*Career Connections* series). Video. Charleston, WV: Cambridge Educational.

Plumber (*Career Connections* series). Video. Charleston, WV: Cambridge Educational.

Welder (*Career Connections* series). Video. Charleston, WV: Cambridge Educational.

The information in this directory was generated from the IPEDS (Integrated Postsecondary Education Data System) database of the U.S. Department of Education. It includes only regionally or nationally accredited institutions offering postsecondary occupational training in administration, business, and the office. Because college catalogs and directories of colleges and universities are readily available elsewhere, this directory does not include institutions that offer only bachelor's and advanced degrees.

Air Conditioning and Refrigeration

ALABAMA

Bessemer State Technical College
P.O. Box 308
Bessemer 35021

Bevill State Community College
P.O. Drawer K
Sumiton 35148

Community College of the Air Force
Maxwell Air Force Base
Montgomery 36112

Douglas MacArthur Technical College
P.O. Box 649
Opp 36467

Harry M Ayers State Technical College
1801 Coleman Rd.
P.O. Box 1647
Anniston 36202

John C Calhoun State Community College
P.O. Box 2216
Decatur 35609-2216

John M Patterson State Technical College
3920 Troy Hwy.
Montgomery 36116

Opelika State Technical College
P.O. Box 2268
Opelika 36803-2268

Shoals Community College
P.O. Box 2545
Muscle Shoals 35662

ARIZONA

Gateway Community College
108 North 40th St.
Phoenix 85034

Pima Community College
2202 West Anklam Rd.
Tucson 85709-0001

Refrigeration School
4210 East Washington
Phoenix 85034

Universal Technical Institute, Inc.
3121 West Weldon Ave.
Phoenix 85017

ARKANSAS

Arkansas Valley Technical Institute
Hwy. 23 N
P.O. Box 506
Ozark 72949

Cotton Boll Technical Institute
P.O. Box 36
Burdette 72321

Foothills Technical Institute
1800 East Moore St., P.O. Box 909
Searcy 72143

Northwest Technical Institute
P.O. Box A
Springdale 72765

Ouachita Technical College
One College Circle, P.O. Box 816
Malvern 72104

Pulaski Technical College
3000 West Scenic Dr.
North Little Rock 72118

Red River Technical College
P.O. Box 140
Hope 71801

CALIFORNIA

Brownson Technical School
1110 Claudina Place
Anaheim 92805

College of the Desert
43-500 Monterey St.
Palm Desert 92260

Contractors License Institute
5777 Madison
Sacramento 95841

Escuelas Leicester
1106 West Olympic Blvd.
Los Angeles 90015

Fresno City College
1101 East University Ave.
Fresno 93741

Hacienda La Puente Unified School
District, Valley Vocational Center
15959 East Gale Ave.
La Puente 91749

Institute for Business and Technology
2550 Scott Blvd.
Santa Clara 95050

Laney College
900 Fallon St.
Oakland 94607

Los Angeles Training Technical College
400 West Washington Blvd.
Los Angeles 90015-4181

Mount San Antonio College
1100 North Grand
Walnut 91789

North America Heating and Air
Conditioning Training Center, Inc.
1598 North H St.
San Bernandino 92405

Oxnard College
4000 South Rose Ave.
Oxnard 93033

Practical Schools
900 East Ball Rd.
Anaheim 92805

Sacramento City College
3835 Freeport Blvd.
Sacramento 95822

San Diego City College
1313 12th Ave.
San Diego 92101

San Joaquin Delta College
5151 Pacific Ave.
Stockton 95207

San Joaquin Valley College
201 New Stine Rd.
Bakersfield 93309

San Joaquin Valley College
3333 North Bond
Fresno 93726

San Jose City College
2100 Moorpark Ave.
San Jose 95128-2798

Sequoia Institute
420 Whitney Place
Fremont 94539

Simi Valley Adult School
3192 Los Angeles Ave.
Simi Valley 93065

COLORADO

Arapahoe Community College
2500 West College Dr.
Littleton 80160-9002

Community College of Denver
P.O. Box 173363
Denver 80217

Denver Institute of Technology
7350 North Broadway
Denver 80221

San Juan Basin Area Vocational School
P.O. Box 970
Cortez 81321

Technical Trades Institute
2315 East Pikes Peak Ave.
Colorado Springs 80909

CONNECTICUT

Baran Institute of Technology
605 Day Hill Rd.
Windsor 06095

New England Technical Institute of
Connecticut, Inc.
200 John Downey Dr.
New Britain 06051

Porter and Chester Institute
138 Weymouth Rd.
Enfield 06082

DELAWARE

Delaware Technical and Community
College, Southern Campus
P.O. Box 610
Georgetown 19947

FLORIDA

ATI Enterprises of Florida, Inc.,
ATI Career Training Center
3501 Northwest Ninth Ave.
Oakland Park 33309

Atlantic Vocational Technical Center
4700 Coconut Creek Pkwy.
Coconut Creek 33063

Brevard Community College
1519 Clearlake Rd.
Cocoa 32922

Central Florida Community College
P.O. Box 1388
Ocala 34478

Charlotte Vocational-Technical
Center
18300 Toledo Blade Blvd.
Port Charlotte 33948-3399

Daytona Beach Community College
1200 Volusia Ave.
Daytona Beach 32114

Florida Community College at
Jacksonville
501 West State St.
Jacksonville 32202

Garces Commercial College
5385 Northwest 36th St.
Miami Springs 33166

Lindsey Hopkins Technical Education
Center
750 Northwest 20th St.
Miami 33127

Manatee Vocational-Technical Center
5603 34th St. W
Bradenton 34210

Miami Lakes Technical Education
Center
5780 Northwest 158th St.
Miami Lakes 33169

North Technical Education Center
7071 Garden Rd.
Riviera Beach 33404

Pinellas Mechanical Pipe Trade
4020 80th Ave. N
Pinellas Park 33565

Pinellas Technical Education Center
Clearwater Campus
6100 154th Ave. N
Clearwater 34620

Robert Morgan Vocational Technical
Center
18180 Southwest 122nd Ave.
Miami 33177

Saint Augustine Technical Center
2980 Collins Ave.
Saint Augustine 32095

Santa Fe Community College
3000 Northwest 83rd St.
Gainesville 32601

Seminole Community College
100 Weldon Blvd.
Sanford 32773-6199

Sheridan Vocational Center
5400 West Sheridan St.
Hollywood 33021

South Florida Community College
600 West College Dr.
Avon Park 33825

Washington-Holmes Area Vocational-
Technical Center
209 Hoyt St.
Chipley 32428

GEORGIA

Altamaha Technical Institute
1777 West Cherry St.
Jesup 31545

Athens Area Technical Institute
U.S. Hwy. 29 N
Athens 30610-0399

Atlanta Area Technical School
1560 Stewart Ave. SW
Atlanta 30310

Augusta Technical Institute
3116 Deans Bridge Rd.
Augusta 30906

Ben Hill-Irwin Technical Institute
P.O. Box 1069
Fitzgerald 31750

Carroll Technical Institute
997 South Hwy. 16
Carrollton 30117

Chattahoochee Technical Institute
980 South Cobb Dr.
Marietta 30060-3398

Coosa Valley Technical Institute
112 Hemlock St.
Rome 30161

Dekalb Technical Institute
495 North Indian Creek Dr.
Clarkston 30021

Griffin Technical Institute
501 Varsity Rd.
Griffin 30223

Gwinnett Technical Institute
1250 Atkinson Rd.
P.O. Box 1505
Lawrenceville 30246-1505

Interactive Learning Systems
Prado Mall, 5600 Roswell Rd.
Atlanta 30342

Lanier Technical Institute
P.O. Box 58
Oakwood 30566

Macon Technical Institute
3300 Macon Tech Dr.
Macon 31206

Moultrie Area Technical Institute
P.O. Box 520
Moultrie 31776

North Georgia Technical Institute
Georgia Hwy. 197, P.O. Box 65
Clarkesville 30523

Okefenokee Technical Institute
1701 Carswell Ave.
Waycross 31501

Swainsboro Technical Institute
201 Kite Rd.
Swainsboro 30401

Thomas Technical Institute
P.O. Box 1578
Thomasville 31799

Valdosta Technical Institute
4089 Valtech Rd.
Valdosta 31602-9796

Walker Technical Institute
265 Bicentennial Trail
Rock Spring 30739

HAWAII

Employment Training Center
UH Community Colleges
33 South King St.
Honolulu 96813

Honolulu Community College
874 Dillingham Blvd.
Honolulu 96817

IDAHO

Boise State University
1910 University Dr.
Boise 83725

College of Southern Idaho
P.O. Box 1238
Twin Falls 83301

North Idaho College
1000 West Garden Ave.
Coeur D'Alene 83814

ILLINOIS

American College of Technology
1300 West Washington
Bloomington 61701

Belleville Area College
2500 Carlyle Rd.
Belleville 62221

Cave Technical Institute
2842 South State St.
Lockport 60441

City College of Chicago, Chicago City-
Wide College
226 West Jackson Blvd.
Chicago 60606-6997

City College of Chicago, Kennedy-King
6800 South Wentworth Ave.
Chicago 60621

College of Du Page
Lambert Rd. and 22nd St.
Glen Ellyn 60137

College of Lake County
19351 West Washington St.
Grays Lake 60030-1198

Coyne American Institute, Inc.
1235 West Fullerton Ave.
Chicago 60614

Elgin Community College
1700 Spartan Dr.
Elgin 60123

Environmental Technical Institute
1054 East Irving Park Rd.
Bensenville 60106

Environmental Technical Institute
13010 South Division St.
Blue Island 60406

Illinois Central College
One College Dr.
East Peoria 61635

Illinois Eastern Community Colleges
Olney Central College
RR 3
Olney 62450

John Wood Community College
150 South 48th St.
Quincy 62301-9147

Lake Land College
5001 Lake Land Blvd.
Mattoon 61938

Lincoln Land Community College
Shepherd Rd.
Springfield 62194-9256

Moraine Valley Community College
10900 South 88th Ave.
Palos Hills 60465-0937

Prairie State College
202 Halsted St.
Chicago Heights 60411

Quincy Technical School
501 North Third St.
Quincy 62301

Rend Lake College
Rte. 1
Ina 62846

Triton College
2000 Fifth Ave.
River Grove 60171

Universal Technical Institute, Inc.
601 Regency Dr.
Glendale Heights 60139

Washburne Trade School
3233 West 31st St.
Chicago 60623

Waubonsee Community College
Rte. 47 at Harter Rd.
Sugar Grove 60554-0901

William Rainey Harper College
1200 West Algonquin Rd.
Palatine 60067-7398

INDIANA

Fort Wayne Regional Vocational School
of Continuing Education
1200 South Barr St.
Fort Wayne 46802

Indiana Vocational Technical College,
Central Indiana
One West 26th St.
Indianapolis 46206-1763

Indiana Vocational Technical College,
Columbus
4475 Central Ave.
Columbus 47203

Indiana Vocational Technical College,
East Central
4301 South Cowan Rd., P.O. Box 3100
Muncie 47302

Indiana Vocational Technical College,
Kokomo
1815 East Morgan St.
Kokomo 46901

Indiana Vocational Technical College,
Lafayette
3208 Ross Rd., P.O. Box 6299
Lafayette 47903

Indiana Vocational Technical College,
North Central
1534 West Sample St.
South Bend 46619

Indiana Vocational Technical College,
Northeast
3800 North Anthony Blvd.
Fort Wayne 46805

Indiana Vocational Technical College,
Northwest
1440 East 35th Ave.
Gary 46409

Indiana Vocational Technical College,
Wabash Valley
7999 U.S. Hwy. 41
Terre Haute 47802-4898

ITT Technical Institute
9511 Angola Ct.
Indianapolis 46268

Oakland City College
Lucretia St.
Oakland City 47660-1099

IOWA

Des Moines Community College
2006 Ankeny Blvd.
Ankeny 50021

Eastern Iowa Community College
District
306 West River Dr.
Davenport 52801-1221

Hawkeye Institute of Technology
1501 East Orange Rd.
Waterloo 50704

Northeast Iowa Community College
Hwy. 150 S, P.O. Box 400
Calmar 52132-0400

North Iowa Area Community College
500 College Dr.
Mason City 50401

Western Iowa Technical Community
College
4647 Stone Ave., P.O. Box 265
Sioux City 51102-0265

KANSAS

Climate Control Institute
3030 North Hillside
Wichita 67219-3902

Kansas City Area Vocational Technical
School
2220 North 59th St.
Kansas City 66104

Kaw Area Vocational-Technical School
5724 Huntoon
Topeka 66604

Liberal Area Vocational Technical
School
P.O. Box 1599
Liberal 67905-1599

Manhattan Area Technical Center
3136 Dickens Ave.
Manhattan 66502

Pittsburg State University
1701 South Broadway
Pittsburg 66762

Salina Area Vocational Technical
School
2562 Scanlan Ave.
Salina 67401

Wichita Area Vocational Technical
School
428 South Broadway
Wichita 67202-3910

KENTUCKY

Ashland State Vocational Technical
School
4818 Roberts Dr.
Ashland 41102

Kentucky Technical, Bowling Green
State Vocational Technical School
1845 Loop Dr., P.O. Box 6000
Bowling Green 42101

Kentucky Technical, Hazard State
Vocational Technical School
101 Vocational-Tech Dr.
Hazard 41701

Kentucky Technical, Jefferson State
Vocational Technical School
727 West Chestnut
Louisville 40203

Northern Kentucky State Vocational-
Technical School
1025 Amsterdam Rd.
Covington 41011

LOUISIANA

Ayers Institute, Inc.
2924 Knight St.
Shreveport 71105

Baton Rouge Regional Technical
Institute
3250 North Acadian Hwy. E
Baton Rouge 70805

Delta School of Business and
Technology
517 Broad St.
Lake Charles 70601

Elaine P Nunez Community College
3700 La Fontaine St.
Chalmette 70043

Gulf Area Technical Institute
1115 Clover St.
Abbeville 70510

ITI Technical College
13944 Airline Hwy.
Baton Rouge 70817

Junionville Memorial Technical
Institute
P.O. Box 725
New Roads 70760

Lafayette Regional Technical Institute
1101 Bertrand Dr.
P.O. Box 4909
Lafayette 70502-4909

Refrigration School of New Orleans
1201 Mazant St.
New Orleans 70117

Ruston Technical Institute
1010 James St.
Ruston 71273-1070

Sabine Valley Vocational-Technical
School
Hwy. 171 S
Many 71449

Shreveport-Bossier Regional Technical
Institute
2010 North Market St., P.O. Box 78527
Shreveport 71137-8527

South Louisiana Regional Technical
Institute
P.O. Box 5033
Houma 70361-5033

Sullivan Technical Institute
1710 Sullivan Dr.
Bogalusa 70427

West Jefferson Technical Institute
475 Manhattan Blvd.
Harvey 70058

Young Memorial Technical Institute
P.O. Box 2148
Morgan City 70381

MAINE

Eastern Maine Technical College
354 Hogan Rd.
Bangor 04401

Southern Maine Technical College
Fort Rd.
South Portland 04106

Washington County Technical College
RR 1, P.O. Box 22C
Calais 04619

MARYLAND

Dundalk Community College
7200 Sollers Point Rd.
Dundalk 21222

Lincoln Technical Institute
7800 Central Ave.
Landover 20785

The Radio Electronic Television
Schools, Inc.
1520 South Caton Ave.
Baltimore 21227-1063

MASSACHUSETTS

Associated Technical Institute
345 West Cummings Park
Woburn 01801

Bay State School of Appliances
225 Turnpike St.
Canton 02021

Massasoit Community College
One Massasoit Blvd.
Brockton 02402

New England Fuel Institute Technical
Training Center
20 Summer St., P.O. Box 9137
Watertown 02272-9137

Northeast Institute of Industrial
Technology
41 Phillips St.
Boston 02114

Peterson School of Steam Engineering
25 Montvale Ave.
Woburn 01801

Springfield Technical Community
College
Armory Square
Springfield 01105

Worcester Technical Institute
251 Belmont St.
Worcester 01605

MICHIGAN

Air-Con Technical Institute K & M
Travel Corp
527 Executive Dr.
Troy 48075

Allstate Vocational Training
15160 West Eight Mile
Oak Park 48237

Ferris State University
901 South State St.
Big Rapids 49307

Grand Rapids Community College
143 Bostwick Ave. NE
Grand Rapids 49505

Henry Ford Community College
5101 Evergreen Rd.
Dearborn 48128

ITT Technical Institute
1225 East Big Beaver Rd.
Troy 48083

Lansing Community College
419 North Capitol Ave.
Lansing 48901-7210

Macomb Community College
14500 Twelve Mile Rd.
Warren 48093-3896

Mott Community College
1401 East Court St.
Flint 48503

Northern Michigan University
1401 Presque Isle
Marquette 49855

Oakland Community College
2480 Opdyke Rd.
Bloomfield Hills 48304-2266

MINNESOTA

Albert Lea-Mankato Technical College
2200 Tech Dr.
Albert Lea 56007

Albert Lea-Mankato Technical College
1920 Lee Blvd.
North Mankato 56003

Hennepin Technical College
1820 North Xenium Ln.
Plymouth 55441

Northwest Technical College,
Moorhead
1900 28th Ave. S
Moorhead 56560

Red Wing-Winona Technical College,
Red Wing Campus
Hwy. 58 at Pioneer Rd.
Red Wing 55066

Saint Cloud Technical College
1540 Northway Dr.
Saint Cloud 56303

Saint Paul Technical College
235 Marshall Ave.
Saint Paul 55102

MISSISSIPPI

Hinds Community College,
Raymond Campus
Raymond 39154

Jones County Junior College
Front St.
Ellisville 39437

Mississippi Delta Community College
P.O. Box 668
Moorhead 38761

Pearl River Community College
Station A
Poplarville 39470

MISSOURI

East Central College
P.O. Box 529
Union 63084

Jefferson College
1000 Viking Dr.
Hillsboro 63050

Linn Technical College
One Technology Dr.
Linn 65051

Macon Area Vocational School
Hwy. 63 N
Macon 63552

Nichols Career Center
609 Union
Jefferson City 65101

Penn Valley Community College
3201 Southwest Trafficway
Kansas City 64111

Ranken Technical College
4431 Finney Ave.
Saint Louis 63113

Rolla Area Vocational-Technical School
1304 East Tenth St.
Rolla 65401

Vattenott College
210 South Main
Independence 64051

Vattenott College
3925 Industrial Dr.
Saint Ann 63074

Vattenott College
1258 East Traffic Way
Springfield 65802

MONTANA

Billings Vocational Technical Center
3803 Central Ave.
Billings 59102

NEBRASKA

Central Community College,
Grand Island
P.O. Box 4903
Grand Island 68802

Metropolitan Community College Area
P.O. Box 3777
Omaha 68103

Mid Plains Community College
416 North Jeffers
North Platte 69101

Northeast Community College
801 East Benjamin,
P.O. Box 469
Norfolk 68702-0469

Universal Technical Institute, Inc.
902 Capitol Ave.
Omaha 68102

NEVADA

Education Dynamics Institute
2635 North Decatur Blvd.
Las Vegas 89108

NEW HAMPSHIRE

New Hampshire Technical College at
Manchester
1066 Front St.
Manchester 03102

NEW JERSEY

Lincoln Technical Institute
Rte. 130 N at Haddonfield Rd.
Pennsauken 08110

Lincoln Technical Institute
2299 Vauxhall Rd.
Union 07083

Mercer County Community College
1200 Old Trenton Rd.
Trenton 08690

Pennco Technical
Erial Rd., P.O. Box 1427
Blackwood 08012

Vinas Refrigeration School
51 Market St.
Paterson 07505

NEW MEXICO

Albuquerque Technical-Vocational
Institute
525 Buena Vista SE
Albuquerque 87106

Clovis Community College
417 Schepps Blvd.
Clovis 88101

New Mexico State University,
Dona Ana Branch
Department 3DA, P.O. Box 30001
Las Cruces 88003-0105

NEW YORK

Apex Technical School
635 Ave. of the Americas
New York 10011

Fegs Trades and Business School
199 Jay St.
Brooklyn 11201

Hudson Valley Community College
80 Vandenburgh Ave.
Troy 12180

Mohawk Valley Community College
1101 Sherman Dr.
Utica 13501

Monroe Community College
1000 East Henrietta Rd.
Rochester 14623

SUNY College of Technology at Alfred
Alfred 14802

SUNY College of Technology at Canton
Canton 13617

SUNY College of Technology at Delhi
Delhi 13753

SUNY College of Technology at
Farmingdale
Melville Rd.
Farmingdale 11735

Turner Trade School, Inc.
35 West 35th St.
New York 10001

NORTH CAROLINA

Alamance Community College
P.O. Box 8000
Graham 27253

Anson Community College
P.O. Box 126
Polkton 28135

Asheville Buncombe Technical
Community College
340 Victoria Rd.
Asheville 28801

Blue Ridge Community College
College Dr.
Flat Rock 28731-9624

Cape Fear Community College
411 North Front St.
Wilmington 28401

Carteret Community College
3505 Arendell St.
Morehead City 28557

Central Piedmont Community College
P.O. Box 35009
Charlotte 28235

Coastal Carolina Community College
444 Western Blvd.
Jacksonville 28546-6877

College of the Albemarle
1208 North Road St.
P.O. Box 2327
Elizabeth City 27906-2327

Davidson County Community College
P.O. Box 1287
Lexington 27293

Fayetteville Technical Community
College
2201 Hull Rd.
Fayetteville 28303

Forsyth Technical Community College
2100 Silas Creek Pkwy.
Winston-Salem 27103

Gaston College
Hwy. 321
Dallas 28034

Guilford Technical Community College
P.O. Box 309
Jamestown 27282

Johnston Community College
P.O. Box 2350
Smithfield 27577-2350

Roanoke-Chowan Community College
Rte. 2
P.O. Box 46A
Ahoskie 27910

Rockingham Community College
P.O. Box 38
Wentworth 27375-0038

Rowan-Cabarrus Community College
P.O. Box 1595
Salisbury 28145-1595

Vance-Granville Community College
State Rd. 1126, P.O. Box 917
Henderson 27536

Wake Technical Community College
9101 Fayetteville Rd.
Raleigh 27603-5696

NORTH DAKOTA

Bismarck State College
1500 Edwards Ave.
Bismarck 58501

North Dakota State College of Science
800 North Sixth St.
Wahpeton 58076

OHIO

Akron Adult Vocational Services
147 Park St.
Akron 44308

American School of Technology
2100 Morse Rd.
Columbus 43229

Belmont Technical College
120 Fox Shannon Place
Saint Clairsville 43950

Columbus State Community College
550 East Spring St., P.O. Box 1609
Columbus 43216

Fairfield Career Center
4000 Columbus Lancaster Rd.
Carroll 43112

Gallia Jackson Vinton JUSD
P.O. Box 157
Rio Grande 45674

ITT Technical Institute, Har Branch
3325 Stop Eight Rd.
Dayton 45414

McKim Technical Institute
1791 South Jacoby Rd.
Copley 44321

RETS Institute of Technology
1606 Laskey Rd.
Toledo 43612

RETS Technical Center
116 Westpark Rd.
Centerville 45459

Terra Technical College
2830 Napoleon Rd.
Fremont 43420

OKLAHOMA

Central Oklahoma Area Vocational
Technical School
Three Court Circle
Drumright 74030

Climate Control Institute
708 South Sheridan Rd.
Tulsa 74112

Indian Meridian Vocational-Technical
School District #16
1312 South Sangre Rd.
Stillwater 74074

Kiamichi AVTS SD #7, Poteau Campus
1509 South McKenna,
P.O. Box 825
Poteau 74953

Metro Tech Vocational Technical Center
1900 Springlake Dr.
Oklahoma City 73111

Oklahoma State University, Okmulgee
1801 East Fourth St.
Okmulgee 74447-3901

Platt College
6125 West Reno
Okc 73127

Southern Oklahoma Area Vocational-
Technical Center
2610 Sam Noble Pkwy.
Ardmore 73401

OREGON

Linn-Benton Community College
6500 Southwest Pacific Blvd.
Albany 97321

West Coast Training, Inc.
P.O. Box 22469
Milwaukie 97222

PENNSYLVANIA

CHI Institute
520 Street Rd.
Southampton 18966

Community College of Allegheny
County
800 Allegheny Ave.
Pittsburgh 15233-1895

Gateway Technical Institute
100 Seventh St.
Pittsburgh 15222

New Castle School of Trades
Youngstown Rd., Rte. 1
Pulaski 16143

Oil Burner Technician School
215 East Lexington St.
Allentown 18103

Orleans Technical Institute
1330 Rhawn St.
Philadelphia 19111-2899

Pennco Technical
3815 Otter St.
Bristol 19007

Pennsylvania College of Technology
One College Ave.
Williamsport 17701

Philadelphia Wireless Technical
Institute
1533 Pine St.
Philadelphia 19102

Thaddeus Stevens State School of
Technology
750 East King St.
Lancaster 17602

Triangle Technical, Greensburg
900 Greengate North Plaza
Greensburg 15601

Triangle Technical School, Inc.
1940 Perrysville Ave.
Pittsburgh 15214

RHODE ISLAND

New England Institute of Technology
2500 Post Rd.
Warwick 02886

SOUTH CAROLINA

Florence-Darlington Technical College
P.O. Box 100548
Florence 29501-0548

Greenville Technical College
Station B, P.O. Box 5616
Greenville 29606-5616

Horry-Georgetown Technical College
P.O. Box 1966
Conway 29526

Midlands Technical College
P.O. Box 2408
Columbia 29202

Piedmont Technical College
P.O. Drawer 1467
Greenwood 29648

York Technical College
452 South Anderson Rd.
Rock Hill 29730

SOUTH DAKOTA

Mitchell Vocational-Technical School
821 North Capital St.
Mitchell 57301

Southeast Vocational Technical Institute
2301 Career Place
Sioux Falls 57107

TENNESSEE

Chattanooga State Technical
Community College
4501 Amnicola Hwy.
Chattanooga 37406

Climate Control Institute, Inc.
568 Colonial Rd.
Memphis 38117

Covington State Area Vocational
Technical School
P.O. Box 249
Covington 38019

Dickson State Area Vocational-
Technical School
740 Hwy. 46
Dickson 37055

Elizabethton State Area Vocational
Technical School
1500 Arney St., P.O. Box 789
Elizabethton 37643

Jacksboro State Area Vocational-
Technical School
Rte. 1
Jacksboro 37757

Knoxville State Area Vocational-
Technical School
1100 Liberty St.
Knoxville 37919

McKenzie State Area Vocational
Technical School
905 Highland Dr. N, P.O. Box 427
McKenzie 38201

McMinnville State Area Vocational
Technical School
Vo Tech Dr.
McMinnville 37110

Memphis Area Vocational-Technical
School
550 Alabama Ave.
Memphis 38105-3799

Morristown State Area Vocational-
Technical School
821 West Louise Ave.
Morristown 37813

Murfreesboro Area Vocational
Technical School
1303 Old Fort Pkwy.
Murfreesboro 37129

Nashville State Area Vocational
Technical School
100 White Bridge Rd.
Nashville 37209

Newbern State Area Vocational-
Technical School
Hwy. 51 N
Newbern 38059

Savannah State Vocational Technical
School
Hwy. 64 W, P.O. Box 89
Crump 38327

Shelbyville State Area Vocational
Technical School
1405 Madison St.
Shelbyville 37160

William Moore School of Technology
1200 Poplar Ave.
Memphis 38104

TEXAS

Alvin Community College
3110 Mustang Rd.
Alvin 77511

American Trades Institute
6627 Maple Ave.
Dallas 75235

Austin Community College
5930 Middle Fiskville Rd.
Austin 78752

Avalon Vocational Technical Institute
4241 Tanglewood
Odessa 79762

Bee County College
3800 Charco Rd.
Beeville 78102

Blinn College
902 College Ave.
Brenham 77833

Capital City Trade and Technical School
205 East Riverside Dr.
Austin 78704

Cedar Valley College
3030 North Dallas Ave.
Lancaster 75134

College of the Mainland
1200 Amburn Rd.
Texas City 77591

Del Mar College
101 Baldwin
Corpus Christi 78404-3897

Eastfield College
3737 Motley Dr.
Mesquite 75150

Houston Community College System
22 Waugh Dr., P.O. Box 7849
Houston 77270-7849

Lee College
511 South Whiting St.
Baytown 77520-4703

Lincoln Technical Institute
2501 East Arkansas Ln.
Grand Prairie 75051

Lindsey-Cooper Refrigeration School,
Inc.
815 South Beltline Rd. at Shady Grove
Rd.
Irving 75060

North Harris Montgomery Community
College District
250 North Sam Houston Pkwy. E
Houston 77060

North Lake College
5001 North MacArthur Blvd.
Irving 75038-3899

Paris Junior College
2400 Clarksville St.
Paris 75460

Saint Philips College
2111 Nevada St.
San Antonio 78203

Southwest Texas Junior College
2401 Garner Field Rd.
Uvalde 78801

Tarrant County Junior College District
1500 Houston St.
Fort Worth 76102

Texas Southmost College
80 Fort Brown
Brownsville 78520

Texas State Technical College,
   Harlingen Campus
2424 Boxwood
Harlingen 78550-3697

Texas State Technical College,
   Sweetwater Campus
300 College Dr.
Sweetwater 79556

Texas State Technical College,
   Waco Campus
3801 Campus Dr.
Waco 76705

Texas Vocational School
1913 South Flores St.
San Antonio 78204

Texas Vocational School, Pharr
P.O. Box 791
Pharr 78577

Trinity Valley Community College
500 South Prairieville
Athens 75751

Tyler Junior College
P.O. Box 9020
Tyler 75711

Tyler School of Business,
   Trade and Technical
Hwy. 64 E & Rte. 14, P.O. Box 176
Tyler 75707

Universal Technical Institute, Inc.
721 Lockhaven Dr.
Houston 77073

Western Technical Institute
1000 Texas St.
El Paso 79901

Wharton County Junior College
911 Boling Hwy.
Wharton 77488

UTAH

Bridgerland Applied Technology Center
1301 North 600 W
Logan 84321

Salt Lake Community College
P.O. Box 30808
Salt Lake City 84130

Utah Valley Community College
800 West 1200 S
Orem 84058

WASHINGTON

Bellingham Technical College
3028 Lindbergh Ave.
Bellingham 98225

North Seattle Community College
9600 College Way N
Seattle 98103

Oil Heat Service Technician School
3820 Stone Way N
Seattle 98103

Perry Technical Institute
2011 West Washington Ave.
Yakima 98903

Spokane Community College
North 1810 Greene Ave.
Spokane 99207

Wenatchee Valley College
1300 Fifth St.
Wenatchee 98801

WEST VIRGINIA

Ben Franklin Career Center
500 28th St.
Dunbar 25064

West Virginia Northern Community
   College
College Square
Wheeling 26003

WISCONSIN

Chippewa Valley Technical College
620 West Clairemont Ave.
Eau Claire 54701

Milwaukee Area Technical College
700 West State St.
Milwaukee 53233

Western Wisconsin Technical College
304 North Sixth St.,
   P.O. Box 908
La Crosse 54602-0908

Wisconsin Area Vocational Training
   and Adult Education System,
   Moraine Park
235 North National Ave., P.O. Box 1940
Fond Du Lac 54936-1940

Architectural Drafting

ALABAMA

Bessemer State Technical College
P.O. Box 308
Bessemer 35021

Bevill State Community College
P.O. Drawer K
Sumiton 35148

Douglas MacArthur Technical College
P.O. Box 649
Opp 36467

George C Wallace State Community
   College, Hanceville
801 Main St. NW
P.O. Box 2000
Hanceville 35077-2000

Harry M Ayers State Technical College
1801 Coleman Rd., P.O. Box 1647
Anniston 36202

Jefferson State Community College
2601 Carson Rd.
Birmingham 35215-3098

J F Drake State Technical College
3421 Meridian St. N
Huntsville 35811

John C Calhoun State Community
   College
P.O. Box 2216
Decatur 35609-2216

John M Patterson State Technical
   College
3920 Troy Hwy.
Montgomery 36116

Lawson State Community College
3060 Wilson Rd. SW
Birmingham 35221

Northwest Alabama Community
   College
Rte. 3, P.O. Box 77
Phil Campbell 35581

Opelika State Technical College
P.O. Box 2268
Opelika 36803-2268

ALASKA

University of Alaska, Anchorage
3211 Providence Dr.
Anchorage 99508

ARIZONA

Arizona Western College
P.O. Box 929
Yuma 85366

Aztech College
1131 West Broadway Rd.
Tempe 85282

Eastern Arizona College
Church St.
Thatcher 85552-0769

High-Technical Institute
1515 East Indian School Rd.
Phoenix 85014

ITT Technical Institute
1840 East Benson Hwy.
Tucson 85714

Mesa Community College
1833 West Southern Ave.
Mesa 85202

National Education Center,
   Arizona Auto Institute Campus
6829 North 46th Ave.
Glendale 85301-3579

Northland Pioneer College
103 First Ave.
Holbrook 86025

Phoenix College
1202 West Thomas Rd.
Phoenix 85013

Pima Community College
2202 West Anklam Rd.
Tucson 85709-0001

ARKANSAS

Arkansas State University,
   Beebe Branch
P.O. Drawer H
Beebe 72012

Cotton Boll Technical Institute
P.O. Box 36
Burdette 72321

Foothills Technical Institute
1800 East Moore St., P.O. Box 909
Searcy 72143

Pulaski Technical College
3000 West Scenic Dr.
North Little Rock 72118

Westark Community College
P.O. Box 3649
Fort Smith 72913

CALIFORNIA

Allan Hancock College
800 South College Dr.
Santa Maria 93454

American River College
4700 College Oak Dr.
Sacramento 95841

Cabrillo College
6500 Soquel Dr.
Aptos 95003

California Career College
123 East Gish Rd.
San Jose 95112

Cerritos College
11110 Alondra Blvd.
Norwalk 90650

College of San Mateo
1700 West Hillsdale Blvd.
San Mateo 94402

College of the Canyons
26455 North Rockwell Canyon Rd.
Santa Clarita 91355

East Los Angeles Skill Center
3921 Selig Place
Los Angeles 90031

Eldorado College
2264 El Camino Real
Oceanside 92054

Evergreen Valley College
3095 Yerba Buena Rd.
San Jose 95135-1598

Fresno City College
1101 East University Ave.
Fresno 93741

Glendale Community College
1500 North Verdugo Rd.
Glendale 91208-2894

Institute for Business and Technology
2550 Scott Blvd.
Santa Clara 95050

ITT Technical Institute
2035 East 223rd
Carson 90810

ITT Technical Institute
9700 Goethe Rd.
Sacramento 95827-5282

ITT Technical Institute
9680 Granite Ridge Dr.
San Diego 92123

ITT Technical Institute
6723 Van Nuys Blvd.
Van Nuys 91405

Los Angeles Training Technical College
400 West Washington Blvd.
Los Angeles 90015-4181

Merced College
3600 M St.
Merced 95348-2898

Mission College
3000 Mission College Blvd.
Santa Clara 95054-1897

Moorpark College
7075 Campus Rd.
Moorpark 93021

MTI College, Colton
760 Via Lata
Colton 92324

Napa Valley College
2277 Napa Vallejo Hwy.
Napa 94558

National Education Center,
   Sawyer Campus
5500 South Eastern
Commerce 90043

Orange Coast College
2701 Fairview Rd.
Costa Mesa 92626

Palomar College
1140 West Mission
San Marcos 92069-1487

Phillips College, Inland Empire Campus
4300 Central Ave.
Riverside 92506

Platt College, San Diego
6250 El Cajon Blvd.
San Diego 92115

Rio Hondo College
3600 Workman Mill Rd.
Whittier 90601-1699

Riverside Community College
4800 Magnolia Ave.
Riverside 92506-1299

Santa Barbara City College
721 Cliff Dr.
Santa Barbara 93109-2394

Sierra College
5000 Rocklin Rd.
Rocklin 95677

Sierra Hi-Tech
7200 Fair Oaks Blvd.
Carmichael 95608

Yuba College
2088 North Beale Rd.
Marysville 95901

COLORADO

Boulder Valley Area Vocational
 Technical Center
6600 East Arapahoe
Boulder 80303

Community College of Denver
P.O. Box 173363
Denver 80217

Denver Institute of Technology
7350 North Broadway
Denver 80221

Front Range Community College
3645 West 112th Ave.
Westminster 80030

ITT Technical Institute
2121 South Blackhawk St., Southeast
 Commons
Aurora 80014

Red Rocks Community College
13300 West Sixth Ave.
Golden 80401

Technical Trades Institute
2315 East Pikes Peak Ave.
Colorado Springs 80909

Technical Trades Institute
772 Horizon Dr.
Grand Junction 81506

CONNECTICUT

Baran Institute of Technology
605 Day Hill Rd.
Windsor 06095

FLORIDA

Brevard Community College
1519 Clearlake Rd.
Cocoa 32922

Florida Community College at
 Jacksonville
501 West State St.
Jacksonville 32202

Florida Technical College
1819 North Semoran Blvd.
Orlando 32807

Florida Technical College of
 Jacksonville, Inc.
8711 Lone Star Rd.
Jacksonville 32211

ITT Technical Institute
4809 Memorial Hwy.
Tampa 33634

Miami Lakes Technical Education
 Center
5780 Northwest 158th St.
Miami Lakes 33169

Okaloosa-Walton Community College
100 College Blvd.
Niceville 32578

Saint Augustine Technical Center
2980 Collins Ave.
Saint Augustine 32095

Santa Fe Community College
3000 Northwest 83rd St.
Gainesville 32601

Sarasota County Technical Institute
4748 Beneva Rd.
Sarasota 34233-1798

Washington-Holmes Area Vocational-
 Technical Center
209 Hoyt St.
Chipley 32428

GEORGIA

Albany Technical Institute
1021 Lowe Rd.
Albany 31708

Athens Area Technical Institute
U.S. Hwy. 29 N
Athens 30610-0399

Bainbridge College
Hwy. 84 E
Bainbridge 31717

Ben Hill-Irwin Technical Institute
P.O. Box 1069
Fitzgerald 31750

Carroll Technical Institute
997 South Hwy. 16
Carrollton 30117

Chattahoochee Technical Institute
980 South Cobb Dr.
Marietta 30060-3398

Clayton State College
5900 Lee St.
P.O. Box 285
Morrow 30260

Coosa Valley Technical Institute
112 Hemlock St.
Rome 30161

Dalton College
213 North College Dr.
Dalton 30720

Dekalb Technical Institute
495 North Indian Creek Dr.
Clarkston 30021

Griffin Technical Institute
501 Varsity Rd.
Griffin 30223

Gwinnett College of Business
4230 Hwy. 29
Lilburn 30247

Gwinnett Technical Institute
1250 Atkinson Rd.
P.O. Box 1505
Lawrenceville 30246-1505

Middle Georgia Technical Institute
1311 Corder Rd.
Warner Robins 31088

Moultrie Area Technical Institute
P.O. Box 520
Moultrie 31776

North Georgia Technical Institute
Georgia Hwy. 197, P.O. Box 65
Clarkesville 30523

North Metro Technical Institute
5198 Ross Rd.
Acworth 30101

Okefenokee Technical Institute
1701 Carswell Ave.
Waycross 31501

Pickens Technical Institute
100 Pickens Tech Dr.
Jasper 30143

South Georgia Technical Institute
728 Souther Field Rd.
Americus 31709

Swainsboro Technical Institute
201 Kite Rd.
Swainsboro 30401

Thomas Technical Institute
P.O. Box 1578
Thomasville 31799

Valdosta Technical Institute
4089 Valtech Rd.
Valdosta 31602-9796

Walker Technical Institute
265 Bicentennial Trail
Rock Spring 30739

West Georgia Technical Institute
303 Fort Dr.
La Grange 30240

HAWAII

Hawaii Community College
200 West Kawili St.
Hilo 96720-4091

Honolulu Community College
874 Dillingham Blvd.
Honolulu 96817

Leeward Community College
96-045 Ala Ike
Pearl City 96782

IDAHO

Boise State University
1910 University Dr.
Boise 83725

College of Southern Idaho
P.O. Box 1238
Twin Falls 83301

Idaho State University
741 South Seventh Ave.
Pocatello 83209

ITT Technical Institute
950 Lusk St.
Boise 83706

ILLINOIS

American College of Technology
1300 West Washington
Bloomington 61701

Associated Design Service School of
 Drafting
11160 Southwest Hwy.
Palos Hills 60465

City College of Chicago,
 Harold Washington
30 East Lake St.
Chicago 60601

City College of Chicago,
 Olive-Harvey College
10001 South Woodlawn Ave.
Chicago 60628

College of Du Page
Lambert Rd. and 22nd St.
Glen Ellyn 60137

Kaskaskia College
27210 College Rd.
Centralia 62801

Quincy Technical School
501 North Third St.
Quincy 62301

Rend Lake College
Rte. 1
Ina 62846

Robert Morris College
180 North Lasalle St.
Chicago 60601

Southeastern Illinois College
3575 College Rd.
Harrisburg 62946

INDIANA

Indiana University, Purdue University
 at Fort Wayne
2101 Coliseum Blvd. E
Fort Wayne 46805

Indiana University,
 Purdue University Indianapolis
355 North Lansing
Indianapolis 46202

Indiana Vocational Technical College,
 Central Indiana
One West 26th St.
Indianapolis 46206-1763

Indiana Vocational Technical College,
 Columbus
4475 Central Ave.
Columbus 47203

Indiana Vocational Technical College,
 East Central
4301 South Cowan Rd., P.O. Box 3100
Muncie 47302

Indiana Vocational Technical College,
 Kokomo
1815 East Morgan St.
Kokomo 46901

Indiana Vocational Technical College,
 North Central
1534 West Sample St.
South Bend 46619

Indiana Vocational Technical College,
 Northeast
3800 North Anthony Blvd.
Fort Wayne 46805

Indiana Vocational Technical College,
 Northwest
1440 East 35th Ave.
Gary 46409

Indiana Vocational Technical College,
 Southwest
3501 First Ave.
Evansville 47710

Indiana Vocational Technical College,
 Wabash Valley
7999 U.S. Hwy. 41
Terre Haute 47802-4898

ITT Technical Institute
5115 Oak Grove Rd.
Evansville 47715

Purdue University, Calumet Campus
2233 171st St.
Hammond 46323

Vincennes University
1002 North First St.
Vincennes 47591

IOWA

American Institute of Commerce
1801 East Kimberly Rd.
Davenport 52807

Des Moines Community College
2006 Ankeny Blvd.
Ankeny 50021

Eastern Iowa Community College
 District
306 West River Dr.
Davenport 52801-1221

Hamilton Business College
2300 Euclid
Des Moines 50310

Hawkeye Institute of Technology
1501 East Orange Rd.
Waterloo 50704

Kirkwood Community College
P.O. Box 2068
Cedar Rapids 52406

Western Iowa Technical Community
 College
4647 Stone Ave.
P.O. Box 265
Sioux City 51102-0265

KANSAS

Flint Hills Technical School
3301 West 18th St.
Emporia 66801

Johnson County Area Vocational-
 Technical School
311 East Park
Olathe 66061

Johnson County Community College
12345 College Blvd.
Overland Park 66210-1299

Kansas City Area Vocational Technical
 School
2220 North 59th St.
Kansas City 66104

Kaw Area Vocational-Technical School
5724 Huntoon
Topeka 66604

Liberal Area Vocational Technical
 School
P.O. Box 1599
Liberal 67905-1599

Manhattan Area Technical Center
3136 Dickens Ave.
Manhattan 66502

Northeast Kansas Area Vocational
Technical School
1501 West Riley St.
P.O. Box 277
Atchison 66002

Northwest Kansas Area Vocational
Technical School
P.O. Box 668
Goodland 67735

Southeast Kansas Area Vocational
Technical School
Sixth and Roosevelt
Coffeyville 67337

Wichita Area Vocational Technical
School
428 South Broadway
Wichita 67202-3910

Wichita Business College
501 East Pawnee
Wichita 67211

KENTUCKY

Kentucky Technical, Bowling Green
State Vocational Technical School
1845 Loop Dr., P.O. Box 6000
Bowling Green 42101

Lexington Community College
Cooper Dr.
Lexington 40506

Louisville Technical Institute
3901 Atkinson Dr.
Louisville 40218

Mayo State Vocational Technical School
Third St.
Paintsville 41240

Northern Kentucky State Vocational-
Technical School
1025 Amsterdam Rd.
Covington 41011

LOUISIANA

Baton Rouge Regional Technical
Institute
3250 North Acadian Hwy. E
Baton Rouge 70805

Delgado Community College
615 City Park Ave.
New Orleans 70119

Delta School of Business and
Technology
517 Broad St.
Lake Charles 70601

Gulf Area Technical Institute
1115 Clover St.
Abbeville 70510

Jefferson Technical Institute
5200 Blair Dr.
Metairie 70001

Ruston Technical Institute
1010 James St.
Ruston 71273-1070

Sabine Valley Vocational-Technical
School
Hwy. 171 S
Many 71449

Slidell Technical Institute
1000 Canulette Rd., P.O. Box 827
Slidell 70459

Southern Technical College
303 Rue Louis XIV
Lafayette 70508

South Louisiana Regional Technical
Institute
P.O. Box 5033
Houma 70361-5033

Sullivan Technical Institute
1710 Sullivan Dr.
Bogalusa 70427

Teche Area Vocational-Technical School
P.O. Box 11057
New Iberia 70562-1057

West Jefferson Technical Institute
475 Manhattan Blvd.
Harvey 70058

Young Memorial Technical Institute
P.O. Box 2148
Morgan City 70381

MAINE

Northern Maine Technical College
33 Edgemont Dr.
Presque Isle 04769

Southern Maine Technical College
Fort Rd.
South Portland 04106

MARYLAND

Anne Arundel Community College
101 College Pkwy.
Arnold 21012

Arundel Institute of Technology
1808 Edison Hwy.
Baltimore 21213

Catonsville Community College
800 South Rolling Rd.
Catonsville 21228

Charles County Community College
Mitchell Rd., P.O. Box 910
La Plata 20646

Montgomery College of Rockville
51 Mannakee St.
Rockville 20850

Prince Georges Community College
301 Largo Rd.
Largo 23701-1243

The Radio Electronic Television
Schools, Inc.
1520 South Caton Ave.
Baltimore 21227-1063

MASSACHUSETTS

Computer Processing Institute
615 Massachusetts Ave.
Cambridge 02139

Franklin Institute of Boston
41 Berkeley St.
Boston 02116

Northern Essex Community College
Elliott Way
Haverhill 01830-2399

Womans Technical Institute
1255 Boylston St.
Boston 02215

MICHIGAN

Alpena Community College
666 Johnson St.
Alpena 49707

Bay De Noc Community College
2001 North Lincoln Rd.
Escanaba 49289

Ferris State University
901 South State St.
Big Rapids 49307

Gogebic Community College
East 4946 Jackson Rd.
Ironwood 49938

Grand Rapids Community College
143 Bostwick Ave. NE
Grand Rapids 49505

Kalamazoo Valley Community College
6767 West O Ave.
Kalamazoo 49009

Kellogg Community College
450 North Ave.
Battle Creek 49017

Kirtland Community College
10775 North St. Helen Rd.
Roscommon 48653

Lake Michigan College
2755 East Napier
Benton Harbor 49022

Lake Superior State University
Sault Sainte Marie 49783

Lansing Community College
419 North Capitol Ave.
Lansing 48901-7210

Macomb Community College
14500 Twelve Mile Rd.
Warren 48093-3896

Monroe County Community College
1555 South Raisinville Rd.
Monroe 48161

Mott Community College
1401 East Court St.
Flint 48503

North Central Michigan College
1515 Howard St.
Petoskey 49770

Northern Michigan University
1401 Presque Isle
Marquette 49855

Northwestern Michigan College
1701 East Front St.
Traverse City 49684

MINNESOTA

Albert Lea-Mankato Technical College
1920 Lee Blvd.
North Mankato 56003

Dakota County Technical College
1300 East 145th St.
Rosemount 55068

Hennepin Technical College
1820 North Xenium Ln.
Plymouth 55441

Hibbing Community College
1515 East 25th St.
Hibbing 55746

Hutchinson-Willmar Technical College,
Willmar Campus
P.O. Box 1097
Willmar 56201

Minneapolis Drafting School
5700 West Broadway
Minneapolis 55428

Northwest Technical College,
Thief River Falls
1301 Hwy. 1 E
Thief River Falls 56701

Northwest Technical Institute
11995 Singletree Ln.
Eden Prairie 55344

Saint Cloud Technical College
1540 Northway Dr.
Saint Cloud 56303

MISSISSIPPI

East Central Community College
Decatur 39327

Hinds Community College,
Raymond Campus
Raymond 39154

Holmes Community College
Hill St.
Goodman 39079

Jones County Junior College
Front St.
Ellisville 39437

Mississippi Gulf Coast Community
College
Central Office, P.O. Box 67
Perkinston 39573

Northeast Mississippi Community
College
Cunningham Blvd.
Booneville 38829

MISSOURI

East Central College
P.O. Box 529
Union 63084

ITT Technical Institute
13505 Lakefront Dr.
Earth City 63045

Linn Technical College
One Technology Dr.
Linn 65051

Northwest Missouri Community College
4315 Pickett Rd.
Saint Joseph 64503-1635

Rolla Area Vocational-Technical School
1304 East Tenth St.
Rolla 65401

Saint Louis Community College,
Forest Park
5600 Oakland Ave.
Saint Louis 63110

Sikeston Area Vocational Technical
School
1002 Virginia
Sikeston 63801

Vattenott College
210 South Main
Independence 64051

Vattenott College
1258 East Traffic Way
Springfield 65802

Waynesville Area Vocational School
810 Roosevelt
Waynesville 65583

MONTANA

Billings Vocational Technical Center
3803 Central Ave.
Billings 59102

Northern Montana College
P.O. Box 7751
Havre 59501

NEBRASKA

Central Community College,
Grand Island
P.O. Box 4903
Grand Island 68802

Metropolitan Community
College Area
P.O. Box 3777
Omaha 68103

Mid Plains Community College
416 North Jeffers
North Platte 69101

Northeast Community College
801 East Benjamin,
P.O. Box 469
Norfolk 68702-0469

Southeast Community College,
Lincoln Campus
8800 O St.
Lincoln 68520

NEVADA

Community College of Southern
Nevada
3200 East Cheyenne Ave.
Las Vegas 89030

NEW HAMPSHIRE

New Hampshire Technical College at
Nashua
505 Amherst St.
Nashua 03061-2052

NEW JERSEY

Brookdale Community College
Newman Springs Rd.
Lincroft 07738-1599

Camden County College
P.O. Box 200
Blackwood 08012

County College of Morris
214 Center Grove Rd.
Randolph 07869

Lincoln Technical Institute
Rte. 130 N at Haddonfield Rd.
Pennsauken 08110

Mercer County Community College
1200 Old Trenton Rd.
Trenton 08690

The Plaza School
Bergen Mall
Paramus 07652

NEW MEXICO

Albuquerque Technical-Vocational
Institute
525 Buena Vista SE
Albuquerque 87106

Luna Vocational Technical Institute
P.O. Drawer K
Las Vegas 87701

New Mexico Junior College
5317 Lovington Hwy.
Hobbs 88240

Northern New Mexico Community
College
1002 North Onate St.
Espanola 87532

Santa Fe Community College
South Richards Ave.
P.O. Box 4187
Santa Fe 87502-4187

NEW YORK

CUNY New York City Technical College
300 Jay St.
Brooklyn 11201

Genesee Community College
One College Rd.
Batavia 14020

Island Drafting and Technical Institute
128 Broadway Rte. 110
Amityville 11701

Mohawk Valley Community College
1101 Sherman Dr.
Utica 13501

Onondaga Community College
Rte. 173
Syracuse 13215

Suffolk County Community College,
Ammerman Campus
533 College Rd.
Selden 11784

SUNY College of Technology at Canton
Canton 13617

SUNY College of Technology at Delhi
Delhi 13753

OHIO

Central Ohio Technical College
1179 University Dr.
Newark 43055-1767

ETI Technical College
4300 Euclid Ave.
Cleveland 44103

ETI Technical College
1320 West Maple St. NW
North Canton 44720

North Central Technical College
2441 Kenwood Circle
P.O. Box 698
Mansfield 44901

Northwest Technical College
22-600 South Rte. 34 & Rte. 1
    P.O. Box 246A
Archbold 43502-9990

Owens Technical College
30335 Oregon Rd.
P.O. Box 10000
Toledo 43699-1947

Owens Technical College,
    Findlay Campus
300 Davis St.
Findlay 45840

Shawnee State University
940 Second St.
Portsmouth 45662

Sinclair Community College
444 West Third St.
Dayton 45402

Southern State Community College
200 Hobart Dr.
Hillsboro 45133

Stark Technical College
6200 Frank Ave. NW
Canton 44720

Technology Education Center
288 South Hamilton Rd.
Columbus 43213

Total Technical Institute
6500 Pearl Rd.
Parma Heights 44130

University of Akron, Main Campus
302 Buchtel Common
Akron 44325-4702

University of Toledo
2801 West Bancroft
Toledo 43606

Wright State University, Lake Campus
7600 Rte. 703E
Celina 45822

OKLAHOMA

Central Oklahoma Area Vocational
    Technical School
Three Court Circle
Drumright 74030

Francis Tuttle Area Vocational-
    Technical Center
12777 North Rockwell Ave.
Oklahoma City 73142-2789

Metro Tech Vocational Technical
    Center
1900 Springlake Dr.
Oklahoma City 73111

Northern Oklahoma College
P.O. Box 310
Tonkawa 74653

Oklahoma City Community College
7777 South May Ave.
Oklahoma City 73159

Oklahoma State University,
    Oklahoma City
900 North Portland
Oklahoma City 73107

Oklahoma State University,
    Okmulgee
1801 East Fourth St.
Okmulgee 74447-3901

Platt College
6125 West Reno
Okc 73127

Platt College
4821 South 72nd East Ave.
Tulsa 74145

Pontotoc Skill Development Center
601 West 33rd
Ada 74820

Southern Oklahoma Area Vocational-
    Technical Center
2610 Sam Noble Pkwy.
Ardmore 73401

Tulsa Junior College
6111 East Skelly Dr.
Tulsa 74135

OREGON

Central Oregon Community College
2600 Northwest College Way
Bend 97701

Chemeketa Community College
P.O. Box 14007
Salem 97309-7070

Clackamas Community College
19600 Molalla Ave.
Oregon City 97045

ITT Technical Institute
6035 Northeast 78th Ct.
Portland 97218

Lane Community College
4000 East 30th Ave.
Eugene 97405

Linn-Benton Community College
6500 Southwest Pacific Blvd.
Albany 97321

Oregon Polytechnic Institute
900 Southeast Sandy Blvd.
Portland 97214

Portland Community College
P.O. Box 19000
Portland 97280-0990

PENNSYLVANIA

American Institute of Design
1616 Orthodox St.
Philadelphia 19124

Berks Technical Institute
832 North Park Rd.,
Four Park Plaza
Wyomissing 19610

Bucks County Community College
Swamp Rd.
Newtown 18940

Butler County Community College
College Dr., Oak Hills
Butler 16003-1203

California University of Pennsylvania
250 University Ave.
California 15419-1394

Community College of Allegheny
    County
800 Allegheny Ave.
Pittsburgh 15233-1895

Community College of Beaver County
One Campus Dr.
Monaca 15061

Dean Institute of Technology
1501 West Liberty Ave.
Pittsburgh 15226-9990

Gateway Technical Institute
100 Seventh St.
Pittsburgh 15222

Lancaster Institute of Drafting, Inc.
3549 Hempland Rd.
Lancaster 17601

Luzerne County Community College
1333 South Prospect St.
Nanticoke 18634

National Education Center,
    Thompson Institute Campus
5650 Derry St.
Harrisburg 17111

Pennsylvania College of Technology
One College Ave.
Williamsport 17701

Thaddeus Stevens State School of
    Technology
750 East King St.
Lancaster 17602

Triangle Technical, Erie
2000 Liberty St.
Erie 16502

Triangle Technical, Greensburg
900 Greengate North Plaza
Greensburg 15601

Triangle Technical School, Inc.
1940 Perrysville Ave.
Pittsburgh 15214

RHODE ISLAND

Johnson and Wales University
Abbott Park Place
Providence 02903-3376

New England Institute of Technology
2500 Post Rd.
Warwick 02886

SOUTH CAROLINA

Trident Technical College
P.O. Box 118067
Charleston 29423-8067

SOUTH DAKOTA

Lake Area Vocational Technical
    Institute
230 11th St. NE
Watertown 57201

Mitchell Vocational-Technical School
821 North Capital St.
Mitchell 57301

Western Dakota Vocational Technical
    Institute
1600 Sedivy
Rapid City 57701

TENNESSEE

Athens State Area Vocational-Technical
    School
1635 Vo Tech Dr.
P.O. Box 848
Athens 37371-0848

Chattanooga State Technical
    Community College
4501 Amnicola Hwy.
Chattanooga 37406

Hohenwald State Area Vocational-
    Technical School
813 West Main
Hohenwald 38462-2201

Jacksboro State Area Vocational-
    Technical School
Rte. 1
Jacksboro 37757

Jackson State Area Vocational
    Technical School
McKellar Airport
Jackson 38301

Knoxville State Area Vocational-
    Technical School
1100 Liberty St.
Knoxville 37919

Livingston State Area Vocational-
    Technical School
P.O. Box 219
Livingston 38570

McKenzie State Area Vocational
    Technical School
905 Highland Dr. N.
P.O. Box 427
McKenzie 38201

McMinnville State Area Vocational
    Technical School
Vo Tech Dr.
McMinnville 37110

Memphis Area Vocational-Technical
    School
550 Alabama Ave.
Memphis 38105-3799

Morristown State Area Vocational-
    Technical School
821 West Louise Ave.
Morristown 37813

Nashville State Area Vocational
    Technical School
100 White Bridge Rd.
Nashville 37209

Newbern State Area Vocational-
Technical School
Hwy. 51 N
Newbern 38059

Northeast State Technical Community
College
P.O. Box 246
Blountville 37617

Pellissippi State Technical Community
College
P.O. Box 22990
Knoxville 37933-0990

Savannah State Vocational Technical
School
Hwy. 64 W, P.O. Box 89
Crump 38327

Shelbyville State Area Vocational
Technical School
1405 Madison St.
Shelbyville 37160

TEXAS

Alvin Community College
3110 Mustang Rd.
Alvin 77511

Amarillo College
P.O. Box 447
Amarillo 79178

American Commercial College
2007 34th St.
Lubbock 79411

American Trades Institute
235 Northeast Loop 820
Hurst 76053

American Trades Institute ATI,
Graphic Arts Institute
11034 Shady Trail
Dallas 75229

Angelina College
P.O. Box 1768
Lufkin 75902-1768

Austin Community College
5930 Middle Fiskville Rd.
Austin 78752

Bee County College
3800 Charco Rd.
Beeville 78102

Brazosport College
500 College Dr.
Lake Jackson 77566

Central Texas College
P.O. Box 1800
Killeen 76540-9990

Cooke County College
1525 West California
Gainesville 76240

Eastfield College
3737 Motley Dr.
Mesquite 75150

El Paso Community College
P.O. Box 20500
El Paso 79998

Four-C College
Eighth and Washington St., P.O. Box 4
Waco 76701

Houston Community College System
22 Waugh Dr., P.O. Box 7849
Houston 77270-7849

ITT Technical Institute
9421 West Sam Houston Pkwy.
Houston 77099

Lamar University, Beaumont
4400 Mlk, P.O. Box 10001
Beaumont 77710

Lee College
511 South Whiting St.
Baytown 77520-4703

Letourneau University
P.O. Box 7001
Longview 75607-7001

Mountain View College
4849 West Illinois
Dallas 75211

North Harris Montgomery Community
College District
250 North Sam Houston Pkwy. E
Houston 77060

Paris Junior College
2400 Clarksville St.
Paris 75460

San Jacinto College, Central Campus
8060 Spencer Hwy.
Pasadena 77505

San Jacinto College, North Campus
5800 Uvalde
Houston 77049

San Jacinto College, South Campus
13735 Beamer Rd.
Houston 77089

South Plains College
1401 College Ave.
Levelland 79336

Saint Philips College
2111 Nevada St.
San Antonio 78203

Temple Junior College
2600 South First St.
Temple 76504-7435

Texas State Technical College,
Amarillo Campus
P.O. Box 11035
Amarillo 79111

Texas State Technical College,
Harlingen Campus
2424 Boxwood
Harlingen 78550-3697

Texas State Technical College,
Sweetwater Campus
300 College Dr.
Sweetwater 79556

Texas State Technical College,
Waco Campus
3801 Campus Dr.
Waco 76705

Trinity Valley Community
College
500 South Prairieville
Athens 75751

Wharton County Junior College
911 Boling Hwy.
Wharton 77488

UTAH

Bridgerland Applied Technology
Center
1301 North 600 W
Logan 84321

Davis Applied Technology Center
550 East 300 S
Kaysville 84037

Dixie College
225 South 700 E
Saint George 84770

ITT Technical Institute
920 West Levoy Dr.
Murray 84123

Odgen-Weber Applied Technology
Center
559 East AVC Ln.
Ogden 84404-6704

Salt Lake Community College
P.O. Box 30808
Salt Lake City 84130

Technical Engineering Institute School
of Drafting
2349 Southwest Temple St.
Salt Lake City 84115

Utah Valley Community College
800 West 1200 S
Orem 84058

WASHINGTON

Big Bend Community College
7662 Chanute St.
Moses Lake 98837

Edmonds Community College
20000 68th Ave. W
Lynnwood 98036

Everett Community College
801 Wetmore Ave.
Everett 98201

Green River Community College
12401 Southeast 320th St.
Auburn 98002

Highline Community College
P.O. Box 98000
Des Moines 98198-9800

Lake Washington Technical College
11605 132nd Ave. NE
Kirkland 98034

Seattle Community College,
South Campus
6000 16th Ave. SW
Seattle 98106

South Puget Sound Community College
2011 Mottman Rd. SW
Olympia 98512

WEST VIRGINIA

Ben Franklin Career Center
500 28th St.
Dunbar 25064

Boone County Career & Technical
Center
P.O. Box 50B
Danville 25053

Cabell County Vocational Technical
Center
1035 Norway Ave.
Huntington 25705

Raleigh County Vocational-Technical
Center
410-½ Stanaford Rd.
Beckley 25801

West Virginia Institute of Technology
Montgomery 25136

West Virginia State College
Rte. 25
Institute 25112

WISCONSIN

Northeast Wisconsin Technical College
2740 West Mason St.
P.O. Box 19042
Green Bay 54307-9042

Wisconsin Indianhead Technical
College
505 Pine Ridge Dr.
P.O. Box 10B
Shell Lake 54871

WYOMING

Casper College
125 College Dr.
Casper 82601

Architectural Technology

ALABAMA

Jefferson State Community College
2601 Carson Rd.
Birmingham 35215-3098

ALASKA

Charter College
2221 East Northern Lights Blvd.
Anchorage 99508

ARKANSAS

Northwest Technical Institute
P.O. Box A
Springdale 72765

CALIFORNIA

City College of San Francisco
50 Phelan Ave.
San Francisco 94112

Cuyamaca College
2950 Jamacha Rd.
El Cajon 92020

East Los Angeles College
1301 Brooklyn Ave.
Monterey Park 91754

Fresno City College
1101 East University Ave.
Fresno 93741

Fullerton College
321 East Chapman Ave.
Fullerton 92632-2095

Golden West College
15744 Golden West
Huntington Beach 92647

Los Angeles City College
855 North Vermont Ave.
Los Angeles 90029

Orange Coast College
2701 Fairview Rd.
Costa Mesa 92626

Pasadena City College
1570 East Colorada Blvd.
Pasadena 91106

San Diego Mesa College
7250 Mesa College Dr.
San Diego 92111-4998

Southwestern College
900 Otay Lakes Rd.
Chula Vista 92010

COLORADO

Arapahoe Community College
2500 West College Dr.
Littleton 80160-9002

Front Range Community College
3645 West 112th Ave.
Westminster 80030

CONNECTICUT

Connecticut Institute of Technology
Two Elizabeth St.
West Haven 06516

Porter and Chester Institute
138 Weymouth Rd.
Enfield 06082

Porter and Chester Institute
670 Lordship Blvd.
Stratford 06497

Porter and Chester Institute
320 Sylvan Lake Rd.
Watertown 06779-1400

Porter and Chester Institute
125 Silas Deane Hwy.
Wethersfield 06109

DELAWARE

Delaware Technical and Community
College, Southern Campus
P.O. Box 610
Georgetown 19947

Delaware Technical Community
College Stanton, Wilmington
400 Stanton-Christiana Rd.
Newark 19702

FLORIDA

Daytona Beach Community College
1200 Volusia Ave.
Daytona Beach 32114

Lindsey Hopkins Technical Education
Center
750 Northwest 20th St.
Miami 33127

Pensacola Junior College
1000 College Blvd.
Pensacola 32504

Pinellas Technical Education Center,
Clearwater Campus
6100 154th Ave. N
Clearwater 34620

IDAHO

Ricks College
Rexburg 83460-4107

ILLINOIS

Southern Illinois University,
Carbondale
Carbondale 62901

INDIANA

ITT Technical Institute
4919 Coldwater Rd.
Fort Wayne 46825

ITT Technical Institute
9511 Angola Ct.
Indianapolis 46268

Purdue University, Main Campus
1076 Freehafer Hall
West Lafayette 47907-1076

IOWA

Western Iowa Technical Community
College
4647 Stone Ave., P.O. Box 265
Sioux City 51102-0265

KENTUCKY

Northern Kentucky University
University Dr.
Highland Heights 41099

MARYLAND

Maryland Drafting Institute
2045 University Blvd.
Langley Park 20783

MASSACHUSETTS

Lincoln Institute of Land Policy
113 Brattle St.
Cambridge 02138

Massasoit Community College
One Massasoit Blvd.
Brockton 02402

Wentworth Institute of Technology
550 Huntington Ave.
Boston 02115

Worcester Technical Institute
251 Belmont St.
Worcester 01605

MICHIGAN

Delta College
University Center 48710

Ferris State University
901 South State St.
Big Rapids 49307

Grand Rapids Community College
143 Bostwick Ave. NE
Grand Rapids 49505

Henry Ford Community College
5101 Evergreen Rd.
Dearborn 48128

Lansing Community College
419 North Capitol Ave.
Lansing 48901-7210

MISSOURI

Jefferson College
1000 Viking Dr.
Hillsboro 63050

Ranken Technical College
4431 Finney Ave.
Saint Louis 63113

Saint Louis Community College,
Forest Park
5600 Oakland Ave.
Saint Louis 63110

NEW HAMPSHIRE

New Hampshire Technical Institute
11 Institute Dr.
Concord 03301

NEW JERSEY

Essex County College
303 University Ave.
Newark 07102

Mercer County Community College
1200 Old Trenton Rd.
Trenton 08690

NEW YORK

Dutchess Community College
Pendell Rd.
Poughkeepsie 12601

Erie Community College, South Campus
4140 Southwestern Blvd.
Orchard Park 14127

New York Institute of Technology,
Old Westbury Campus
P.O. Box 170
Old Westbury 11568-0170

Onondaga Community College
Rte. 173
Syracuse 13215

Orange County Community College
115 South St.
Middletown 10940

Suffolk County Community College,
Ammerman Campus
533 College Rd.
Selden 11784

SUNY College of Technology at Alfred
Alfred 14802

SUNY College of Technology at Delhi
Delhi 13753

SUNY College of Technology at
Farmingdale
Melville Rd.
Farmingdale 11735

NORTH CAROLINA

Catawba Valley Community College
2550 Hwy. 70 SE
Hickory 28602-0699

Central Piedmont Community College
P.O. Box 35009
Charlotte 28235

Coastal Carolina Community College
444 Western Blvd.
Jacksonville 28546-6877

Forsyth Technical Community College
2100 Silas Creek Pkwy.
Winston-Salem 27103

Guilford Technical Community College
P.O. Box 309
Jamestown 27282

Pitt Community College
Hwy. 11 S
P.O. Drawer 7007
Greenville 27835-7007

Sandhills Community College
2200 Airport Rd.
Pinehurst 28374

Wake Technical Community College
9101 Fayetteville Rd.
Raleigh 27603-5696

NORTH DAKOTA

North Dakota State College of Science
800 North Sixth St.
Wahpeton 58076

OHIO

Columbus State Community College
550 East Spring St.
P.O. Box 1609
Columbus 43216

Owens Technical College
30335 Oregon Rd.
P.O. Box 10000
Toledo 43699-1947

Sinclair Community College
444 West Third St.
Dayton 45402

Terra Technical College
2830 Napoleon Rd.
Fremont 43420

University of Cincinnati,
Main Campus
2624 Clifton Ave.
Cincinnati 45221-0127

PENNSYLVANIA

American Institute of Design
1616 Orthodox St.
Philadelphia 19124

Community College of Philadelphia
1700 Spring Garden St.
Philadelphia 19130

Delaware County Community College
901 South Media Line Rd.
Media 19063

Harrisburg Area Community College,
Harrisburg Campus
One HACC Dr.
Harrisburg 17110

Johnson Technical Institute
3427 North Main Ave.
Scranton 18508

Northampton County Area Community
College
3835 Green Pond Rd.
Bethlehem 18017

Pennsylvania College of Technology
One College Ave.
Williamsport 17701

Pennsylvania Institute of Technology
800 Manchester Ave.
Media 19063

Pennsylvania State University,
Fayette Campus
One University Dr.
Uniontown 15401

Pennsylvania State University,
Worthington Scranton Campus
120 Ridge View Dr.
Dunmore 18512

Triangle Technical, Dubois
P.O. Box 551
Dubois 15801

SOUTH CAROLINA

Greenville Technical College
Station B
P.O. Box 5616
Greenville 29606-5616

SOUTH DAKOTA

Southeast Vocational Technical
Institute
2301 Career Place
Sioux Falls 57107

TENNESSEE

Nashville State Technical Institute
120 White Bridge Rd.
Nashville 37209

State Technical Institute of Memphis
5983 Macon Cove
Memphis 38134

UTAH

Snow College
150 East College Ave.
Ephraim 84627

VERMONT

Vermont Technical College
Randolph Center 05061

VIRGINIA

Dabney S Lancaster Community
College
P.O. Box 1000
Clifton Forge 24422-1000

John Tyler Community College
13101 Jefferson Davis Hwy.
Chester 23831-5399

Maryland Drafting Institute
8001 North Forbes Place
Springfield 22151

New River Community College
P.O. Drawer 1127
Dublin 24084

Northern Virginia Community College
4001 Wakefield Chapel Rd.
Annandale 22003

Patrick Henry Community College
P.O. Box 5311
Martinsville 24115-5311

Thomas Nelson Community College
P.O. Box 9407
Hampton 23670

Tidewater Community College
Rte. 135
Portsmouth 23703

Virginia Western Community College
3095 Colonial Ave.
Roanoke 24015

WISCONSIN

North Central Technical College
1000 Campus Dr.
Wausau 54401-1899

Northeast Wisconsin Technical College
2740 West Mason St.
P.O. Box 19042
Green Bay 54307-9042

Wisconsin Area Vocational Training
and Adult Education System District
Number Four
3550 Anderson St.
Madison 53704

Carpentry

ALABAMA

Atmore State Technical College
P.O. Box 1119
Atmore 36504

Chauncey Sparks State Technical
College
P.O. Drawer 580
Eufaula 36027

Douglas MacArthur Technical College
P.O. Box 649
Opp 36467

Gadsden State Community College
P.O. Box 227
Gadsden 35902-0227

George C Wallace State Community
College, Hanceville
801 Main St. NW
P.O. Box 2000
Hanceville 35077-2000

Harry M Ayers State Technical College
1801 Coleman Rd.
P.O. Box 1647
Anniston 36202

J F Ingram State Technical College
P.O. Box 209
Deatsville 36022

John C Calhoun State Community
College
P.O. Box 2216
Decatur 35609-2216

Lawson State Community College
3060 Wilson Rd. SW
Birmingham 35221

Opelika State Technical College
P.O. Box 2268
Opelika 36803-2268

ARIZONA

Central Arizona College
8470 North Overfield Rd.
Coolidge 85228-9778

Eastern Arizona College
Church St.
Thatcher 85552-0769

ARKANSAS

Black River Technical College
Hwy. 304
P.O. Box 468
Pocahontas 72455

Crowley's Ridge Technical School
P.O. Box 925
Forrest City 72335

Northwest Technical Institute
P.O. Box A
Springdale 72765

Pulaski Technical College
3000 West Scenic Dr.
North Little Rock 72118

Quapaw Technical Institute
201 Vocational-Tech Dr.
Hot Springs 71913

Red River Technical College
P.O. Box 140
Hope 71801

CALIFORNIA

College of the Redwoods
7351 Tompkins Hill Rd.
Eureka 95501-9302

El Camino College
16007 Crenshaw Blvd.
Torrance 90506

Fresno City College
1101 East University Ave.
Fresno 93741

Laney College
900 Fallon St.
Oakland 94607

Los Angeles Training Technical College
400 West Washington Blvd.
Los Angeles 90015-4181

San Joaquin Delta College
5151 Pacific Ave.
Stockton 95207

Sierra College
5000 Rocklin Rd.
Rocklin 95677

FLORIDA

Manatee Vocational-Technical Center
5603 34th St. W
Bradenton 34210

Miami Lakes Technical Education
Center
5780 Northwest 158th St.
Miami Lakes 33169

Pinellas Technical Education Center,
Clearwater Campus
6100 154th Ave. N
Clearwater 34620

Saint Augustine Technical Center
2980 Collins Ave.
Saint Augustine 32095

Washington-Holmes Area Vocational-
Technical Center
209 Hoyt St.
Chipley 32428

GEORGIA

Atlanta Area Technical School
1560 Stewart Ave. SW
Atlanta 30310

Columbus Technical Institute
928 45th St.
Columbus 31904-6572

Griffin Technical Institute
501 Varsity Rd.
Griffin 30223

Gwinnett Technical Institute
1250 Atkinson Rd., P.O. Box 1505
Lawrenceville 30246-1505

Lanier Technical Institute
P.O. Box 58
Oakwood 30566

North Georgia Technical Institute
Georgia Hwy. 197, P.O. Box 65
Clarkesville 30523

Pickens Technical Institute
100 Pickens Tech Dr.
Jasper 30143

HAWAII

Hawaii Community College
200 West Kawili St.
Hilo 96720-4091

Honolulu Community College
874 Dillingham Blvd.
Honolulu 96817

IDAHO

College of Southern Idaho
P.O. Box 1238
Twin Falls 83301

North Idaho College
1000 West Garden Ave.
Coeur D'Alene 83814

ILLINOIS

Black Hawk College, Quad-Cities
6600 34th Ave.
Moline 61265

Washburne Trade School
3233 West 31st St.
Chicago 60623

IOWA

Des Moines Community College
2006 Ankeny Blvd.
Ankeny 50021

Indian Hills Community College
525 Grandview
Ottumwa 52501

Iowa Central Community College
330 Ave. M
Fort Dodge 50501

Iowa Valley Community College
P.O. Box 536
Marshalltown 50158

Northeast Iowa Community College
Hwy. 150 S, P.O. Box 400
Calmar 52132-0400

Southwestern Community College
1501 Townline
Creston 50801

Western Iowa Technical Community
College
4647 Stone Ave., P.O. Box 265
Sioux City 51102-0265

KANSAS

Hutchinson Community College
1300 North Plum St.
Hutchinson 67501

Johnson County Area Vocational-
Technical School
311 East Park
Olathe 66061

Kansas City Area Vocational Technical
School
2220 North 59th St.
Kansas City 66104

Kaw Area Vocational-Technical School
5724 Huntoon
Topeka 66604

Liberal Area Vocational Technical
School
P.O. Box 1599
Liberal 67905-1599

Manhattan Area Technical Center
3136 Dickens Ave.
Manhattan 66502

North Central Kansas Area Vocational
Technical School
Hwy. 24, P.O. Box 507
Beloit 67420

Northeast Kansas Area Vocational
Technical School
1501 West Riley St.
P.O. Box 277
Atchison 66002

Northwest Kansas Area Vocational
Technical School
P.O. Box 668
Goodland 67735

Salina Area Vocational Technical
School
2562 Scanlan Ave.
Salina 67401

Southeast Kansas Area Vocational
Technical School
Sixth and Roosevelt
Coffeyville 67337

Wichita Area Vocational Technical
School
428 South Broadway
Wichita 67202-3910

KENTUCKY

Ashland State Vocational Technical
School
4818 Roberts Dr.
Ashland 41102

Kentucky Technical-Madisonville State
Vocational Technical School
150 School Ave.
Madisonville 42431

Mayo State Vocational Technical School
Third St.
Paintsville 41240

Northern Kentucky State Vocational-
Technical School
1025 Amsterdam Rd.
Covington 41011

LOUISIANA

Alexandria Regional Technical Institute
4311 South MacArthur Dr.
Alexandria 71302-3137

Junionville Memorial Technical
Institute
P.O. Box 725
New Roads 70760

Sullivan Technical Institute
1710 Sullivan Dr.
Bogalusa 70427

West Jefferson Technical Institute
475 Manhattan Blvd.
Harvey 70058

MAINE

Eastern Maine Technical College
354 Hogan Rd.
Bangor 04401

Landing School of Boat Building and
Design
P.O. Box 1490
Kennebunkport 04046

Northern Maine Technical College
33 Edgemont Dr.
Presque Isle 04769

Southern Maine Technical College
Fort Rd.
South Portland 04106

Washington County Technical College
RR 1, P.O. Box 22C
Calais 04619

MARYLAND

Howard Community College
Little Patuxent Pkwy.
Columbia 21044

MASSACHUSETTS

North Bennet Street School
39 North Bennet St.
Boston 02113

MICHIGAN

Bay De Noc Community College
2001 North Lincoln Rd.
Escanaba 49289

Macomb Community College
14500 Twelve Mile Rd.
Warren 48093-3896

Northern Michigan University
1401 Presque Isle
Marquette 49855

MINNESOTA

Alexandria Technical College
1601 Jefferson St.
Alexandria 56308

Hennepin Technical College
1820 North Xenium Ln.
Plymouth 55441

Hutchinson-Willmar Technical College,
Willmar Campus
P.O. Box 1097
Willmar 56201

Minneapolis Technical College
1415 Hennepin Ave.
Minneapolis 55403

Minnesota Riverland Technical College,
Austin Campus
1900 Eighth Ave. NW
Austin 55912

Minnesota Riverland Technical College,
Faribault Campus
1225 Southwest Third St.
Faribault 55021

Minnesota Riverland Technical College,
Rochester Campus
1926 College View Rd. SE
Rochester 55904

Northwest Technical College,
Detroit Lakes
900 Hwy. 34 E
Detroit Lakes 56501

Northwest Technical College,
East Grand Forks
Hwy. 220 N
East Grand Forks 56721

Northwest Technical College, Moorhead
1900 28th Ave. S
Moorhead 56560

Red Wing-Winona Technical College,
Red Wing Campus
Hwy. 58 at Pioneer Rd.
Red Wing 55066

Saint Cloud Technical College
1540 Northway Dr.
Saint Cloud 56303

Saint Paul Technical College
235 Marshall Ave.
Saint Paul 55102

Southwestern Technical College,
Jackson Campus
401 West St.
Jackson 56143

Southwestern Technical College,
Pipestone Campus
P.O. Box 250
Pipestone 56164

MISSISSIPPI

East Central Community College
Decatur 39327

Hinds Community College,
Raymond Campus
Raymond 39154

MISSOURI

Macon Area Vocational School
Hwy. 63 N
Macon 63552

Ranken Technical College
4431 Finney Ave.
Saint Louis 63113

Rolla Area Vocational-Technical School
1304 East Tenth St.
Rolla 65401

Waynesville Area Vocational School
810 Roosevelt
Waynesville 65583

MONTANA

Helena Vocational-Technical Center
1115 North Roberts St.
Helena 59601

NEBRASKA

Mid Plains Community College
416 North Jeffers
North Platte 69101

NEW HAMPSHIRE

New Hampshire Technical College at
Manchester
1066 Front St.
Manchester 03102

NEW MEXICO

Albuquerque Technical-Vocational
Institute
525 Buena Vista SE
Albuquerque 87106

Crownpoint Institute of Technology
P.O. Box 849
Crownpoint 87313

NEW YORK

Mohawk Valley Community College
1101 Sherman Dr.
Utica 13501

SUNY College of Technology at Delhi
Delhi 13753

NORTH CAROLINA

Alamance Community College
P.O. Box 8000
Graham 27253

Cleveland Community College
137 South Post Rd.
Shelby 28150

Rockingham Community College
P.O. Box 38
Wentworth 27375-0038

Vance-Granville Community College
State Rd. 1126, P.O. Box 917
Henderson 27536

NORTH DAKOTA

United Tribes Technical College
3315 University Dr.
Bismarck 58501

OHIO

Eastland Career Center
4465 South Hamilton Rd.
Groveport 43125

Tri-County Vocational School
15675 SR 691
Nelsonville 45764

OKLAHOMA

Central Oklahoma Area Vocational
Technical School
Three Court Circle
Drumright 74030

Great Plains Area Vocational-Technical
School
4500 West Lee Blvd.
Lawton 73505

Kiamichi AVTS SD #7, Talihina Campus
Rte. 2 & Hwy. 63A, P.O. Box 1800
Talihina 74571

Metro Tech Vocational Technical Center
1900 Springlake Dr.
Oklahoma City 73111

Southern Oklahoma Area Vocational-
Technical Center
2610 Sam Noble Pkwy.
Ardmore 73401

PENNSYLVANIA

Bucks County Community College
Swamp Rd.
Newtown 18940

Community College of Allegheny
County
800 Allegheny Ave.
Pittsburgh 15233-1895

Pennsylvania College of Technology
One College Ave.
Williamsport 17701

Thaddeus Stevens State School of
Technology
750 East King St.
Lancaster 17602

Triangle Technical, Dubois
P.O. Box 551
Dubois 15801

RHODE ISLAND

New England Institute of Technology
2500 Post Rd.
Warwick 02886

SOUTH CAROLINA

Bob Jones University
Greenville 29614

Greenville Technical College
Station B, P.O. Box 5616
Greenville 29606-5616

SOUTH DAKOTA

Lake Area Vocational Technical
Institute
230 11th St. NE
Watertown 57201

TEXAS

Texas State Technical College,
Harlingen Campus
2424 Boxwood
Harlingen 78550-3697

UTAH

Odgen-Weber Applied Technology
Center
559 East AVC Ln.
Ogden 84404-6704

Salt Lake Community College
P.O. Box 30808
Salt Lake City 84130

Utah Valley Community College
800 West 1200 S
Orem 84058

WASHINGTON

Bates Technical College
1101 South Yakima Ave.
Tacoma 98405

Northwest School of Wooden
Boatbuilding
251 Otto St.
Port Townsend 98368

Olympic College
1600 Chester Ave.
Bremerton 98310-1699

Seattle Central Community College
1701 Broadway
Seattle 98122

Seattle Vocational Institute
315 22nd Ave. S
Seattle 98144

WEST VIRGINIA

Raleigh County Vocational-Technical
Center
410-½ Stanaford Rd.
Beckley 25801

WISCONSIN

Chippewa Valley Technical College
620 West Clairemont Ave.
Eau Claire 54701

Gateway Technical College
3520 30th Ave.
Kenosha 53144-1690

Milwaukee Area Technical College
700 West State St.
Milwaukee 53233

Northeast Wisconsin Technical College
2740 West Mason St.
P.O. Box 19042
Green Bay 54307-9042

Wisconsin Area Vocational Training
and Adult Education System District
Number Four
3550 Anderson St.
Madison 53704

Wisconsin Indianhead Technical
College
505 Pine Ridge Dr.
P.O. Box 10B
Shell Lake 54871

WYOMING

Laramie County Community College
1400 East College Dr.
Cheyenne 82007

Civil Technology

CALIFORNIA

Antelope Valley College
3041 West Ave. K
Lancaster 93534

CONNECTICUT

Connecticut Institute of Technology
Two Elizabeth St.
West Haven 06516

DELAWARE

Delaware Technical Community
College Stanton, Wilmington
400 Stanton-Christiana Rd.
Newark 19702

IDAHO

Idaho State University
741 South Seventh Ave.
Pocatello 83209

ILLINOIS

Lake Land College
5001 Lake Land Blvd.
Mattoon 61938

INDIANA

Indiana University,
Purdue University at Fort Wayne
2101 Coliseum Blvd. E
Fort Wayne 46805

Indiana University,
Purdue University Indianapolis
355 North Lansing
Indianapolis 46202

Vincennes University
1002 North First St.
Vincennes 47591

IOWA

Iowa Western Community College
2700 College Rd., P.O. Box 4C
Council Bluffs 51502

KENTUCKY

Kentucky Technical, Hazard State
Vocational Technical School
101 Vocational-Tech Dr.
Hazard 41701

Kentucky Technical, West Kentucky
State Vocational Technical School
P.O. Box 7408
Paducah 42002-7408

LOUISIANA

T H Harris Technical Institute
337 East South St., P.O. Box 713
Opelousas 70570

MAINE

University of Maine
Office of Institutional Studies
Orono 04469

MARYLAND

Catonsville Community College
800 South Rolling Rd.
Catonsville 21228

MASSACHUSETTS

Franklin Institute of Boston
41 Berkeley St.
Boston 02116

Massasoit Community College
One Massasoit Blvd.
Brockton 02402

Springfield Technical Community
College
Armory Square
Springfield 01105

Wentworth Institute of Technology
550 Huntington Ave.
Boston 02115

MICHIGAN

Alpena Community College
666 Johnson St.
Alpena 49707

Ferris State University
901 South State St.
Big Rapids 49307

Lansing Community College
419 North Capitol Ave.
Lansing 48901-7210

Michigan Technological University
1400 Townsend Dr.
Houghton 49931-1295

MINNESOTA

Duluth Technical College
2101 Trinity Rd.
Duluth 55811

Saint Paul Technical College
235 Marshall Ave.
Saint Paul 55102

MISSISSIPPI

Northeast Mississippi Community
College
Cunningham Blvd.
Booneville 38829

NEW HAMPSHIRE

University of New Hampshire,
Main Campus
Thompson Hall
Durham 03824

NEW JERSEY

Middlesex County College
155 Mill Rd., P.O. Box 3050
Edison 08818-3050

Ocean County College
College Dr.
Toms River 08753

NEW MEXICO

Albuquerque Technical-Vocational
Institute
525 Buena Vista SE
Albuquerque 87106

NEW YORK

Broome Community College
P.O. Box 1017
Binghamton 13902

CUNY New York City Technical College
300 Jay St.
Brooklyn 11201

Erie Community College,
North Campus
Main St. and Youngs Rd.
Williamsville 14221

Hudson Valley Community College
80 Vandenburgh Ave.
Troy 12180

Mohawk Valley Community College
1101 Sherman Dr.
Utica 13501

Monroe Community College
1000 East Henrietta Rd.
Rochester 14623

Nassau Community College
One Education Dr.
Garden City 11530

Paul Smith's College of Arts and
Science
New York 12970

SUNY College of Technology at Canton
Canton 13617

SUNY College of Technology at Delhi
Delhi 13753

SUNY College of Technology at
Farmingdale
Melville Rd.
Farmingdale 11735

SUNY Westchester Commmunity
College
75 Grasslands Rd.
Valhalla 10595

NORTH CAROLINA

Central Piedmont Community College
P.O. Box 35009
Charlotte 28235

Gaston College
Hwy. 321
Dallas 28034

Guilford Technical Community College
P.O. Box 309
Jamestown 27282

Wake Technical Community College
9101 Fayetteville Rd.
Raleigh 27603-5696

NORTH DAKOTA

North Dakota State College of Science
800 North Sixth St.
Wahpeton 58076

OHIO

Cincinnati Technical College
3520 Central Pkwy.
Cincinnati 45223

Columbus State Community College
550 East Spring St., P.O. Box 1609
Columbus 43216

Lakeland Community College
7700 Clocktower Dr.
Mentor 44060-7594

Sinclair Community College
444 West Third St.
Dayton 45402

Stark Technical College
6200 Frank Ave. NW
Canton 44720

University of Cincinnati, Main Campus
2624 Clifton Ave.
Cincinnati 45221-0127

University of Toledo
2801 West Bancroft
Toledo 43606

Youngstown State University
410 Wick Ave.
Youngstown 44555

OREGON

Mount Hood Community College
26000 Southeast Stark St.
Gresham 97030

Oregon Institute of Technology
3201 Campus Dr.
Klamath Falls 97601-8801

PENNSYLVANIA

Community College of Allegheny
County
800 Allegheny Ave.
Pittsburgh 15233-1895

Pennsylvania College of Technology
One College Ave.
Williamsport 17701

Pennsylvania Institute of Technology
800 Manchester Ave.
Media 19063

SOUTH CAROLINA

Central Carolina Technical College
506 North Guignard Dr.
Sumter 29150

Florence-Darlington Technical College
P.O. Box 100548
Florence 29501-0548

Horry-Georgetown Technical College
P.O. Box 1966
Conway 29526

Spartanburg Technical College
Hwy. I-85, P.O. Drawer 4386
Spartanburg 29305

Trident Technical College
P.O. Box 118067
Charleston 29423-8067

York Technical College
452 South Anderson Rd.
Rock Hill 29730

SOUTH DAKOTA

Southeast Vocational Technical Institute
2301 Career Place
Sioux Falls 57107

TENNESSEE

Nashville State Technical Institute
120 White Bridge Rd.
Nashville 37209

Pellissippi State Technical Community
College
P.O. Box 22990
Knoxville 37933-0990

State Technical Institute of Memphis
5983 Macon Cove
Memphis 38134

TEXAS

Texas State Technical College,
Waco Campus
3801 Campus Dr.
Waco 76705

VERMONT

Vermont Technical College
Randolph Center 05061

VIRGINIA

Tidewater Community College
Rte. 135
Portsmouth 23703

Wytheville Community College
1000 East Main St.
Wytheville 24382

WASHINGTON

Bates Technical College
1101 South Yakima Ave.
Tacoma 98405

Centralia College
600 West Locust St.
Centralia 98531

Spokane Community College
North 1810 Greene Ave.
Spokane 99207

Walla Walla Community College
500 Tausick Way
Walla Walla 99362

Yakima Valley Community College
P.O. Box 1647
Yakima 98907

WEST VIRGINIA

Bluefield State College
219 Rock St.
Bluefield 24701

WISCONSIN

Mid-State Technical College, Main
Campus
500 32nd St. N
Wisconsin Rapids 54494

Northeast Wisconsin Technical College
2740 West Mason St., P.O. Box 19042
Green Bay 54307-9042

Wisconsin Area Vocational Training
and Adult Education System,
Moraine Park
235 North National Ave., P.O. Box 1940
Fond Du Lac 54936-1940

Construction and Building Technology

ALASKA

Alaska Vocational-Technical Center
P.O. Box 889
Seward 99664

ARIZONA

Center for Employment Training,
Tucson
2750 South Fourth Ave.
Tucson 85713

Center for Employment Training,
Yuma
301 South Main St.
Yuma 85364

Central Arizona College
8470 North Overfield Rd.
Coolidge 85228-9778

Eastern Arizona College
Church St.
Thatcher 85552-0769

Northland Pioneer College
103 First Ave.
Holbrook 86025

Pima Community College
2202 West Anklam Rd.
Tucson 85709-0001

ARKANSAS

Arkansas Valley Technical Institute
Hwy. 23 N, P.O. Box 506
Ozark 72949

Red River Technical College
P.O. Box 140
Hope 71801

CALIFORNIA

Butte College
3536 Butte Campus Dr.
Oroville 95965

California Human Development
Corporation, Center for
Employment Training
3273 Airway Dr.
Santa Rosa 95403

Career Management Institute
1855 West Katella Ave.
Orange 92667

Center for Employment Training,
Bloomington
19059 West Valley Blvd.
Bloomington 92316

Center for Employment Training,
El Centro
380 South Third St.
El Centro 92243

Center for Employment Training,
Escondido
1131 Washington Ave. E
Escondido 92025

Center for Employment Training,
Gilroy
7800 Arroyo Circle
Gilroy 95020

Center for Employment Training, Indio
44105 Jackson St.
Indio 92201

Center for Employment Training,
Oxnard
730 South A St.
Oxnard 93030

Center for Employment Training,
Riverside
9327 Narnia Dr.
Riverside 92503

Center for Employment Training,
San Diego
3295 Market St.
San Diego 92102

Center for Employment Training,
San Francisco
180 Fair Oaks St.
San Francisco 94110

Center for Employment Training,
San Jose-McGinness
1212 McGinness Ave.
San Jose 95127

Center for Employment Training,
San Jose-Vine
701 Vine St.
San Jose 95110

Center for Employment Training,
Santa Ana
120 West Fifth St.
Santa Ana 92701

Center for Employment Training,
Santa Maria
211 West Main St.
Santa Maria 93454

Center for Employment Training,
Watsonville
24 Menker St.
Watsonville 95076

Chabot College
25555 Hesperian Blvd.
Hayward 94545

Coastline Community College
11460 Warner Ave.
Fountain Valley 92708

College of San Mateo
1700 West Hillsdale Blvd.
San Mateo 94402

Contractors License Courses
of Modesto
3300 Tully Rd.
Modesto 95350

Contractors License Institute
5777 Madison
Sacramento 95841

Cosumnes River College
8401 Center Pkwy.
Sacramento 95823-5799

Don Bosco Technical Institute
1151 San Gabriel Blvd.
Rosemead 91770-4299

Fresno City College
1101 East University Ave.
Fresno 93741

Fullerton College
321 East Chapman Ave.
Fullerton 92632-2095

Laborers Training and Retraining Fund
of Southern California
P.O. Box 391667
Anza 92539-1667

Lassen College
Hwy. 139
P.O. Box 3000
Susanville 96130

Palomar College
1140 West Mission
San Marcos 92069-1487

Pasadena City College
1570 East Colorada Blvd.
Pasadena 91106

Santa Rosa Junior College
1501 Mendocino Ave.
Santa Rosa 95401-4395

Sierra College
5000 Rocklin Rd.
Rocklin 95677

Southwestern College
900 Otay Lakes Rd.
Chula Vista 92010

COLORADO

Precision Safety and Services, Inc.
1045 Garden of the Gods Rd.
Colorado Springs 80907

San Luis Valley Area Vocational School
1011 Main St.
Alamosa 81101

DELAWARE

Wilmington Skills Center
13th and Poplar St.
Wilmington 19801

FLORIDA

Miami Lakes Technical Education
Center
5780 Northwest 158th St.
Miami Lakes 33169

Pinellas Mechanical Pipe Trade
4020 80th Ave. N
Pinellas Park 33565

Saint Augustine Technical Center
2980 Collins Ave.
Saint Augustine 32095

GEORGIA

Valdosta Technical Institute
4089 Valtech Rd.
Valdosta 31602-9796

HAWAII

Employment Training Center,
UH Community Colleges
33 South King St.
Honolulu 96813

IDAHO

Ricks College
Rexburg 83460-4107

ILLINOIS

Belleville Area College
2500 Carlyle Rd.
Belleville 62221

College of Lake County
19351 West Washington St.
Grays Lake 60030-1198

Danville Area Community College
2000 East Main St.
Danville 61832

Illinois Central College
One College Dr.
East Peoria 61635

John Wood Community College
150 South 48th St.
Quincy 62301-9147

Joliet Junior College
1216 Houbolt Ave.
Joliet 60436

Lake Land College
5001 Lake Land Blvd.
Mattoon 61938

MacMurray College
East College Ave.
Jacksonville 62650

McDowell Business Training Center
1313 South Michigan Ave.
Chicago 60605

Parkland College
2400 West Bradley Ave.
Champaign 61821

Rend Lake College
Rte. 1
Ina 62846

Rock Valley College
3301 North Mulford Rd.
Rockford 61114

Southern Illinois University,
Carbondale
Carbondale 62901

Spoon River College
RR 1
Canton 61520

Triton College
2000 Fifth Ave.
River Grove 60171

Washburne Trade School
3233 West 31st St.
Chicago 60623

INDIANA

Fort Wayne Regional Vocational School
of Continuing Education
1200 South Barr St.
Fort Wayne 46802

Vincennes University
1002 North First St.
Vincennes 47591

IOWA

Kirkwood Community College
P.O. Box 2068
Cedar Rapids 52406

Northwest Iowa Technical College
603 West Park St.
Sheldon 51201

Western Iowa Technical Community
College
4647 Stone Ave., P.O. Box 265
Sioux City 51102-0265

KANSAS

Flint Hills Technical School
3301 West 18th St.
Emporia 66801

Kansas City Area Vocational Technical
School
2220 North 59th St.
Kansas City 66104

Kaw Area Vocational-Technical School
5724 Huntoon
Topeka 66604

Salina Area Vocational Technical
School
2562 Scanlan Ave.
Salina 67401

Wichita Area Vocational Technical
School
428 South Broadway
Wichita 67202-3910

KENTUCKY

Kentucky Technical, Bowling Green
State Vocational Technical School
1845 Loop Dr.
P.O. Box 6000
Bowling Green 42101

LOUISIANA

Jefferson Technical Institute
5200 Blair Dr.
Metairie 70001

West Jefferson Technical Institute
475 Manhattan Blvd.
Harvey 70058

MAINE

Central Maine Technical College
1250 Turner St.
Auburn 04210

MARYLAND

All-State Career School
201 South Arlington Ave.
Baltimore 21223

Catonsville Community College
800 South Rolling Rd.
Catonsville 21228

MASSACHUSETTS

Dean Junior College
99 Main St.
Franklin 02038

Wentworth Institute of Technology
550 Huntington Ave.
Boston 02115

MICHIGAN

Allstate Vocational Training
15160 West Eight Mile
Oak Park 48237

Delta College
University Center 48710

Lawrence Institute of Technology
21000 Ten Mile Rd.
Southfield 48075

Macomb Community College
14500 Twelve Mile Rd.
Warren 48093-3896

NCI Associates, Ltd.
27637 John Rd.
Madison Heights 48071

MINNESOTA

Duluth Technical College
2101 Trinity Rd.
Duluth 55811

Inver Hills Community College
5445 College Trail
Inver Grove Heights 55076

Minnesota Riverland Technical College,
Rochester Campus
1926 College View Rd. SE
Rochester 55904

Northeast Metro Technical College
3300 Century Ave. N
White Bear Lake 55110

North Hennepin Community College
7411 85th Ave. N
Brooklyn Park 55445

Northwest Technical College,
Detroit Lakes
900 Hwy. 34 E
Detroit Lakes 56501

Opportunities Industrialization Center,
Twin Cities
935 Olson Memorial Hwy.
Minneapolis 55405

Range Technical College,
Hibbing Campus
2900 East Beltline
Hibbing 55746

Southwestern Technical College,
Jackson Campus
401 West St.
Jackson 56143

MISSOURI

East Central College
P.O. Box 529
Union 63084

Jefferson College
1000 Viking Dr.
Hillsboro 63050

Vattenott Educational Centers
3854 Washington St.
Saint Louis 63108

MONTANA

Missoula Vocational Technical Center
909 South Ave. W
Missoula 59801

NEBRASKA

Metropolitan Community College Area
P.O. Box 3777
Omaha 68103

Northeast Community College
801 East Benjamin
P.O. Box 469
Norfolk 68702-0469

NEW MEXICO

University of New Mexico,
    Gallup Branch
200 College Rd.
Gallup 87301

NEW YORK

CUNY College of Staten Island
2800 Victory Blvd.
Staten Island 10314

CUNY New York City Technical College
300 Jay St.
Brooklyn 11201

Erie Community College,
    City Campus
121 Ellicott St.
Buffalo 14203

Erie Community College,
    North Campus
Main St. and Youngs Rd.
Williamsville 14221

Fegs Trades and Business School
199 Jay St.
Brooklyn 11201

Fulton-Montgomery Community
    College
2805 State Hwy. 67
Johnstown 12095

Herkimer County Community College
Reservoir Rd.
Herkimer 13350-1598

Hudson Valley Community College
80 Vandenburgh Ave.
Troy 12180

Institute of Design and Construction
141 Willoughby St.
Brooklyn 11201

SUNY College of Technology &
    Agriculture at Morrisville
Morrisville 13408

SUNY College of Technology at Alfred
Alfred 14802

SUNY College of Technology at Canton
Canton 13617

SUNY College of Technology at Delhi
Delhi 13753

Technical Career Institutes
320 West 31st St.
New York 10001

Tompkins-Cortland Community
    College
170 North St.
Dryden 13053

NORTH CAROLINA

Halifax Community College
P.O. Drawer 809
Weldon 27890

NORTH DAKOTA

Little Hoop Community College
P.O. Box 269
Fort Totten 58335

OHIO

Auburn Career Center
8140 Auburn Rd.
Painesville 44077

Columbus State Community College
550 East Spring St., P.O. Box 1609
Columbus 43216

D E3, Inc.
19701 South Miles Pkwy.
Cleveland 44128-4257

Mahoning County Joint Vocational
    School District
7300 North Palmyra Rd.
Canfield 44406

Southern Hills Joint Vocational School
    District
9193 Hamer Rd.
Georgetown 45121

University of Akron, Main Campus
302 Buchtel Common
Akron 44325-4702

U.S. Grant Joint Vocational School
3046 Rte. 125
Bethel 45106

OKLAHOMA

Carl Albert State College
1507 South McKenna
Poteau 74953-5208

Central Oklahoma Area Vocational
    Technical School
Three Court Circle
Drumright 74030

Oklahoma State University, Okmulgee
1801 East Fourth St.
Okmulgee 74447-3901

Pontotoc Skill Development Center
601 West 33rd
Ada 74820

OREGON

Chemeketa Community College
P.O. Box 14007
Salem 97309-7070

PENNSYLVANIA

Community College of Allegheny
    County
800 Allegheny Ave.
Pittsburgh 15233-1895

Community College of Philadelphia
1700 Spring Garden St.
Philadelphia 19130

Dean Institute of Technology
1501 West Liberty Ave.
Pittsburgh 15226-9990

Delaware County Institute of Training
615 Ave. of the States
Chester 19013

Harrisburg Area Community College,
    Harrisburg Campus
One HACC Dr.
Harrisburg 17110

Johnson Technical Institute
3427 North Main Ave.
Scranton 18508

New Castle School of Trades
Youngstown Rd., Rte. 1
Pulaski 16143

Orleans Technical Institute
1330 Rhawn St.
Philadelphia 19111-2899

Pennsylvania College of Technology
One College Ave.
Williamsport 17701

Pennsylvania State University,
    Main Campus
201 Old Main
University Park 16802

PTC Career Institute
40 North Second St.
Philadelphia 19106

SOUTH CAROLINA

Piedmont Technical College
P.O. Drawer 1467
Greenwood 29648

Technical College of the Low Country
100 South Ribaut Rd.
Beaufort 29902

SOUTH DAKOTA

Southeast Vocational Technical
    Institute
2301 Career Place
Sioux Falls 57107

Western Dakota Vocational Technical
    Institute
1600 Sedivy
Rapid City 57701

TENNESSEE

Elizabethton State Area Vocational
    Technical School
1500 Arney St.
    P.O. Box 789
Elizabethton 37643

Oneida State Area Vocational Technical
    School
120 Eli Ln.
Oneida 37841

TEXAS

Blinn College
902 College Ave.
Brenham 77833

Odessa College
201 West University
Odessa 79764

San Antonio Training Division
9350 South Presa
San Antonio 78223-4799

Texas State Technical College,
    Waco Campus
3801 Campus Dr.
Waco 76705

UTAH

Bridgerland Applied Technology Center
1301 North 600 W
Logan 84321

VERMONT

Vermont Technical College
Randolph Center 05061

VIRGINIA

Industrial Training Company
511 West Grace St.
Richmond 23220

WASHINGTON

Bates Technical College
1101 South Yakima Ave.
Tacoma 98405

Bellingham Technical College
3028 Lindbergh Ave.
Bellingham 98225

Lake Washington Technical College
11605 132nd Ave. NE
Kirkland 98034

Lower Columbia College
P.O. Box 3010
Longview 98632

Peninsula College
1502 East Lauridsen Blvd.
Port Angeles 98362

Spokane Community College
North 1810 Greene Ave.
Spokane 99207

WEST VIRGINIA

Roane-Jackson Technical Center
4800 Spencer Rd.
Leroy 25252-9700

WISCONSIN

Good Armstrong and Associates, Ltd.
2142 South 55th St.
Milwaukee 53219

North Central Technical College
1000 Campus Dr.
Wausau 54401-1899

Wisconsin Area Vocational Training
    and Adult Education System District
    Number Four
3550 Anderson St.
Madison 53704

Wisconsin Indianhead Technical
    College
505 Pine Ridge Dr.
    P.O. Box 10B
Shell Lake 54871

Construction Equipment Maintenance and Operation

ALABAMA

Alabama Aviation and Technical
    College
P.O. Box 1209
Ozark 36361

Community College of the Air Force
Maxwell Air Force Base
Montgomery 36112

Douglas MacArthur Technical College
P.O. Box 649
Opp 36467

J F Ingram State Technical College
P.O. Box 209
Deatsville 36022

ALASKA

Alaska Vocational-Technical Center
P.O. Box 889
Seward 99664

University of Alaska, Anchorage
3211 Providence Dr.
Anchorage 99508

ARIZONA

Central Arizona College
8470 North Overfield Rd.
Coolidge 85228-9778

Cochise College
4190 West Hwy. 80
Douglas 85607-9724

Universal Technical Institute, Inc.
3121 West Weldon Ave.
Phoenix 85017

ARKANSAS

Crowley's Ridge Technical School
P.O. Box 925
Forrest City 72335

Gateway Technical College
P.O. Box 3350
Batesville 72503

Northwest Technical Institute
P.O. Box A
Springdale 72765

Ozarka Technical College
218 South Dr.,
P.O. Box 10
Melbourne 72556-0010

Phillips County Community College
P.O. Box 785
Helena 72342

Pulaski Technical College
3000 West Scenic Dr.
North Little Rock 72118

Red River Technical College
P.O. Box 140
Hope 71801

Westark Community College
P.O. Box 3649
Fort Smith 72913

CALIFORNIA

College of San Mateo
1700 West Hillsdale Blvd.
San Mateo 94402

Institute of Industrial Sewing Machine
Engineering and Mechanical
Training
11128 Balboa Blvd.
Granada Hills 91344

Los Angeles Training Technical College
400 West Washington Blvd.
Los Angeles 90015-4181

Solano County Community College
District
4000 Suisun Valley Rd.
Suisun 94585

COLORADO

Denver Automotive & Diesel College
460 South Lipan St.
Denver 80223-9366

Pueblo College of Business &
Technology
330 Lake Ave.
Pueblo 81004

San Juan Basin Area Vocational School
P.O. Box 970
Cortez 81321

San Luis Valley Area Vocational School
1011 Main St.
Alamosa 81101

T H Pickens Technical Center
500 Buckley Rd.
Aurora 80011

DELAWARE

Delaware Technical and Community
College, Southern Campus
P.O. Box 610
Georgetown 19947

FLORIDA

Broward Community College
225 East Las Olas Blvd.
Fort Lauderdale 33301

Lee County Vocational-Technical
Center
3800 Michigan Ave.
Fort Myers 33916

Miami Lakes Technical Education
Center
5780 Northwest 158th St.
Miami Lakes 33169

Pensacola Junior College
1000 College Blvd.
Pensacola 32504

Pinellas Technical Education Center,
Clearwater Campus
6100 154th Ave. N
Clearwater 34620

Saint Augustine Technical Center
2980 Collins Ave.
Saint Augustine 32095

Washington-Holmes Area Vocational-
Technical Center
209 Hoyt St.
Chipley 32428

GEORGIA

Atlanta Area Technical School
1560 Stewart Ave. SW
Atlanta 30310

Augusta Technical Institute
3116 Deans Bridge Rd.
Augusta 30906

Ben Hill-Irwin Technical Institute
P.O. Box 1069
Fitzgerald 31750

Carroll Technical Institute
997 South Hwy. 16
Carrollton 30117

Columbus Technical Institute
928 45th St.
Columbus 31904-6572

Coosa Valley Technical Institute
112 Hemlock St.
Rome 30161

Heart of Georgia Technical Institute
Rte. 5, P.O. Box 136
Dublin 31021

Lanier Technical Institute
P.O. Box 58
Oakwood 30566

Pickens Technical Institute
100 Pickens Tech Dr.
Jasper 30143

Savannah Technical Institute
5717 White Bluff Rd.
Savannah 31499

West Georgia Technical Institute
303 Fort Dr.
La Grange 30240

HAWAII

Honolulu Community College
874 Dillingham Blvd.
Honolulu 96817

IDAHO

Boise State University
1910 University Dr.
Boise 83725

North Idaho College
1000 West Garden Ave.
Coeur D'Alene 83814

ILLINOIS

John A Logan College
Carterville 62918

Rend Lake College
Rte. 1
Ina 62846

Triton College
2000 Fifth Ave.
River Grove 60171

Universal Technical Institute, Inc.
601 Regency Dr.
Glendale Heights 60139

INDIANA

Indiana Vocational Technical College,
Northwest
1440 East 35th Ave.
Gary 46409

Indiana Vocational Technical College,
South Central
8204 Hwy. 311
Sellersburg 47172

Indiana Vocational Technical College,
Southwest
3501 First Ave.
Evansville 47710

Indiana Vocational Technical College,
Wabash Valley
7999 U.S. Hwy. 41
Terre Haute 47802-4898

IOWA

Hawkeye Institute of Technology
1501 East Orange Rd.
Waterloo 50704

Northwest Iowa Technical College
603 West Park St.
Sheldon 51201

KANSAS

Kansas State University of Agriculture
and Applied Science
Anderson Hall
Manhattan 66506

North Central Kansas Area Vocational
Technical School
Hwy. 24, P.O. Box 507
Beloit 67420

KENTUCKY

Kentucky Technical, Bowling Green
State Vocational Technical School
1845 Loop Dr.
P.O. Box 6000
Bowling Green 42101

Kentucky Technical, Hazard State
Vocational Technical School
101 Vocational-Tech Dr.
Hazard 41701

Mayo State Vocational Technical School
Third St.
Paintsville 41240

LOUISIANA

Delta-Ouachita Regional-Technical
Institute
609 Vocational Pkwy.
West Monroe 71291

MAINE

Eastern Maine Technical College
354 Hogan Rd.
Bangor 04401

Northern Maine Technical College
33 Edgemont Dr.
Presque Isle 04769

Washington County Technical College
RR 1
P.O. Box 22C
Calais 04619

MARYLAND

Dundalk Community College
7200 Sollers Point Rd.
Dundalk 21222

MICHIGAN

Henry Ford Community College
5101 Evergreen Rd.
Dearborn 48128

Michigan Institute of Aeronautics
Willow Run Airport East Side
47884 D St.
Belleville 48111

Ram Technical Institute, Inc.
21700 Greenfield
Oak Park 48237

MINNESOTA

Albert Lea-Mankato Technical College
2200 Tech Dr.
Albert Lea 56007

Brainerd-Staples Technical College,
Staples Campus
1830 Airport Rd.
Staples 56479

Dakota County Technical College
1300 East 145th St.
Rosemount 55068

Inver Hills Community College
5445 College Trail
Inver Grove Heights 55076

North Hennepin Community College
7411 85th Ave. N
Brooklyn Park 55445

Northwest Technical College,
East Grand Forks
Hwy. 220 N
East Grand Forks 56721

Saint Paul Technical College
235 Marshall Ave.
Saint Paul 55102

Southwestern Technical College,
Canby Campus
1011 First St. W
Canby 56220

MISSISSIPPI

Copiah-Lincoln Junior College
P.O. Box 457
Wesson 39191

Jones County Junior College
Front St.
Ellisville 39437

Northwest Mississippi Community
College
Hwy. 51 N
Senatobia 38668

MISSOURI

Linn Technical College
One Technology Dr.
Linn 65051

Maple Woods Community College
2601 Northeast Barry Rd.
Kansas City 64156

MONTANA

Missoula Vocational Technical Center
909 South Ave. W
Missoula 59801

NEBRASKA

Central Community College,
Grand Island
P.O. Box 4903
Grand Island 68802

Western Nebraska Community College
1601 East 27th St. NE
Scottsbluff 69361-1899

NEW HAMPSHIRE

New Hampshire Technical College at
Laconia
Prescott Hill Rte. 106
Laconia 03246

NEW YORK

Mahanna Career Institute
1821 Broad St.
Utica 13501

NORTH CAROLINA

Alamance Community College
P.O. Box 8000
Graham 27253

Brunswick Community College
P.O. Box 30
Supply 28462

Central Carolina Community College
1105 Kelly Dr.
Sanford 27330

Davidson County Community College
P.O. Box 1287
Lexington 27293

Halifax Community College
P.O. Drawer 809
Weldon 27890

Pitt Community College
Hwy. 11 S, P.O. Drawer 7007
Greenville 27835-7007

Richmond Community College
P.O. Box 1189
Hamlet 28345

Rockingham Community College
P.O. Box 38
Wentworth 27375-0038

Southeastern Community College
P.O. Box 151
Whiteville 28472

Wilkes Community College
Collegiate Dr.
Wilkesboro 28697

Wilson Technical Community College
902 Herring Ave.
Wilson 27893

OHIO

Akron Adult Vocational Services
147 Park St.
Akron 44308

Butler County JVS District, D Russel
Lee Career Center
3603 Hamilton Middletown Rd.
Hamilton 45011

Eastland Career Center
4465 South Hamilton Rd.
Groveport 43125

Gallia Jackson Vinton JUSD
P.O. Box 157
Rio Grande 45674

Ohio Diesel Technical Institute,
Ohio Auto Diesel Technical
1421 East 49th St.
Cleveland 44103

Pickaway Ross Joint Vocational School
District
895 Crouse Chapel Rd.
Chillicothe 45601-9010

Pioneer Joint Vocational School
District
27 Ryan Rd., P.O. Box 309
Shelby 44875

Tri-County Vocational School
15675 SR 691
Nelsonville 45764

OREGON

Lane Community College
4000 East 30th Ave.
Eugene 97405

West Coast Training, Inc.
P.O. Box 22469
Milwaukie 97222

PENNSYLVANIA

Machine Shop Technologies Institute,
Inc.
110 South Main St. West End
Pittsburgh 15220

National Education Center,
Vale Technical Institute Campus
135 West Market St.
Blairsville 15717

Pennco Technical
3815 Otter St.
Bristol 19007

Pennsylvania College of Technology
One College Ave.
Williamsport 17701

SOUTH CAROLINA

Aiken Technical College
P.O. Drawer 696
Aiken 29802

Greenville Technical College
Station B, P.O. Box 5616
Greenville 29606-5616

Spartanburg Technical College
Hwy. I-85, P.O. Drawer 4386
Spartanburg 29305

Trident Technical College
P.O. Box 118067
Charleston 29423-8067

York Technical College
452 South Anderson Rd.
Rock Hill 29730

TENNESSEE

Chattanooga State Technical
Community College
4501 Amnicola Hwy.
Chattanooga 37406

Covington State Area Vocational
Technical School
P.O. Box 249
Covington 38019

Crossville State Area Vocational
Technical School
P.O. Box 2959
Crossville 38557

Dickson State Area Vocational-
Technical School
740 Hwy. 46
Dickson 37055

Hohenwald State Area Vocational-
Technical School
813 West Main
Hohenwald 38462-2201

Jackson State Area Vocational
Technical School
McKellar Airport
Jackson 38301

Livingston State Area Vocational-
Technical School
P.O. Box 219
Livingston 38570

Memphis Area Vocational-Technical
School
550 Alabama Ave.
Memphis 38105-3799

Murfreesboro Area Vocational
Technical School
1303 Old Fort Pkwy.
Murfreesboro 37129

Newbern State Area Vocational-
Technical School
Hwy. 51 N
Newbern 38059

Northeast State Technical Community
College
P.O. Box 246
Blountville 37617

Paris State Area Vocational-Technical
School
312 South Wilson St.
Paris 38242

Shelbyville State Area Vocational
Technical School
1405 Madison St.
Shelbyville 37160

State Technical Institute of Memphis
5983 Macon Cove
Memphis 38134

TEXAS

Dalfort Aircraft Technical
7701 Lemmon Ave.
Dallas 75209

Texas Aero Tech
6911 Lemmon Ave.
Dallas 75209

Texas State Technical College,
Waco Campus
3801 Campus Dr.
Waco 76705

Universal Technical Institute, Inc.
721 Lockhaven Dr.
Houston 77073

Wharton County Junior College
911 Boling Hwy.
Wharton 77488

UTAH

Bridgerland Applied Technology Center
1301 North 600 W
Logan 84321

Davis Applied Technology Center
550 East 300 S
Kaysville 84037

VIRGINIA

Commonwealth College
4160 Virginia Beach Blvd.
Virginia Beach 23452

Danville Community College
1008 South Main St.
Danville 24541

J Sargeant Reynolds Community
College
P.O. Box 85622
Richmond 23285-5622

Northern Virginia Community College
4001 Wakefield Chapel Rd.
Annandale 22003

Thomas Nelson Community College
P.O. Box 9407
Hampton 23670

Tidewater Community College
Rte. 135
Portsmouth 23703

WASHINGTON

Lake Washington Technical College
11605 132nd Ave. NE
Kirkland 98034

Seattle Community College,
South Campus
6000 16th Ave. SW
Seattle 98106

Spokane Community College
North 1810 Greene Ave.
Spokane 99207

Spokane Falls Community College
West 3410 Fort George Wright Dr.
Spokane 99204

WISCONSIN

Chippewa Valley Technical College
620 West Clairemont Ave.
Eau Claire 54701

Gateway Technical College
3520 30th Ave.
Kenosha 53144-1690

North Central Technical College
1000 Campus Dr.
Wausau 54401-1899

Northeast Wisconsin Technical College
2740 West Mason St.
P.O. Box 19042
Green Bay 54307-9042

Wisconsin Area Vocational Training
and Adult Education System,
Moraine Park
235 North National Ave.
P.O. Box 1940
Fond Du Lac 54936-1940

WYOMING

Career Development Center
525 West Lakeway
Gillette 82716

Laramie County Community College
1400 East College Dr.
Cheyenne 82007

Western Wyoming Community College
P.O. Box 428
Rock Springs 82902

Electricity

ALABAMA

Chauncey Sparks State Technical
College
P.O. Drawer 580
Eufaula 36027

Gadsden State Community College
P.O. Box 227
Gadsden 35902-0227

G C Wallace State Community College
P.O. Drawer 1049
Selma 36702-1049

J F Ingram State Technical College
P.O. Box 209
Deatsville 36022

Lawson State Community College
3060 Wilson Rd. SW
Birmingham 35221

Opelika State Technical College
P.O. Box 2268
Opelika 36803-2268

ARIZONA

Refrigeration School
4210 East Washington
Phoenix 85034

ARKANSAS

Arkansas Valley Technical Institute
Hwy. 23 N
P.O. Box 506
Ozark 72949

Northwest Technical Institute
P.O. Box A
Springdale 72765

CALIFORNIA

College of the Redwoods
7351 Tompkins Hill Rd.
Eureka 95501-9302

Educorp Career College
230 East Third St.
Long Beach 90802

Los Angeles Training Technical
College
400 West Washington Blvd.
Los Angeles 90015-4181

San Joaquin Delta College
5151 Pacific Ave.
Stockton 95207

COLORADO

Mesa State College
P.O. Box 2647
Grand Junction 81502

CONNECTICUT

New England Technical Institute of
Connecticut, Inc.
200 John Downey Dr.
New Britain 06051

FLORIDA

Atlantic Vocational Technical Center
4700 Coconut Creek Pkwy.
Coconut Creek 33063

Central Florida Community College
P.O. Box 1388
Ocala 34478

Charlotte Vocational-Technical Center
18300 Toledo Blade Blvd.
Port Charlotte 33948-3399

Florida Community College at
 Jacksonville
501 West State St.
Jacksonville 32202

Garces Commercial College
5385 Northwest 36th St.
Miami Springs 33166

Manatee Vocational-Technical Center
5603 34th St. W
Bradenton 34210

North Technical Education Center
7071 Garden Rd.
Riviera Beach 33404

Sarasota County Technical Institute
4748 Beneva Rd.
Sarasota 34233-1798

Washington-Holmes Area Vocational-
 Technical Center
209 Hoyt St.
Chipley 32428

GEORGIA

Albany Technical Institute
1021 Lowe Rd.
Albany 31708

Atlanta Area Technical School
1560 Stewart Ave. SW
Atlanta 30310

Augusta Technical Institute
3116 Deans Bridge Rd.
Augusta 30906

Bainbridge College
Hwy. 84 E
Bainbridge 31717

Chattahoochee Technical Institute
980 South Cobb Dr.
Marietta 30060-3398

Coosa Valley Technical Institute
112 Hemlock St.
Rome 30161

Lanier Technical Institute
P.O. Box 58
Oakwood 30566

Macon Technical Institute
3300 Macon Tech Dr.
Macon 31206

North Georgia Technical Institute
Georgia Hwy. 197
P.O. Box 65
Clarkesville 30523

Savannah Technical Institute
5717 White Bluff Rd.
Savannah 31499

Swainsboro Technical Institute
201 Kite Rd.
Swainsboro 30401

HAWAII

Hawaii Community College
200 West Kawili St.
Hilo 96720-4091

Honolulu Community College
874 Dillingham Blvd.
Honolulu 96817

IDAHO

Boise State University
1910 University Dr.
Boise 83725

Idaho State University
741 South Seventh Ave.
Pocatello 83209

ILLINOIS

Belleville Area College
2500 Carlyle Rd.
Belleville 62221

Illinois Eastern Community Colleges,
 Olney Central College
RR 3
Olney 62450

Prairie State College
202 Halsted St.
Chicago Heights 60411

IOWA

Northeast Iowa Community College
Hwy. 150 S
P.O. Box 400
Calmar 52132-0400

Northwest Iowa Technical College
603 West Park St.
Sheldon 51201

Western Iowa Technical Community
 College
4647 Stone Ave., P.O. Box 265
Sioux City 51102-0265

KANSAS

Kaw Area Vocational-Technical School
5724 Huntoon
Topeka 66604

Manhattan Area Technical Center
3136 Dickens Ave.
Manhattan 66502

North Central Kansas Area Vocational
 Technical School
Hwy. 24, P.O. Box 507
Beloit 67420

Northeast Kansas Area Vocational
 Technical School
1501 West Riley St., P.O. Box 277
Atchison 66002

Southeast Kansas Area Vocational
 Technical School
Sixth and Roosevelt
Coffeyville 67337

Wichita Area Vocational Technical
 School
428 South Broadway
Wichita 67202-3910

KENTUCKY

Ashland State Vocational Technical
 School
4818 Roberts Dr.
Ashland 41102

Kentucky Department for Adult &
 Technical Education,
 Central Kentucky SVTS
104 Vo Tech Rd.
Lexington 40510

Kentucky Technical, Bowling Green
 State Vocational Technical School
1845 Loop Dr., P.O. Box 6000
Bowling Green 42101

Kentucky Technical, Rowan State
 Vocational Technical School
100 Vocational-Tech Dr.
Morehead 40351

Mayo State Vocational Technical School
Third St.
Paintsville 41240

LOUISIANA

Alexandria Regional Technical Institute
4311 South MacArthur Dr.
Alexandria 71302-3137

Delgado Community College
615 City Park Ave.
New Orleans 70119

Delta School of Business and
 Technology
517 Broad St.
Lake Charles 70601

ITI Technical College
13944 Airline Hwy.
Baton Rouge 70817

Shreveport-Bossier Regional Technical
 Institute
2010 North Market St., P.O. Box 78527
Shreveport 71137-8527

West Jefferson Technical Institute
475 Manhattan Blvd.
Harvey 70058

MAINE

Kennebec Valley Technical College
92 Western Ave.
Fairfield 04937-1367

Northern Maine Technical College
33 Edgemont Dr.
Presque Isle 04769

Southern Maine Technical College
Fort Rd.
South Portland 04106

Washington County Technical College
RR 1, P.O. Box 22C
Calais 04619

MASSACHUSETTS

Franklin Institute of Boston
41 Berkeley St.
Boston 02116

Mount Ida College
777 Dedham St.
Newton Centre 02159

Woburn Electrical School of Code and
 Theory
P.O. Box 1127
Groton 01450

MICHIGAN

Air-Con Technical Institute K & M
 Travel Corp
527 Executive Dr.
Troy 48075

Alpena Community College
666 Johnson St.
Alpena 49707

Kellogg Community College
450 North Ave.
Battle Creek 49017

MINNESOTA

Albert Lea-Mankato Technical College
2200 Tech Dr.
Albert Lea 56007

Dakota County Technical College
1300 East 145th St.
Rosemount 55068

Minneapolis Technical College
1415 Hennepin Ave.
Minneapolis 55403

Northwest Technical College, Moorhead
1900 28th Ave. S
Moorhead 56560

Northwest Technical College, Wadena
405 Southwest Colfax Ave., P.O. Box 566
Wadena 56482

Range Technical College,
 Hibbing Campus
2900 East Beltline
Hibbing 55746

Saint Cloud Technical College
1540 Northway Dr.
Saint Cloud 56303

Saint Paul Technical College
235 Marshall Ave.
Saint Paul 55102

Southwestern Technical College,
 Canby Campus
1011 First St. W
Canby 56220

Southwestern Technical College,
 Jackson Campus
401 West St.
Jackson 56143

MISSISSIPPI

East Central Community College
Decatur 39327

East Mississippi Community College
P.O. Box 158
Scooba 39358

Hinds Community College,
 Raymond Campus
Raymond 39154

Mississippi Delta Community College
P.O. Box 668
Moorhead 38761

Mississippi Gulf Coast Community
 College
Central Office
P.O. Box 67
Perkinston 39573

Pearl River Community College
Station A
Poplarville 39470

Southwest Mississippi Community
 College
College Dr.
Summit 39666

MISSOURI

Vattenott College
3925 Industrial Dr.
Saint Ann 63074

Waynesville Area Vocational School
810 Roosevelt
Waynesville 65583

NEBRASKA

Central Community College,
 Grand Island
P.O. Box 4903
Grand Island 68802

Mid Plains Community College
416 North Jeffers
North Platte 69101

Northeast Community College
801 East Benjamin
P.O. Box 469
Norfolk 68702-0469

NEW HAMPSHIRE

New Hampshire Technical College at
 Laconia
Prescott Hill Rte. 106
Laconia 03246

NEW JERSEY

Hudson County Area Vocational
 Technical School,
 North Hudson Center
8511 Tonnelle Ave.
North Bergen 07047

NEW MEXICO

Albuquerque Technical-Vocational
 Institute
525 Buena Vista SE
Albuquerque 87106

Crownpoint Institute of Technology
P.O. Box 849
Crownpoint 87313

Northern New Mexico Community
 College
1002 North Onate St.
Espanola 87532

NEW YORK

Berk Trade and Business School
311 West 35th St.
New York 10001

Hudson Valley Community College
80 Vandenburgh Ave.
Troy 12180

Monroe Community College
1000 East Henrietta Rd.
Rochester 14623

SUNY College of Technology at Alfred
Alfred 14802

SUNY College of Technology at Canton
Canton 13617

SUNY College of Technology at Delhi
Delhi 13753

NORTH CAROLINA

Cape Fear Community College
411 North Front St.
Wilmington 28401

Central Carolina Community College
1105 Kelly Dr.
Sanford 27330

Cleveland Community College
137 South Post Rd.
Shelby 28150

Coastal Carolina Community College
444 Western Blvd.
Jacksonville 28546-6877

College of the Albemarle
1208 North Road St., P.O. Box 2327
Elizabeth City 27906-2327

Forsyth Technical Community College
2100 Silas Creek Pkwy.
Winston-Salem 27103

Gaston College
Hwy. 321
Dallas 28034

Guilford Technical Community College
P.O. Box 309
Jamestown 27282

Haywood Community College
Freedlander Dr.
Clyde 28721

Isothermal Community College
P.O. Box 804
Spindale 28160

Johnston Community College
P.O. Box 2350
Smithfield 27577-2350

Martin Community College
Kehukee Park Rd.
Williamston 27892-9988

Mitchell Community College
500 West Broad
Statesville 28677

Pitt Community College
Hwy. 11 S, P.O. Drawer 7007
Greenville 27835-7007

Randolph Community College
P.O. Box 1009
Asheboro 27204

Richmond Community College
P.O. Box 1189
Hamlet 28345

Rockingham Community College
P.O. Box 38
Wentworth 27375-0038

Rowan-Cabarrus Community College
P.O. Box 1595
Salisbury 28145-1595

Surry Community College
South Main St.
Dobson 27017-0304

Wake Technical Community College
9101 Fayetteville Rd.
Raleigh 27603-5696

Wilson Technical Community College
902 Herring Ave.
Wilson 27893

NORTH DAKOTA

Bismarck State College
1500 Edwards Ave.
Bismarck 58501

OHIO

Owens Technical College
30335 Oregon Rd.
P.O. Box 10000
Toledo 43699-1947

Scioto County Joint Vocational School
District
Rte. 2 and Houston Hollow Rd.
Lucasville 45648

Tri-County Vocational School
15675 SR 691
Nelsonville 45764

OKLAHOMA

Metro Tech Vocational Technical Center
1900 Springlake Dr.
Oklahoma City 73111

PENNSYLVANIA

Dean Institute of Technology
1501 West Liberty Ave.
Pittsburgh 15226-9990

Eastern Montgomery County Area
Vocational Technical School
3075 Terwood Rd.
Willow Grove 19090

Luzerne County Community College
1333 South Prospect St.
Nanticoke 18634

Orleans Technical Institute
1330 Rhawn St.
Philadelphia 19111-2899

Pennsylvania College of Technology
One College Ave.
Williamsport 17701

Triangle Technical, Dubois
P.O. Box 551
Dubois 15801

Triangle Technical School, Inc.
1940 Perrysville Ave.
Pittsburgh 15214

SOUTH DAKOTA

Mitchell Vocational-Technical School
821 North Capital St.
Mitchell 57301

Western Dakota Vocational Technical
Institute
1600 Sedivy
Rapid City 57701

TENNESSEE

Knoxville State Area Vocational-
Technical School
1100 Liberty St.
Knoxville 37919

McKenzie State Area Vocational
Technical School
Highland Dr. N
P.O. Box 427 905
McKenzie 38201

Nashville State Area Vocational
Technical School
100 White Bridge Rd.
Nashville 37209

Nashville State Technical Institute
120 White Bridge Rd.
Nashville 37209

TEXAS

Brazosport College
500 College Dr.
Lake Jackson 77566

Saint Philips College
2111 Nevada St.
San Antonio 78203

San Antonio Trades School
120 Playmoor St.
San Antonio 78210

San Jacinto College, Central Campus
8060 Spencer Hwy.
Pasadena 77505

Texarkana College
2500 North Robison Rd.
Texarkana 75501

Texas State Technical College,
Waco Campus
3801 Campus Dr.
Waco 76705

Texas Vocational School, Pharr
P.O. Box 791
Pharr 78577

UTAH

Bridgerland Applied Technology Center
1301 North 600 W
Logan 84321

Salt Lake Community College
P.O. Box 30808
Salt Lake City 84130

VIRGINIA

Apprentice School Newport News
Shipbuilding
4101 Washington Ave.
Newport News 23607

Southside Training Skill Center,
Nottoway County
P.O. Box 258
Crewe 23930

WASHINGTON

Bellingham Technical College
3028 Lindbergh Ave.
Bellingham 98225

WEST VIRGINIA

James Rumsey Vocational Technical
Center
Rte. 6
P.O. Box 268
Martinsburg 25401

WISCONSIN

Chippewa Valley Technical College
620 West Clairemont Ave.
Eau Claire 54701

Milwaukee Area Technical College
700 West State St.
Milwaukee 53233

Northeast Wisconsin Technical College
2740 West Mason St., P.O. Box 19042
Green Bay 54307-9042

Wisconsin Area Vocational Training
and Adult Education System,
Moraine Park
235 North National Ave.
P.O. Box 1940
Fond Du Lac 54936-1940

Glazing

ARKANSAS

Arkansas Valley Technical Institute
Hwy. 23 N, P.O. Box 506
Ozark 72949

Red River Technical College
P.O. Box 140
Hope 71801

CALIFORNIA

Career Management Institute
1855 West Katella Ave.
Orange 92667

Contractors License Courses of Modesto
3300 Tully Rd.
Modesto 95350

Contractors License Institute
5777 Madison
Sacramento 95841

Laborers Training and Retraining Fund
of Southern California
P.O. Box 391667
Anza 92539-1667

COLORADO

Precision Safety and Services, Inc.
1045 Garden of the Gods Rd.
Colorado Springs 80907

San Luis Valley Area Vocational School
1011 Main St.
Alamosa 81101

DELAWARE

Wilmington Skills Center
13th and Poplar St.
Wilmington 19801

FLORIDA

Miami Lakes Technical Education
Center
5780 Northwest 158th St.
Miami Lakes 33169

Pinellas Mechanical Pipe Trade
4020 80th Ave. N
Pinellas Park 33565

ILLINOIS

Belleville Area College
2500 Carlyle Rd.
Belleville 62221

College of Lake County
19351 West Washington St.
Grays Lake 60030-1198

Danville Area Community College
2000 East Main St.
Danville 61832

Illinois Central College
One College Dr.
East Peoria 61635

John Wood Community College
150 South 48th St.
Quincy 62301-9147

Joliet Junior College
1216 Houbolt Ave.
Joliet 60436

McDowell Business Training Center
1313 South Michigan Ave.
Chicago 60605

Parkland College
2400 West Bradley Ave.
Champaign 61821

Rock Valley College
3301 North Mulford Rd.
Rockford 61114

Triton College
2000 Fifth Ave.
River Grove 60171

MASSACHUSETTS

Dean Junior College
99 Main St.
Franklin 02038

MICHIGAN

Delta College
University Center 48710

Macomb Community College
14500 Twelve Mile Rd.
Warren 48093-3896

NCI Associates, Ltd.
27637 John Rd.
Madison Heights 48071

MINNESOTA

Opportunities Industrialization Center,
Twin Cities
935 Olson Memorial Hwy.
Minneapolis 55405

NEW YORK

Erie Community College,
North Campus
Main St. and Youngs Rd.
Williamsville 14221

Fulton-Montgomery Community
College
2805 State Hwy. 67
Johnstown 12095

Herkimer County Community College
Reservoir Rd.
Herkimer 13350-1598

Hudson Valley Community College
80 Vandenburgh Ave.
Troy 12180

SUNY College of Technology &
Agriculture at Morrisville
Morrisville 13408

SUNY College of Technology at Alfred
Alfred 14802

SUNY College of Technology at Canton
Canton 13617

SUNY College of Technology at Delhi
Delhi 13753

Tompkins-Cortland Community
College
170 North St.
Dryden 13053

OHIO

D E3, Inc.
19701 South Miles Pkwy.
Cleveland 44128-4257

OKLAHOMA

Oklahoma State University, Okmulgee
1801 East Fourth St.
Okmulgee 74447-3901

Pontotoc Skill Development Center
601 West 33rd
Ada 74820

PENNSYLVANIA

Community College of Allegheny
County
800 Allegheny Ave.
Pittsburgh 15233-1895

Orleans Technical Institute
1330 Rhawn St.
Philadelphia 19111-2899

SOUTH DAKOTA

Southeast Vocational Technical
Institute
2301 Career Place
Sioux Falls 57107

TENNESSEE

Elizabethton State Area Vocational
Technical School
1500 Arney St.
P.O. Box 789
Elizabethton 37643

Oneida State Area Vocational Technical
School
120 Eli Ln.
Oneida 37841

TEXAS

Blinn College
902 College Ave.
Brenham 77833

UTAH

Bridgerland Applied Technology Center
1301 North 600 W
Logan 84321

VERMONT

Vermont Technical College
Randolph Center 05061

VIRGINIA

Industrial Training Company
511 West Grace St.
Richmond 23220

WISCONSIN

Good Armstrong and Associates, Ltd.
2142 South 55th St.
Milwaukee 53219

North Central Technical College
1000 Campus Dr.
Wausau 54401-1899

Masonry

ALABAMA

Atmore State Technical College
P.O. Box 1119
Atmore 36504

Chauncey Sparks State Technical
College
P.O. Drawer 580
Eufaula 36027

J F Ingram State Technical College
P.O. Box 209
Deatsville 36022

ARIZONA

Central Arizona College
8470 North Overfield Rd.
Coolidge 85228-9778

ARKANSAS

Arkansas Valley Technical Institute
Hwy. 23 N, P.O. Box 506
Ozark 72949

Red River Technical College
P.O. Box 140
Hope 71801

CALIFORNIA

Career Management Institute
1855 West Katella Ave.
Orange 92667

Contractors License Courses of Modesto
3300 Tully Rd.
Modesto 95350

Contractors License Institute
5777 Madison
Sacramento 95841

Laborers Training and Retraining Fund
of Southern California
P.O. Box 391667
Anza 92539-1667

COLORADO

Precision Safety and Services, Inc.
1045 Garden of the Gods Rd.
Colorado Springs 80907

San Luis Valley Area Vocational School
1011 Main St.
Alamosa 81101

DELAWARE

Wilmington Skills Center
13th and Poplar St.
Wilmington 19801

FLORIDA

Miami Lakes Technical Education
Center
5780 Northwest 158th St.
Miami Lakes 33169

Pinellas Mechanical Pipe Trade
4020 80th Ave. N
Pinellas Park 33565

Saint Augustine Technical Center
2980 Collins Ave.
Saint Augustine 32095

ILLINOIS

Belleville Area College
2500 Carlyle Rd.
Belleville 62221

College of Lake County
19351 West Washington St.
Grays Lake 60030-1198

Danville Area Community College
2000 East Main St.
Danville 61832

Illinois Central College
One College Dr.
East Peoria 61635

John Wood Community College
150 South 48th St.
Quincy 62301-9147

Joliet Junior College
1216 Houbolt Ave.
Joliet 60436

McDowell Business Training Center
1313 South Michigan Ave.
Chicago 60605

Parkland College
2400 West Bradley Ave.
Champaign 61821

Rock Valley College
3301 North Mulford Rd.
Rockford 61114

Triton College
2000 Fifth Ave.
River Grove 60171

KANSAS

North Central Kansas Area Vocational
Technical School
Hwy. 24
P.O. Box 507
Beloit 67420

KENTUCKY

Kentucky Technical, Bowling Green
State Vocational Technical School
1845 Loop Dr.
P.O. Box 6000
Bowling Green 42101

Northern Kentucky State Vocational-
Technical School
1025 Amsterdam Rd.
Covington 41011

MAINE

Northern Maine Technical College
33 Edgemont Dr.
Presque Isle 04769

MASSACHUSETTS

Dean Junior College
99 Main St.
Franklin 02038

MICHIGAN

Delta College
University Center 48710

Macomb Community College
14500 Twelve Mile Rd.
Warren 48093-3896

NCI Associates, Ltd.
27637 John Rd.
Madison Heights 48071

MINNESOTA

Opportunities Industrialization Center,
Twin Cities
935 Olson Memorial Hwy.
Minneapolis 55405

MISSISSIPPI

East Central Community College
Decatur 39327

Mississippi Gulf Coast Community
College
Central Office
P.O. Box 67
Perkinston 39573

NEW YORK

Erie Community College,
North Campus
Main St. and Youngs Rd.
Williamsville 14221

Fulton-Montgomery Community
College
2805 State Hwy. 67
Johnstown 12095

Herkimer County Community College
Reservoir Rd.
Herkimer 13350-1598

Hudson Valley Community College
80 Vandenburgh Ave.
Troy 12180

SUNY College of Technology &
Agriculture at Morrisville
Morrisville 13408

SUNY College of Technology at Alfred
Alfred 14802

SUNY College of Technology at Canton
Canton 13617

SUNY College of Technology at Delhi
Delhi 13753

Tompkins-Cortland Community
College
170 North St.
Dryden 13053

NORTH CAROLINA

Central Carolina Community College
1105 Kelly Dr.
Sanford 27330

Johnston Community College
P.O. Box 2350
Smithfield 27577-2350

OHIO

Akron Adult Vocational Services
147 Park St.
Akron 44308

D E3, Inc.
19701 South Miles Pkwy.
Cleveland 44128-4257

OKLAHOMA

Kiamichi AVTS SD #7,
McCurtain Campus
Hwy. 70 N & Rte. 3
P.O. Box 177
Idabel 74745

Oklahoma State University,
Okmulgee
1801 East Fourth St.
Okmulgee 74447-3901

Pontotoc Skill Development Center
601 West 33rd
Ada 74820

PENNSYLVANIA

Community College of Allegheny
County
800 Allegheny Ave.
Pittsburgh 15233-1895

Orleans Technical Institute
1330 Rhawn St.
Philadelphia 19111-2899

SOUTH DAKOTA

Southeast Vocational Technical
Institute
2301 Career Place
Sioux Falls 57107

TENNESSEE

Elizabethton State Area Vocational
Technical School
1500 Arney St.
P.O. Box 789
Elizabethton 37643

Morristown State Area Vocational-
Technical School
821 West Louise Ave.
Morristown 37813

Oneida State Area Vocational Technical
School
120 Eli Ln.
Oneida 37841

TEXAS

Blinn College
902 College Ave.
Brenham 77833

Texas State Technical College,
Waco Campus
3801 Campus Dr.
Waco 76705

Trinity Valley Community College
500 South Prairieville
Athens 75751

UTAH

Bridgerland Applied Technology Center
1301 North 600 W
Logan 84321

Odgen-Weber Applied Technology
Center
559 East AVC Ln.
Ogden 84404-6704

VERMONT

Vermont Technical College
Randolph Center 05061

VIRGINIA

Industrial Training Company
511 West Grace St.
Richmond 23220

WISCONSIN

Good Armstrong and Associates, Ltd.
2142 South 55th St.
Milwaukee 53219

North Central Technical College
1000 Campus Dr.
Wausau 54401-1899

Painting and Decoration

ARKANSAS

Arkansas Valley Technical Institute
Hwy. 23 N, P.O. Box 506
Ozark 72949

Red River Technical College
P.O. Box 140
Hope 71801

CALIFORNIA

Career Management Institute
1855 West Katella Ave.
Orange 92667

Contractors License Courses of Modesto
3300 Tully Rd.
Modesto 95350

Contractors License Institute
5777 Madison
Sacramento 95841

Laborers Training and Retraining Fund
of Southern California
P.O. Box 391667
Anza 92539-1667

San Joaquin Delta College
5151 Pacific Ave.
Stockton 95207

COLORADO

Precision Safety and Services, Inc.
1045 Garden of the Gods Rd.
Colorado Springs 80907

San Luis Valley Area Vocational School
1011 Main St.
Alamosa 81101

DELAWARE

Wilmington Skills Center
13th and Poplar St.
Wilmington 19801

FLORIDA

Miami Lakes Technical Education Center
5780 Northwest 158th St.
Miami Lakes 33169

Pinellas Mechanical Pipe Trade
4020 80th Ave. N
Pinellas Park 33565

ILLINOIS

Belleville Area College
2500 Carlyle Rd.
Belleville 62221

College of Lake County
19351 West Washington St.
Grays Lake 60030-1198

Danville Area Community College
2000 East Main St.
Danville 61832

Illinois Central College
One College Dr.
East Peoria 61635

John Wood Community College
150 South 48th St.
Quincy 62301-9147

Joliet Junior College
1216 Houbolt Ave.
Joliet 60436

McDowell Business Training Center
1313 South Michigan Ave.
Chicago 60605

Parkland College
2400 West Bradley Ave.
Champaign 61821

Rock Valley College
3301 North Mulford Rd.
Rockford 61114

Triton College
2000 Fifth Ave.
River Grove 60171

Washburne Trade School
3233 West 31st St.
Chicago 60623

MAINE

Washington County Technical College
RR 1, P.O. Box 22C
Calais 04619

MASSACHUSETTS

Dean Junior College
99 Main St.
Franklin 02038

MICHIGAN

Delta College
University Center 48710

Macomb Community College
14500 Twelve Mile Rd.
Warren 48093-3896

NCI Associates, Ltd.
27637 John Rd.
Madison Heights 48071

MINNESOTA

Hennepin Technical College
1820 North Xenium Ln.
Plymouth 55441

Opportunities Industrialization Center,
Twin Cities
935 Olson Memorial Hwy.
Minneapolis 55405

Saint Paul Technical College
235 Marshall Ave.
Saint Paul 55102

NEW YORK

Erie Community College,
North Campus
Main St. and Youngs Rd.
Williamsville 14221

Fulton-Montgomery Community
College
2805 State Hwy. 67
Johnstown 12095

Herkimer County Community College
Reservoir Rd.
Herkimer 13350-1598

Hudson Valley Community College
80 Vandenburgh Ave.
Troy 12180

SUNY College of Technology &
Agriculture at Morrisville
Morrisville 13408

SUNY College of Technology at Alfred
Alfred 14802

SUNY College of Technology at Canton
Canton 13617

SUNY College of Technology at Delhi
Delhi 13753

Tompkins-Cortland Community
College
170 North St.
Dryden 13053

OHIO

D E3, Inc.
19701 South Miles Pkwy.
Cleveland 44128-4257

OKLAHOMA

Oklahoma State University, Okmulgee
1801 East Fourth St.
Okmulgee 74447-3901

Pontotoc Skill Development Center
601 West 33rd
Ada 74820

PENNSYLVANIA

Community College of Allegheny
County
800 Allegheny Ave.
Pittsburgh 15233-1895

Orleans Technical Institute
1330 Rhawn St.
Philadelphia 19111-2899

SOUTH DAKOTA

Southeast Vocational Technical
Institute
2301 Career Place
Sioux Falls 57107

TENNESSEE

Elizabethton State Area Vocational
Technical School
1500 Arney St.
P.O. Box 789
Elizabethton 37643

Oneida State Area Vocational Technical
School
120 Eli Ln.
Oneida 37841

TEXAS

Blinn College
902 College Ave.
Brenham 77833

UTAH

Bridgerland Applied Technology Center
1301 North 600 W
Logan 84321

VERMONT

Vermont Technical College
Randolph Center 05061

VIRGINIA

Industrial Training Company
511 West Grace St.
Richmond 23220

WISCONSIN

Good Armstrong and Associates, Ltd.
2142 South 55th St.
Milwaukee 53219

North Central Technical College
1000 Campus Dr.
Wausau 54401-1899

Plumbing and Pipe Fitting

ALABAMA

J F Ingram State Technical College
P.O. Box 209
Deatsville 36022

ARIZONA

Central Arizona College
8470 North Overfield Rd.
Coolidge 85228-9778

Eastern Arizona College
Church St.
Thatcher 85552-0769

ARKANSAS

Arkansas Valley Technical Institute
Hwy. 23 N
P.O. Box 506
Ozark 72949

Northwest Technical Institute
P.O. Box A
Springdale 72765

CALIFORNIA

Brownson Technical School
1110 Claudina Place
Anaheim 92805

Contractors License Institute
5777 Madison
Sacramento 95841

Educorp Career College
230 East Third St.
Long Beach 90802

Los Angeles Training Technical College
400 West Washington Blvd.
Los Angeles 90015-4181

DELAWARE

Wilmington Skills Center
13th and Poplar St.
Wilmington 19801

FLORIDA

Atlantic Vocational Technical Center
4700 Coconut Creek Pkwy.
Coconut Creek 33063

Pinellas Mechanical Pipe Trade
4020 80th Ave. N
Pinellas Park 33565

Seminole Community College
100 Weldon Blvd.
Sanford 32773-6199

INDIANA

Charles A Prosser Vocational Center
4202 Charlestown Rd.
New Albany 47150

IOWA

Northeast Iowa Community College
Hwy. 150 S, P.O. Box 400
Calmar 52132-0400

Western Iowa Technical Community
College
4647 Stone Ave., P.O. Box 265
Sioux City 51102-0265

KANSAS

Kansas City Area Vocational Technical
School
2220 North 59th St.
Kansas City 66104

Kaw Area Vocational-Technical School
5724 Huntoon
Topeka 66604

North Central Kansas Area Vocational
Technical School
Hwy. 24, P.O. Box 507
Beloit 67420

Wichita Area Vocational Technical
School
428 South Broadway
Wichita 67202-3910

KENTUCKY

Kentucky Technical, Bowling Green
State Vocational Technical School
1845 Loop Dr., P.O. Box 6000
Bowling Green 42101

Kentucky Technical, Jefferson State
Vocational Technical School
727 West Chestnut
Louisville 40203

MAINE

Northern Maine Technical College
33 Edgemont Dr.
Presque Isle 04769

Southern Maine Technical College
Fort Rd.
South Portland 04106

Washington County Technical College
RR 1, P.O. Box 22C
Calais 04619

MASSACHUSETTS

Peterson School of Steam Engineering
25 Montvale Ave.
Woburn 01801

MINNESOTA

Saint Cloud Technical College
1540 Northway Dr.
Saint Cloud 56303

Saint Paul Technical College
235 Marshall Ave.
Saint Paul 55102

Southwestern Technical College,
Jackson Campus
401 West St.
Jackson 56143

MISSISSIPPI

Mississippi Gulf Coast Community
College
Central Office
P.O. Box 67
Perkinston 39573

MISSOURI

Ranken Technical College
4431 Finney Ave.
Saint Louis 63113

NEW MEXICO

Albuquerque Technical-Vocational
Institute
525 Buena Vista SE
Albuquerque 87106

NEW YORK

Berk Trade and Business School
311 West 35th St.
New York 10001

SUNY College of Technology at Alfred
Alfred 14802

SUNY College of Technology at Delhi
Delhi 13753

NORTH CAROLINA

Cleveland Community College
137 South Post Rd.
Shelby 28150

Forsyth Technical Community College
2100 Silas Creek Pkwy.
Winston-Salem 27103

Johnston Community College
P.O. Box 2350
Smithfield 27577-2350

Southeastern Community College
P.O. Box 151
Whiteville 28472

Wake Technical Community College
9101 Fayetteville Rd.
Raleigh 27603-5696

NORTH DAKOTA

North Dakota State College of Science
800 North Sixth St.
Wahpeton 58076

PENNSYLVANIA

Community College of Allegheny
County
800 Allegheny Ave.
Pittsburgh 15233-1895

Eastern Montgomery County Area
Vocational Technical School
3075 Terwood Rd.
Willow Grove 19090

Luzerne County Community College
1333 South Prospect St.
Nanticoke 18634

Thaddeus Stevens State School of
Technology
750 East King St.
Lancaster 17602

RHODE ISLAND

New England Institute of Technology
2500 Post Rd.
Warwick 02886

TEXAS

North Lake College
5001 North MacArthur Blvd.
Irving 75038-3899

San Antonio Trades School
120 Playmoor St.
San Antonio 78210

UTAH

Bridgerland Applied Technology Center
1301 North 600 W
Logan 84321

Odgen-Weber Applied Technology
Center
559 East AVC Ln.
Ogden 84404-6704

VIRGINIA

Apprentice School Newport News
Shipbuilding
4101 Washington Ave.
Newport News 23607

WISCONSIN

Gateway Technical College
3520 30th Ave.
Kenosha 53144-1690

North Central Technical College
1000 Campus Dr.
Wausau 54401-1899

Welding and Cutting

ALABAMA

Community College of the Air Force
Maxwell Air Force Base
Montgomery 36112

Harry M Ayers State Technical College
1801 Coleman Rd., P.O. Box 1647
Anniston 36202

ARKANSAS

Arkansas State University,
Beebe Branch
P.O. Drawer H
Beebe 72012

Arkansas Valley Technical Institute
Hwy. 23 N
P.O. Box 506
Ozark 72949

Garland County Community College
100 College Dr.
Hot Springs 71913

CALIFORNIA

San Diego City College
1313 12th Ave.
San Diego 92101

DELAWARE

Delaware Technical Community
College Stanton, Wilmington
400 Stanton-Christiana Rd.
Newark 19702

IDAHO

Ricks College
Rexburg 83460-4107

ILLINOIS

MacMurray College
East College Ave.
Jacksonville 62650

INDIANA

Indiana Vocational Technical College,
Central Indiana
One West 26th St.
Indianapolis 46206-1763

Indiana Vocational Technical College,
Northwest
1440 East 35th Ave.
Gary 46409

Indiana Vocational Technical College,
Wabash Valley
7999 U.S. Hwy. 41
Terre Haute 47802-4898

IOWA

Iowa Lakes Community College
19 South Seventh St.
Estherville 51334

Kirkwood Community College
P.O. Box 2068
Cedar Rapids 52406

KANSAS

Allen County Community College
1801 North Cottonwood
Iola 66749

MICHIGAN

Alpena Community College
666 Johnson St.
Alpena 49707

Bay De Noc Community College
2001 North Lincoln Rd.
Escanaba 49289

Ferris State University
901 South State St.
Big Rapids 49307

Kellogg Community College
450 North Ave.
Battle Creek 49017

Lansing Community College
419 North Capitol Ave.
Lansing 48901-7210

MINNESOTA

Alexandria Technical College
1601 Jefferson St.
Alexandria 56308

Hennepin Technical College
1820 North Xenium Ln.
Plymouth 55441

NEW MEXICO

New Mexico State University,
Dona Ana Branch
Department 3DA
P.O. Box 30001
Las Cruces 88003-0105

NEW YORK

Erie Community College, City Campus
121 Ellicott St.
Buffalo 14203

Erie Community College,
North Campus
Main St. and Youngs Rd.
Williamsville 14221

Fashion Institute of Technology
227 West 27th St.
New York 10001

Mohawk Valley Community College
1101 Sherman Dr.
Utica 13501

Schenectady County Community
    College
Washington Ave.
Schenectady 12305

SUNY College of Technology at Delhi
Delhi 13753

NORTH CAROLINA

Cape Fear Community College
411 North Front St.
Wilmington 28401

Durham Technical Community College
1637 Lawson St.
Durham 27703

OHIO

Sinclair Community College
444 West Third St.
Dayton 45402

University of Cincinnati, Main Campus
2624 Clifton Ave.
Cincinnati 45221-0127

OKLAHOMA

Oklahoma State University, Okmulgee
1801 East Fourth St.
Okmulgee 74447-3901

OREGON

Clackamas Community College
19600 Molalla Ave.
Oregon City 97045

PENNSYLVANIA

Dean Institute of Technology
1501 West Liberty Ave.
Pittsburgh 15226-9990

Westmoreland County Community
    College
Youngwood 15697-1895

SOUTH CAROLINA

Tri-County Technical College
P.O. Box 587
Pendleton 29670

TEXAS

Brazosport College
500 College Dr.
Lake Jackson 77566

UTAH

Bridgerland Applied Technology Center
1301 North 600 W
Logan 84321

VIRGINIA

Danville Community College
1008 South Main St.
Danville 24541

New River Community College
P.O. Drawer 1127
Dublin 24084

Thomas Nelson Community College
P.O. Box 9407
Hampton 23670

Tidewater Community College
Rte. 135
Portsmouth 23703

WEST VIRGINIA

West Virginia University at Parkersburg
Rte. 5, P.O. Box 167A
Parkersburg 26101

WISCONSIN

Gateway Technical College
3520 30th Ave.
Kenosha 53144-1690

North Central Technical College
1000 Campus Dr.
Wausau 54401-1899

Wisconsin Area Vocational Training
    and Adult Education System District
    Number Four
3550 Anderson St.
Madison 53704

Wisconsin Area Vocational Training
    and Adult Education System,
    Moraine Park
235 North National Ave.
P.O. Box 1940
Fond Du Lac 54936-1940

Index

All jobs mentioned in this volume are listed and cross-referenced in the index. Entries that appear in all capital letters have separate occupational profiles. For example, AIR-CONDITIONING AND HEATING TECHNICIAN, AIR-CONDITIONING, HEATING, AND REFRIGERATION MECHANIC, ARCHITECT, and so on are profiles in this volume. Entries that are not capitalized refer to jobs that do not have a separate profile but for which information is given.

Under some capitalized entries there is a section entitled "Profile includes." This lists all jobs that are mentioned in the profile. For example, in the case of AIR-CONDITIONING, HEATING, AND REFRIGERATION MECHANIC, jobs that are described in the profile are: Air-conditioning and refrigeration mechanic, Furnace installer, Gas burner mechanic, and Oil burner mechanic.

Some entries are followed by a job title in parentheses after the page number on which it can be found. This job title is the occupational profile in which the entry is discussed. For instance, the Construction engineer entry is followed by the profile title (Civil engineer).

Photographic Credits

Bethlehem Steel 59; Burlington Northern Railroad 85; Earl Dotter 1, 35, 39, 41, 43, 75, 100; Tom Dunham 72, 77, 92, 95, 106, 111; IBM 119; Sara Matthews 9; RTKL 115; Steven Silvers/Texas Instruments 79; Martha Tabor 4, 5, 45, 47, 51, 53, 57, 61, 64, 66, 68, 81, 89, 97, 104, 109, 117, 121, 127, 132, 134; The Terry Wild Studio 6; Visual Education Corporation 30, 33, 37, 55, 70; Shirley Zeiberg 62